OBJECTIONS

TO

CALVINISM AS IT IS,

IN

A SERIES OF LETTERS

ADDRESSED TO

Rev. N. L. Rice, D. D.,

BY

Rev. R. S. Foster.

WITH AN APPENDIX,

CONTAINING

REPLIES AND REJOINDERS

Cincinnati:
PUBLISHED BY SWORMSTEDT & POE,
FOR THE METHODIST EPISCOPAL CHURCH, AT THE WESTERN BOOK CONCERN, CORNER OF MAIN AND EIGHTH STREETS.

R. P. THOMPSON, PRINTER.
1856.

INTRODUCTION.

THE subject of Predestination has, for many ages, engaged the attention of theologians and philosophers. That the world is governed by fixed and permanent laws, is evident, even to the casual observer. But by whom those laws are established, and how far they extend, have been matters of controversy. In the Christian world, all admit that the will of God is the great source of law. In the arrangements of the vast systems of worlds, as well as in the formation of the earth, with all its varied tribes, we recognize the hand of Him who doeth "his will in the heavens above and in the earth beneath." All acknowledge the existence of a Divine decree; but the questions arise, Do all things thus come to pass? Are human actions the result of laws as fixed and unalterable as those which govern the movements of the planets? Is the destiny of every human being unchangeably determined before his birth, without reference to foreseen conduct? Or has the mind a power of choice? can it move freely within certain specified limits? and will the nature of its movements and choice influence its eternal happiness? These are questions which, in some form, have exercised the highest powers of the human intellect.

The Atheistical school of philosophers, ancient as well as modern, taught the doctrine of necessity. With them, matter is eternal; and no designing mind superintending its movements, there must be a necessity in nature. This has been differently expressed in different ages. Sometimes it appears as the atomic theory of Democritus and Leucippus, and, again, as the Pantheism of Spinoza. But, whatever form it may assume, it teaches that all actions come to pass by necessity, and denies the responsibility of all beings. It annihilates the freedom of the human will, and degrades intelligence to mechanism.

Another class of philosophers admits the existence of a Diety, but denies his special, superintending providence. Such imagine the great First Cause to be, according to the Hindoo mythology, in a state of beatific repose, or to be employed in movements so transcendently important, that the affairs of earth are neglected, or that he is himself subject to fate.

The third great class is composed of such as not only admit the existence of God, but who worship him as the supreme Governor, and as invested with all moral as well as natural perfections. They reject the doctrine of fate and all necessity, other than that which springs from the Divine decree. But they differ as to the extent of that decree. This difference has given rise to the formation of sects and parties in all ages, and to controversies of the most exciting character. Milton, in his Paradise Lost, fancies the fallen angels engaged in discussions of this nature. They

> "Reasoned high
> Of providence, foreknowledge, will, and fate;
> Fixed fate, free will, foreknowledge, absolute,
> And found no end, in wandering mazes lost."

Such, too, has been the character of many human controversies. One party maintains that God decrees whatever comes to pass, and that the number of those who are to be saved and of those who are to be lost, is definitely and unalterably determined from eternity; while others teach that some actions flow from man's free will, and that God gives man the power to choose between life and death—decreeing salvation to those who obey his Gospel, and denouncing death upon the disobedient; or, in other words, that *characters*, and not *persons*, are elected. The latter sentiment, so far as a heathen, ignorant of gracious influences, could perceive, is expressed by Plato, when, in his treatise against the Atheists, he says that God "devises this in reference to the whole, namely, what kind of a situation every thing which becomes of a certain quality must receive and inhabit; but the causes of becoming of such a quality, he hath left to our own wills."

The Jewish sects differed upon these, as well as upon other points of doctrine. The Essenes taught predestination in its most severe form. The Sadducees held the freedom of the will in nearly the same manner as the Pelagians have since taught; while the Pharisees endeavored to combine the two systems. Prideaux says, "They ascribed to God and fate all that is done, and yet left to man the freedom of his will. But how they made these two apparent incompatibles consist together, is nowhere sufficiently explained; perchance they meant no more than that every man freely chooseth what he is unalterably predestinated to. But if he be predestinated to that choice, how freely soever he may seem to choose, certainly he hath no free will, because he is, according to this scheme, unalterably necessitated to all that he doth, and cannot possibly choose otherwise."

The Mohammedans were, generally, rigid predestinarians. With them, every event in nature was fixed by an absolute decree. The soldier could neither be killed nor wounded until his time had come. Hence, they acquired a recklessness of all physical danger, as well as of moral feeling. But, even with them, the mind rebelled against fatalism, and the sect of the Motazalites, and portions of other sects, held the freedom of the human will.

In the early ages of Christianity, the doctrine of predestination, as extending to every act and fixing the destiny of every individual, without reference to foreseen faith or works, was unknown. The early fathers teach no such creed. They occasionally use the terms foreordain, predestinate, elect, etc., but they invariably use these expressions in the Scriptural signification as employed by St. Paul, and not in the predestinarian, or what has since been termed the Calvinistic sense. This continued to be the case for the first four centuries of the Christian era; but, at the commencement of the fifth century, the Pelagian controversy arose. As usual in controversies, each party ran into an extreme. Pelagius was right in teaching that God willed all men to be saved, and in denying the doctrine of infant damnation, which had crept into the Church; but he erred greatly in teaching man's ability, without grace, to commence a religious life, or to keep the commandments of God. Augustine, perceiving his errors, held correctly, that man's salvation is of grace, and that, apart from grace, he has no power to commence or continue a religious career. But he erred in teaching the unconditional election to life of a part of the race, and the damnation of the rest, including some infants. Augustine was sustained, and his works remain to this day standards in the Catholic Church.

It must, however, be remarked, that Augustine is not at all times consistent in his statements. Hence, Calvin alledges that he had attributed to foreknowledge that which pertains only to decrees. His writings thus gave rise to discussions almost interminable. During the progress of the century in which he lived, a number, who were termed Predestinarians, advocated the doctrine of unconditional election and reprobation, to the utter denial of free will. Again: in the ninth century, Godeschalcus, a Saxon monk, having taught that God had predestinated some to eternal death, a violent controversy arose, heightened by the enmity which existed between him and Rabanus, who was his abbot. The doctrines of Godeschalcus were condemned by three councils, and he was cruelly cast into prison. But, afterward, his sentiments were approved by three councils, and at his death the controversy ceased.

The Dominicans, who were for many centuries among the strongest pillars of the Catholic Church, and to whom the machinery of the Inquisition was committed, were strict predestinarians. So, also, were the Augustinians and the Jansenists. On the other hand, the Jesuits, who became the most indefatigable enemies of the Reformation, while they professed to believe with Augustine, yet were the advocates of free will. With all its professed unity, the Roman Church has been as much divided upon these questions as the Protestant. At present the Jesuitic theology is prevalent. They deny that they are either Calvinistic or Arminian. But, while they profess to accord with St. Augustine, they have, no doubt, departed far from his views.

At the time of the Reformation, the great reformers drew much from St. Augustine. Luther was an Augustinian friar; and he found the great doctrine of justification by faith so well established by that father against all opposers, that he received for a time his views on predestination also. On free will he had a sharp contest with Erasmus, but afterward kept almost silent on these perplexing questions, and, in the latter part of his life, strongly recommended Melancthon's works, which taught a different doctrine. The Lutheran Church, receiving their impress from him, hold only a predestination based upon foreknowledge; in this, strictly agreeing with the Arminian view. Melancthon, in the commencement of his career, was a rigid Predestinarian. In 1525, writing of the decrees, he says: "Lastly, Divine predestination takes away human liberty; for all things come to pass according to Divine predestination—not only external works, but also internal thoughts, in all creatures." He, however, in a few years changed his opinion, and struck out such passages from his works. To Cranmer he observed that there had been, among the reformers, "Stoical disputations respecting fate, offensive in their nature, and noxious in their tendency." In writing to

Peucer he compares Calvin to Zeno, saying, "Lælius writes to me, that the controversy respecting the Stoical fate is agitated with such uncommon fervor at Geneva, that one individual is cast into prison because he happened to differ from Zeno." And near his death, referring to the doctrines of predestination, he says they are "monstrous opinions, which are contumelious against God, and pernicious to morals."

Calvin became, among the reformers, the great champion of the decrees, and hence the system bears his name. So much importance did he attach to these peculiar views, that he scrupled not to apply the most opprobrious epithets to those who refused to receive them. In one of his sermons he says, "The enemies of God's predestination are stupid and ignorant, and the devil hath plucked out their eyes." Again: "Such men fight against the Holy Ghost, like mad beasts, and endeavor to abolish the holy Scripture. There is more honesty in the Papists than in these men; for the doctrine of the Papists is a great deal better, more holy, and more agreeable to the sacred Scriptures, than the doctrine of those vile and wicked men, who cast down God's holy election—these dogs that bark at it, and swine that root it up." And in another sermon he says, "The devil hath no fitter instruments than those who fight against predestination."

Sentiments such as these, taught to the youth preparing for the ministry, could not fail to have an influence in promoting a persecuting spirit. These ministers were scattered among the reformed Churches over Europe, and soon began to exhibit their disposition. Liberty of opinion was tolerated for a time; but, early in the succeeding century, the famous Synod of Dort was assembled, in which the opinions of the Remonstrants, or Arminians, were condemned as heresy. Pious and influential ministers were banished from the land, many were thrown into prison, while some of their patrons were put to death. Macaulay well characterizes the proceedings of this synod, as manifesting "gross injustice, insolence, and cruelty."

A reaction followed. Arminianism and a modified Calvinism, known afterward as Baxterianism, gained ground upon the Continent, and rapidly pervaded the Anglican Church. In the days of Wesley, a strong effort was made to suppress Arminian views. Calvinism being made a test of office in the college in which they were engaged, Mr. Benson was removed, and Mr. Fletcher resigned. A distinguished clergyman, Mr. Shirley, issued a circular, requesting a meeting of ministers, to go in a body to Mr. Wesley's ensuing conference, and demand that he and his preachers should retract their sentiments. But, though the spirit of the Synod of Dort was aroused, the civil power to punish could not be employed. Mr. W. continued to preach, and Mr. Fletcher, in his defense, issued those masterly Checks, which displayed at once his superior genius, and the strength of the cause which he had espoused.

In America, in early days, the religious sentiment was, generally, Calvinistic. Such Churches were supported by law, in the New England states, until a late period. The colleges and seminaries were, also, principally under their control. Hence, the introduction of Methodism gave rise to numerous controversies. In the midst, however, of repeated conflicts, Arminianism has increased, until now a majority of members in the Union belong to Churches which reject the Calvinistic faith. Of the Churches, too, which are called Calvinistic, at least one-half have embraced what is termed "New School" theology. Whatever may be the merits or demerits of that system, the "Old School" assert that it is a departure, not only to Arminianism, but to Pelagianism.

For some years past there had been a growing union among Christians; controversies were less frequent; and the Presbyterian and Methodist Churches were living in peace and harmony. Recently, however, repeated attacks, of the most virulent character, have been made upon the doctrines and usages of the Methodist Episcopal Church. For a time this was patiently borne; but as forbearance only seemed to increase the frequency and severity of the attacks, a notice of the principles involved became necessary.

The letters contained in the present volume were written by Rev. R. S. Foster, A. M., a member of the Ohio annual conference, who has charge of Wesley Chapel in this city. A number of them appeared in the columns of the Western Christian Advocate; and, at the earnest solicitations of many readers, he was induced to present them in a more permanent form. Their style is clear and forcible, and the process of argumentation strictly logical. As the reader will perceive, he has limited himself to two principal points. First, to show what are the doctrines of Calvinism; and, secondly, to state the prominent objections to them. This work has been well executed, by giving the standard authors in their own language, and thus preventing any candid opponent from making the charge of misrepresentation. The book will thus be very valuable to such as have not access to extensive libraries, or who have not time to examine for themselves the various writers here quoted. The objections are distinctly and explicitly stated, and the intelligent reader will, we think, be fully convinced that they are well sustained. We commend the volume as one of great merit, to such as are perplexed upon the subject of predestination. We doubt not that many, after perusing these pages, will fully acquiesce with Calvin, in terming, as he did, the decree of predestination, a "HORRIBLE DECREE."

M. SIMPSON.

CONTENTS.

OBJECTIONS

TO

CALVINISM AS IT IS.

CHAPTER I.

ORIGIN AND DESIGN OF THE WORK.

STAY, reader, for a moment. The author would speak with you. Some explanations may be of service, before you commence the perusal of the following pages. They shall be brief and few.

This book is the creature of circumstance. It had never existed, but for reasons over which the author himself had no control. He wrote because it seemed necessary to write—not because he had any ambition for authorship. He made a book, not with "intention of forethought," but almost before he was aware of it, and without any prepense whatever. The Church, of which he is a humble and obscure minister, had been long and grievously assailed by one of the principal organs of a sister denomination—her doctrines and usages held up to public odium, as perverted by the pen of misrepresentation—her influence for piety questioned, and whatever was peculiar to her organization ridiculed and calumniated. And this ungenerous course was commenced and pursued by an accredited champion, at a time when peace and Christian union had long existed—against remonstrances on our part, and published deprecations of the consequences which were certain to ensue. We endured for a time. But this only seemed to whet the envenomed appetite of an adversary who seemed intent to devour us. The greater our reluctance, the greater his ferocity. It now seemed, that to remain longer silent would not only be a reproach to ourselves—a matter which, alone considered, gave us little concern—but must, also, weaken the force, if not peril the interests, of truth itself. It was, under such circumstances that the substance of what is contained in this volume was given to the public, through one of the journals of our Church, in a series of letters, addressed to the reverend gentleman who seemed so anxious to discuss our respective differences. This is our apology, if any is necessary, for sending to the public a volume which, it may be, some unacquainted with the facts might conclude was uncalled for. *Truth and religion required it.* The time had come when the real issues needed to be stated, and truth vindicated.

The object of the author has not been to discuss fully the doctrines peculiar to Calvinism—not to present the counter views of Arminians—nothing of the kind: *it was simply to present a statement of Calvinism, and objections thereto*—not to examine its defense—not to build up an opposite system—not to contrast it with other schemes—simply to state it, and deduce its consequences—believing that these consequences are sufficient to overthrow and destroy it. Had it been our plan to examine the arguments by which Calvinists are wont to defend themselves, we could have desired no easier a task than their refutation. But this has been so ably and so often done, that we find no occasion to repeat it. The scheme falls under the weight of its consequences—it matters not what its defense is. Its consequences prove that it is utterly false; and no argument can, therefore, prove it true.

The statement herein made of Calvinism, you will find in the progress of your examination, is in no single instance the prejudiced and *ex parte* statement of the author himself, but always the statement of the Confession of Faith, and the renowned and distinguished advocates of the system, in their own language, fully and fairly quoted. No author has been at the pains to quote so largely and variously. Having derived our statements from their own standards, we deduce the consequences. You will judge whether the consequences are legitimate or not; and whether, if legitimate, they are fatal to the system. This is all you have to do. If Calvinism is what its friends here represent it to be, and its consequences what I show them to be, you must decide in your own mind upon the merits of the system.

It may be that this volume will find its way into the hands of some who have long cherished, and still do cherish, respect for the system it is intended to expose. To such may I say a word. Read this book, if you shall be induced to read it at all, candidly and without feelings of resentment or prejudice. Be assured that, however plainly the author may have spoken, toward you he entertains none but sentiments of kindness; his object is not to wound and afflict, but purely to defend the truth. Let not the charge of misrepresentation blind you. You are men—judge for yourselves. You will find that the author has made no representations at all—that these are all and wholly taken from your own standards. He is only responsible for the construction he has given to them, and the consequences he has drawn. You will judge of these. I admit that you have been taught different views, and you have heard these consequences denied; but, will this satisfy you? Do you not see that, though disclaimed and denied, they still stand against you, unanswered—unanswerable? The premises are yours—the conclusions you cannot escape. Read as a Christian only desirous for the truth, and dare nobly to follow the truth wherever she points the way.

Toward the Presbyterian Church, I have cherished sentiments of the profoundest attachment from my early boyhood. These sentiments have grown up with me to manhood—they remain to this hour. In her communion are many personal friends and relatives, and among her ministers are some dear to me as my own brothers. In despite of her errors, I here record my firm persuasion that she has many surpassing excellences—many which my own Church may well and wisely emulate. But that her creed is essentially erroneous, and that in important points, I have always believed, and now believe more firmly than ever before, having examined the subject more thoroughly. My reasons for this belief are hereafter given. Because of this attachment, and lest it might wound personal friends, but much more, lest it might wound some friend of the Savior, I have regretted constantly the necessity of discussing the subject; but, still believing that truth is better than error—more pleasing to God and more beneficial to the world, however painful the process of quarrying it—I have spoken plainly, and, I trust, in the fear of God, on its behalf.

If, on examination, you shall find Calvinism liable to the charges herein preferred against it, and if your reason, and conscience, and religion, and nature itself revolt at it, then it becomes you to inquire whether, through the pretense of not believing it yourself, of its not being taught by your ministers generally, of its being greatly modified—whether, because of any or all of these reasons, you can safely continue, with your influence, to bolster the system, and propagate its existence and influence among men. May the great Head of the Church bless you with right views and feelings, and bring you to a wise and judicious conclusion!

The plan of this book, it is believed, is entirely new, at least so far as the writer is informed; and so supplies a desideratum on the controverted questions introduced. The subject is brought more directly before the reader by copious quotations, and the objections presented in a more condensed and direct form, than in any other of the numerous and superior works written on it. The reader is thus enabled to see what Calvinism is—without being confused and distracted by prejudiced statements—as held and taught by its own expounders, and, at the same time, what are the difficulties alledged by its opposers, as sufficient to discredit it, and, whether friendly or hostile to it, will be aided to come to a candid conclusion on the merits of the question.

It will be found that the difficulties brought against the system in these pages, are mainly derived from the logical consequences resulting from it, and the undoubted antagonism of such consequences to the word of God, the nature of man, and the universal persuasion and consciousness of mankind. This course was preferred by the author, because it was less trodden, and, upon the whole, as he believes, more convincing and conclusive. It could have been shown, as it has been triumphantly many times—confining the argument to the Scripture limits—that Calvinism is not taught therein, and that an opposite system is; but this was made incidental to our main object—which was to show that consequences so revolting inevitably result from it, as to prove him guilty of blasphemy who charges it upon the word of God; or, rather, as to make it impossible for any to believe or pretend any thing so dreadful. It is assumed that what is logically false cannot be Scripturally true; and, therefore, that by involving Calvinism in logical dilemmas, it is overthrown, and proved to be unscriptural, as the Scriptures cannot teach what is logically false and contradictory. Whatever may be the seeming, the text *cannot* teach what is logically untrue; or teaching it, it teaches what is false, and cannot be the word of God. Whoever, therefore, derives a system from the Bible which is false, and demonstrably so to human reason by the processes of conclusive logic, either derives from the Bible what it does not authorize, or he proves it false: in other words, he is mistaken, or the Bible is not true. We attempt, in the following pages, to show that Calvinists do this; and if our reasoning is conclusive, it will not be difficult for our readers to decide which horn of the dilemma to choose.

It may be proper to state here, that, to avoid repetition, we have been compelled to leave off many strong objections, bearing against each of the several points discussed; and even after much care, there may seem to be some sameness. The reason of this is manifest. I have singled out eight distinct points of the Calvinistic creed, as objectionable. Now, these points are related, and, to a great extent, are susceptible of the same proof, and liable to the same objections. Hence, in treating of them separately, I have necessarily, in some measure, used the same or similar objections against each. If the same objection disproves all the points separately, it is legitimate and proper to employ it against each: the interest of truth requires that it should be repeated whenever it bears against error. We have, however, varied the argument as much as possible, and have not repeated the same point except where it was absolutely necessary.

To enable you to determine the force of our argument, as a whole, against the system we oppose, I make this additional suggestion: if one single point of the eight specified is disproved, Calvinism is irreparably injured—if one point is removed, the system is destroyed—it is proved false, not only in that particular point, but, also, in all correlative points—its dependencies fall with it. If, then, I have shown difficulties bearing upon any one point, such as to convince you that it cannot be true, the system is irretrievably involved. But, I ask you, has not, not only one, but every point named, been successfully assailed? Is it not so? Can you see an escape, not for all, but for a single one? But, again: I have introduced a score of objections, or approximating this, upon each point. Now, one objection is sufficient. If nineteen out of twenty are worthless, and a single one is good, the objection stands—the system falls. A proposition cannot be true against one valid objection, any more than it can against fifty. If one resist successful assault, the proposition is ruined. But, I ask you in all candor, can a single one be assailed? I have no need of many of them; but can any one take them from my support? You will readily perceive that I have introduced a great excess of proof. But this shows you how hopeless the system against which such weight of objection bears—how much it will have to do, before it is saved. It must rescue every point against every separate objection. And I assert that it cannot rescue a single point from a single objection. Let my readers, as they proceed, attempt for themselves to find an escape from the consequences urged, and abide the honest result, whatever it may be. If Calvinism is true, embrace it. If not, discard it. But, be not misled by the pretense that, notwithstanding its difficulties, it is found in the word of God. This is a subterfuge to escape the necessity of examining logical consequences—a lesson, which, you will perceive in the appendix, my friend of the defense has learned. Your own judgment convinces you, that if the system is logically liable, it cannot be taught in the word of God.

The references made to authors in quotations, has, in every instance, with few exceptions, been taken by the writer himself directly from them; and to those who cannot examine for themselves, he insures their correctness. Those charged to Piscator and Twisse are taken from Mr. Wesley; but their correctness is not questioned. I have sought, in every instance, to quote enough to give the full meaning of the author, and have never put a construction, knowingly, not intended by him. The consequences deduced, I admit, have been disclaimed; but my readers must judge whether this can be done or not. I give you the premises—you must decide upon the correctness of the deductions.

It is not presumed by the author, either that he has succeeded in finding all, or the strongest objections, bearing against the system he attempts to refute. Doubtless there are many other and stronger ones, which a better mind could have discovered, and which, with more time and leisure, the author himself might have found; but what is given will, we think, be sufficient, and we have no fear but what the candid reader will agree with us, when he shall have thoroughly perused the work. The book was prepared amid the numerous and weighty labors of a large pastoral charge, and that when ordinary duties were greatly exceeded by a season of unparalleled affliction—during the prevalence of the cholera—at a time when, from day to day and week to week, the author was ministering to many of those who were dying with that most dreaded scourge, and when his own life, as the life of all, seemed uncertain from hour to hour. This, with the fact that it never was intended for publication in volume form, will serve to palliate its defects and extenuate its faults.

The reader is now prepared to set forward with us in the discussion of the following pages. If he shall be entertained for a few brief hours, and profited in any degree in his noble pursuit of truth, we shall be more than compensated for all the toil we have bestowed in the preparation. And may God, the great Father of us all, bring both writer and reader to that world of happiness and glory, where truth shall be no more invested with shade, but appear in its own brightness, and all shall see eye to eye, and know even as we are known!

CHAPTER II.

GOD'S ETERNAL DECREES.

If the reader has not considered the previous chapter, he will do himself a service to turn back and give it a perusal, before he proceeds to read what follows.

When one man proposes to discuss the opinions of another man, or company of men, it is of first importance that he understand the opinions which he thus proposes to discuss, and, understanding them himself, that he clearly and distinctly state them to his readers. In every discussion, the first thing to be settled is the precise point in dispute; and if this be omitted, the controversy must needs degenerate into a mere idle logomachy—an unprofitable strife of words.

And it is not always sufficient that the opinions of an opponent be clearly stated—when practicable, they should be stated in precisely his own language, that the chances of misrepresentation may be as few as possible, and that the reader may see the grounds upon which the particular construction is based. This is due an opponent—it is due the reader—it is due the cause of truth.

In accordance with these views, I shall proceed at once to state the point, in Calvinian theology, to which I am about to object. And, to give the system, and its advocates, the benefit of a candid and unprejudiced statement, I shall first quote the sections of the Confession of Faith which regard it, and then the interpretations given thereto by the most eminent and accredited of its defenders. If the reference to authors shall be large, it will be that we may gain the very best possible light upon the point in question. The subject to be treated of in this chapter is "God's Eternal Decrees;" and upon this subject the Confession of Faith, chapter iii, sections i and ii, holds the following language:

"God, from all eternity, did, by the most wise and holy counsel of his own will, freely and unchangeably ordain whatsoever comes to pass; yet so as thereby neither is God the author of sin, nor is violence offered to the will of the creatures, nor is the liberty or contingency of second causes taken away, but rather established.

"Although God knows whatsoever may or can come to pass upon all supposed conditions, yet hath he not decreed any thing because he foresaw it as future, or as that which would come to pass upon such conditions."

This is the article of faith. In corroboration and exegesis of it, I read from the Larger Catechism:

"What are the decrees of God?

"God's decrees are the wise, free, and holy acts of the counsel of his will, whereby, from all eternity, he hath, for his own glory, unchangeably foreordained whatsoever comes to pass in time, especially concerning angels and men."

In the exposition of the Confession of Faith, by Rev. R. Shaw, "revised and published by the Presbyterian Board of Publication," I read, treating of the article of faith, "That God must have decreed all future things, is a conclusion which necessarily flows from his foreknowledge, independence, and immutability. The foreknowledge of God will, necessarily, infer a decree; for God could not foreknow that things would be, unless he had decreed they *should* be." (Exposition of the Confession, p. 58.)

"If God would be an independent being, all creatures must have an entire dependence upon him; but this dependence proves, undeniably, that all *their acts* must be regulated by his sovereign will." (Ib.)

"If God be of one mind, which none can change, he must have *unalterably fixed every thing* in his purpose, which he *effects* in his providence." (Ib., p. 59.)

"The decree of God relates to all *future things, without*

exceptions. Whatsoever is done in time, was foreordained before the beginning of time." (Ib., p. 59.)

"The decrees of God are absolute and unconditional: he has not decreed any thing because he foresaw it as future, and the execution of his decree is not suspended upon any condition which may or may not be performed." (Ib., p. 60.)

"Nothing can happen but what is subject to his knowledge, and *decreed by his will.*" (Calvin's Institutes, book i, chap. xiv, sec. iii.)

"If God simply foresaw the fates of men, and did not also dispose and fix them by his determination, there would be room to agitate the question, whether his providence or foresight rendered them at all necessary. But, since he foresees future events only in consequence of his decree that they shall happen, it is useless to contend about foreknowledge, while it is evident that all things come to pass, rather by ordination and decree." (Calvin's Institutes, book iii, chap. xiii, sec. vi.)

"But what reason shall we assign for his permitting it, but because it is his will? It is not probable, however, that man procured his own destruction by the mere permission, and without the appointment of God, as though God had determined what he would choose to be the condition of the principal of his creatures.

"I shall not hesitate, therefore, to confess plainly, with Augustine, that the will of God is the necessity of things, and that what he has willed will necessarily come to pass." (Calvin's Institutes, vol ii, p. 171.)

"All things, both *beings* and *events*, exist in exact accordance with the purpose, pleasure, and what is commonly called the decree of God." (Dwight's Theology.)

"The decrees of God relate to all future things, without exception. Whatsoever is done in time, was foreordained before time." (Dr. J. Dick's Theology.)

"Decrees of God are his settled purpose, whereby he foreordained whatsoever comes to pass. The opinion that whatever occurs in the world at large, or the lot of private individuals, is the result of previous and unalterable arrangement by that supreme Power which presides over nature, has always been held by many of the vulgar, and has been believed by speculative men. The ancient Stoics, Zeno and Chrysippus, whom the Jewish Essenes seem to have followed, asserted the existence of a Deity, that, acting wisely, but *necessarily*, contrived the general system of the world; from which, by a series of causes, whatever is now done in it, unavoidably results. Mohammed introduced into his Koran the doctrine of absolute predestination of the course of human affairs. He represents life and death, prosperity and adversity, and every event that befalls a man in this world, as the result of a previous determination of the one God, who rules over all. Augustine, and the whole of the earliest reformers, but *especially Calvin, favored this doctrine.*" (Buck.)

"The characteristical feature of the Calvinistic system is that entire dependence of the creature upon the Creator, which it *uniformly* asserts, by considering the will of the supreme Being as the cause of every thing that now exists or that is to exist at any future time." (Hill's Divinity.)

"The supreme Being selects those single objects and those combinations of objects which he chooses to bring into existence; and every circumstance in the manner of the existence of that which is to be, thus depending entirely on his will, is known to him, because he decreed it should be." (Hill.)

"Every action and motion of every creature is governed by the hidden counsel of God, so that nothing can come to pass, but was ordained of him.

"All things come to pass by his ordination and decree." (Calvin.)

"But, since he forsees future events only in consequence of his decree that they shall happen, it is useless to contend about foreknowledge, while it is evident that all things come to pass rather by ordination and decree." (Calvin's Institutes, vol. i, p. 170.)

"Reason and revelation are in perfect unison in assuring us, that God is the supreme, independent, first cause, of whom all secondary and inferior causes are no more than the effects." (Toplady on Predestination, p. 17.)

In this, and the following quotations from Toplady, we have also the sentiments of Zanchius, as Toplady but translates Zanchius.

"It may seem absurd to human wisdom, that God should harden, blind, and deliver up some men to a reprobate sense—that he should first deliver them over to evil, and then condemn them for that evil; but the believing, spiritual man sees no absurdity in all this, knowing that God would be never a whit less good, even though he should destroy all men." (Toplady on Predestination, p. 53.)

"Though he [God] may be said to be author of all the actions done by the wicked, yet he is not the author of them, in a moral, compound sense, as they are sinful, but physically simply, and *sensu diviso,* as they are mere actions, abstractly from all consideration of the goodness or badness of them." (Ib., p. 54.)

"Hence, we see that God does not immediately and *per se* infuse iniquity into the wicked, but powerfully excites them to action, and withholds those gracious influences of his Spirit, without which every action is necessarily evil." (Ib., p. 55.)

"Every action, as such, is undoubtedly good, it being an actual exertion of those operative powers given us by God for that very end. God may, therefore, be the author of all actions, and yet not be the author of evil." (Ib., p. 56.)

"Whatever things God wills or does, are not willed and

done by him, because they were, in their own nature, and previously to his willing them, just and right, or because, from their intrinsic fitness, he ought to will and do them; but they are, therefore, just, right, and proper, because he is holiness itself, wills and does them." (Ib., p. 63.)

"We make God the arbiter and governor of all things, who, in his own wisdom, has, from the remotest eternity, decreed what he would do, and now, by *his own power, executes* what he has decreed. Whence we assert, that not only the heavens, and the earth, and inanimate creatures, but also the deliberations and volitions of men, are so governed by his providence as to be directed to the end appointed by it." (Calvin's Institutes, vol. i, p. 191.)

"It should be considered as indubitably certain, that all the revolutions visible in the world proceed from the secret exertion of the Divine power. What God decrees must necessarily come to pass." (Ib., vol i, p. 194.)

"I admit more than this: even that thieves, homicides, and other malefactors, are instruments of Divine providence, whom the Lord uses for the execution of the judgments which he has appointed." (Ib., p. 200.)

"They consider it absurd [they whose views Calvin opposes] that a man should be blinded by the will and command of God, and afterward be punished for his blindness. They, therefore, evade the difficulty, that it happens only by the permission, and not by the will of God; but God himself, by the most unequivocal declarations, rejects this subterfuge. That men, however, can effect nothing, but by the secret will of God, and can deliberate on nothing, but what he has previously decreed, and determined by his secret direction, is proved by express and innumerable testimonies." (Ib., p. 211.)

"The whole may be summed up thus: that, as the will of God is said to be the cause of all things, his providence is established as the governor in all the counsels and works of men; so that it not only exerts its power in the elect, who are influenced by the Holy Spirit, but also *compels the compliance of the reprobates*." (Ib., p. 215.)

"God's sovereign decree is the first link, his unalterable decree the second, and his all active providence the third, in the great chain of causes. What his will determined, that his decree established, and his providence, either mediately or immediately, effects. His will was the adorable spring of all, his decree marked out the channel, and his providence directs the stream. If so, it may be objected, that whatever is, is right. Consequences cannot be helped." (Toplady on Predestination, p. 19.)

"But does not this doctrine tend to the establishment of fatality? Supposing it even did, were it not better to be a Christian fatalist, than to avow a set of loose Arminian principles, which, if pushed to their full extent, will inevitably terminate in the rankest Atheism? For without predestination there can be no providence; and without a providence, no God. After all, what do you mean by fate? If you mean a regular succession of determined events, from the beginning to the end of time—an uninterrupted chain, without a single chasm—all depending on the eternal will and continued influence of the great first cause—if this is fate, it must be owned that it and the Scripture predestination are, at most, very thinly divided, or, rather, entirely coalesce." (Ib., p. 22.)

"God's foreknowledge, taken abstractedly, is not the sole cause of beings and *events; but his will and foreknowledge together*." (Ib., p. 27.)

"Whatever comes to pass, comes to pass by virtue of the absolute, omnipotent will of God, which is the primary and supreme cause of all things." (Ib., p. 32.)

"The will of God is so the cause of all things as to be itself without cause; for nothing can be the cause of that which is the cause of every thing. So that the Divine will is the *ne plus ultra* of all our inquiries. When we ascend to that, we can go no further. Hence, we find every matter resolved, ultimately, into the mere sovereign pleasure of God, as the spring and occasion of whatsoever is done in heaven and earth. And no wonder that the will of God should be the mainspring that sets all inferior wheels in motion, and should likewise be the rule by which he goes in all his dealings with his creatures, since nothing out of God, exterior to himself, can possibly induce him to will or nill one thing rather than another." (Ib., p. 34.)

"God is a being whose will acknowledges no cause; neither is it for us to prescribe rules to his sovereign pleasure, or call him to account for what he does. He has neither superior nor equal; and his will is the rule of all things. He did not will such and such things, because they were, in themselves, right, and he was bound to will them; but, therefore, equitable and right, because he wills them." (Ib., p. 35.)

"Whatever man does he does necessarily, though not with any sensible compulsion; and that we can only do what God, from eternity, willed and foreknew we should." (Ib., p. 41.)

"That man fell in consequence of the Divine decree, we prove thus. . . . Surely, if God had not willed the fall, he could, and no doubt would, have prevented it. But he did not prevent it: *ergo*, he willed it. And if he willed it, he certainly decreed it; for the decree is nothing else but the seal and ratification of his will. He does nothing but what he decreed, and he decreed nothing which he did not will; and both will and decree are absolutely eternal, though the execution of them both be in time." (Ib., p. 84.)

"Now, it is self-evident, that if he [God] knows all things beforehand, he either doth approve of them, or he doth not approve of them; that is, he either is willing they should be, or he is not willing they should be. But to will that they should be, is to decree them.

"The Arminians ridicule the distinctions between the secret and revealed will of, or, more properly expressed, between the decree and law of God; because we say he may decree one thing and command another. However, if they will call this a contradiction of wills, we know that there is such a thing; so that it is the greatest absurdity to dispute about it. We know that God willed that Pharoah's heart should be hardened, and yet that the hardness of his heart was sin." (Edwards, vol. v, p. 25.)

"All the actions of men, even those which the Scripture holds forth to our abhorrence, are represented as being comprehended in the great plan of Divine providence. I do not mean merely that all the actions of men are foreseen by God—of this the predictions in Scripture offer evidence which even the Arminians admit to be incontrovertible—but I mean that the actions of men are foreseen by God, not as events independent of his will, but as originating in his determination, and fulfilling his purpose." (Hill, vol. v, p. 71.

Any number, almost, of similar quotations might be added to the list, but it is unnecessary: all the standard Calvinistic authors since the days of Augustine, some with greater and others with less caution, express themselves upon this point in about the same manner. We cannot say so much for their uniformity when it comes to the details of explanation and defense—here, indeed, truth constrains us to say, we find what appears to our mind great confusion, perplexity, and contradiction, arising out of the difficulties of the doctrine; and if we should be unfortunate in not precisely apprehending it, I hope it will not be ascribed to willful blindness, seeing that its friends differ so much in regard to it.

If I understand the meaning of the above quotations at all—and the language is so plain and unambiguous that it would certainly be difficult to misunderstand, particularly when taken in connection with other parts of the Calvinistic system—it may thus be summed up:

1. Whatsoever comes to pass in time was decreed unconditionally and unalterably before time.

2. Whatsoever comes to pass in time, comes to pass because it was decreed before time.

3. Nothing can be, but what was decreed; and what was decreed cannot fail to be; and it cannot fail to be, because decreed.

Having defined what we understand to be the doctrine of decrees, as held by Presbyterians—a definition derived from their own Confession of Faith, and numerous Calvinistic authors of great respectability and authority—I shall now proceed to alledge objections thereto.

And, first, I object: it renders the conclusion inevitable that God is the author of sin. I employ the term author in the sense of *originator* or cause.

Do not, I pray you, turn away from this point. I know it has been often urged. I know you have as steadily denied it. I know, indeed, that you have expressly incorporated your protest in the article of faith itself: "God, from all eternity, did, by the most wise and holy counsel of his own will, freely and unchangeably ordain whatsoever comes to pass; [and now your disclaimer,] yet so as thereby neither is God the author of sin, nor is violence offered to the will of the creature." But this disclaimer by no means relieves my embarrassment—it greatly increases it, by placing you in the attitude, to my mind, of believing a palpable contradiction, namely, that God did cause all things, sin included, yet in such a way that he did not cause sin. It is as though you should say, Lycurgus made all the laws of Sparta, yet in such a way, that there were many laws of Sparta which Lycurgus did not make. But supposing that the absurdity does not strike your mind with the same force it does mine—or of course you could not embrace it—I shall more particularly present the reasons; and perhaps you can assist me in my conclusions.

I reason thus, and the process is exceedingly brief and simple: "God decreed whatsoever comes to pass;" but sin comes to pass; therefore, God decreed sin. "What God decrees, must necessarily come to pass;" but he decreed sin; therefore, sin necessarily comes to pass. "God's decree is the necessity of things;" but sin is something; therefore, God's decree is the necessity, or necessitating cause of sin. God's decree, being from eternity, precedes all things; and whatever is in time results from God's decree, as its cause; but sin is in time; therefore, sin results from God's decree, as its cause.

Let me particularize now. The doctrine is, that God decreed, from eternity, whatsoever comes to pass in time—and that according to his own good pleasure—every particular thing, event, and act. I must insist, according to this, that he decreed the sin of every sinful man—nay, each particular sin of each particular man, and all the sins of all men, long before the human race was created; for if there be any sin which was not decreed, then something has come to pass in time which was not decreed from eternity; but then your system is in error, when it says whatsoever comes to pass in time was decreed from eternity.

Do men murder, rob, blaspheme, commit adultery, incest, idolatry? It was so decreed before they were born: they could no more avoid it than they could resist the fiat of Omnipotence, or subvert the purposes of the Almighty. Indeed, the decree to create them was connected with a decree, that when, and as certainly as, created, they should commit these sins, and their creation was in order to their sins.

Shall I be told, that, though all things come to pass by decree, yet that the decree is not the cause of their occurrence—not the efficient reason why they occur? Then I desire to know precisely what Calvinists mean by the terms, decree, predestinate, foreordain—whether any thing can, or could possibly come to pass without being decreed—whether, after being decreed, any thing can fail to come to pass—whether decree proceeds upon foreknowledge that certain things will come to pass, and are, therefore, decreed simply as certain because foreknown—whether, in a word, there is any connection between God's decree and the thing decreed, and what that connection is. I understand, from the most respectable Calvinistic authorities, already quoted, that the decree of God, and the event decreed, stand related as cause and effect—that the event necessarily answers the decree—that the whole universe, indeed, including all beings, events, and acts, arises out of the decree or predetermination of God. This being the case, it will be perceived, inevitably, by the simplest process of reasoning, that sin results, as an effect, from the Divine decree, as its cause.

Shall I be told, that, though God, by his decree, is the cause of sinful acts, yet he causes not the sin of the act? This seems to be the view of the expositor of the Confession. He says, "The decree of God is either effective or permissive." He does not tell us in what sense he employs the term permissive—a point I should like to have explained—but he proceeds to tell what his permissive decree respects. "His effective decree respects all the good that comes to pass—his permissive decree all *the evil that is in* sinful actions." Now observe: "We must distinguish between actions purely as such, and the sinfulness of the actions. The decree of God is effective (causal) with respect to the action itself, abstractly considered; it is permissive with respect to the sinfulness of the act as a moral evil." The same sentiment I find in various other authors; and, indeed, I find it a common and favorite mode of explanation. It is thus stated by Hermin Witsius, a learned German, in an elaborate defense of his favorite tenets: "As these things are universally true, they may be applied to those free actions of rational creatures in which there is a moral evil inherent, namely, *that creatures may be determined to their actions by the efficacious influence of God, so far as they are actions according to their physical entity.*" (The various quotations from Witsius are, with few exceptions, from book i, chap. viii, sec. xii, to the end.) What am I to understand by all this? There is a discrimination between the sinful act and the sin of the act. This is correct: an act and its sinfulness are certainly distinct. Sin resides in the intention, not in the act. A man ruins his friend, or murders his father: the question of his guilt turns upon his intention. Well, then, is this the meaning of our Calvinistic brethren, that, though God's decree is the efficient cause of the sinful act, as an act, it is not the cause of its sin? for the sin is in the sinner's intention in committing it. But, then, a question arises right here, Was not the sinner's intention decreed, also, as well as the act? If you answer no, then here is something which comes to pass in time which was not decreed before time. If you answer yes, and the sin was in the intention, then God, who was the author of the intention, was the author of the sin; for the sin and the intention are the same.

Again: did not God decree that certain acts, if committed with certain intentions, should be sinful? but did he not, also, decree that those very acts and intentions should exist? If so, is he not the author of the sin, both with respect to the act and intention? If not, is not here something coming to pass in time which was not decreed before time? There may be some way of escape from this difficulty: I cannot myself perceive it, and must wait patiently for further light.

And again: is not intention an essential part of a moral act? Can there be a moral act without intention, as an element of it? if not, then God did not decree moral acts, or he decreed the intention, with all else that constitutes them moral acts. If he did not decree all moral acts, then here is a class of acts which he did not decree; and so your doctrine is in error, when it asserts that he decreed all things. But if he did decree all moral acts, then he decreed all sins, without exception, and as sins, essentially with all that constitutes their sin—the sin itself.

Still again: am I told that God is not the author of sin, because he cannot sin—he is under no law, and, therefore, he cannot transgress? Is this the idea? I believe some learned Calvinists take this course to escape the difficulty. If this means any thing, it must mean to discriminate between God's proper, personal acts, and those acts which he causes other beings to put forth. In regard to the first, it is not pretended that God breaks the law personally, by himself personally transgressing it; but this is meant, God is the author of sin in this sense: 1. He makes a law, the transgression of which is sin. 2. He places creatures under the law. 3. He impels them to those acts of transgression which are sinful. Thus he causes sin, by causing his creatures to transgress the law under which they were placed. The act of transgression, in this case, is God's own proper, though not personal, act; and if there be any sin, he is not only the author of the sin, but the sinner himself. This is so palpable I hesitate to dwell upon it, lest it might seem an imputation upon the good sense of my readers.

Will you be so kind, then, dear sir, as to tell me how you escape the conclusion to which I am thus impelled—that God is, in the true and proper sense, the author of sin?

All Calvinistic authors, with whose writings I am conversant, perceive and admit the liability of their scheme to this objection, and do their utmost to escape it; and, I will add, they certainly display great genius and skill, in contending with the difficulty, and do as much to make error seem like the truth as the most gifted intellects can do.

The argument may be summed up thus: Whatsoever comes to pass in time, was unconditionally and unalterably decreed before time. But sin comes to pass in time; therefore, sin was unconditionally—and of course purely of the pleasure of God, and for its own sake—and unalterably decreed before time. God's decrees are the cause of all things that come to pass in time; but sin comes to pass in time; therefore, God's decrees are the cause of sin.

What results from a decree as a necessary sequence, results from the author of the decree; but sin results from the decree of God as a necessary sequence; therefore, sin results from himself.

According to this dogma, no man ever did or ever can do any thing, but what it was ordained he should do from eternity; to avoid which is as impossible as to overthrow the decree of God, and which, if possible, would be rebellion against God, punishable with death. When I sin, I am instrumentally doing what God chose should be done before I was born; the thing I do was his choice, and he made me for no other purpose but to accomplish it—decreed it for me, and me for it.

From the foregoing argument I can conceive of no escape, unless it be by one of the following method:

1. A denial of the premise, "God decrees whatsoever comes to pass." Will Dr. Rice deny?

2. A denial that God's decree necessarily procures the thing decreed. Will Dr. Rice deny?

3. A denial that God is author of that which is solely procured by his decree. Will Dr. Rice deny?

For it is undeniable; no skill can escape the conclusion. If whatever comes to pass was decreed beforehand, and if this preceding decree was the sole necessitating cause of things so decreed, then the author of the decree is the author of all things included therein; and as all things that occur in time are included in the decree, and caused by it, so sin, which occurs in time, was included in, and caused by, the decree. It is by a process of reasoning of the foregoing description, that we are impelled to the conclusion, that the Calvinistic system renders God the author of sin. If we have misunderstood the system, will the Doctor point out in what particular? If our reasoning is illogical or unfair, will he show us in what respect?

I am only conscious of a desire to ascertain the truth, and would not, if I could, resort to unfairness, to criminate the system I oppose. And if I were capable of so unchristian a disposition, I certainly could not do it successfully, observed as I am. May the great Head of the Church himself give us light, and lead us into the unity of the faith, and the truth, as it is in Jesus!

2. I object to the doctrine of decrees, as held by Calvinists, in the second place, because it is inconsistent with, and destructive to the free agency of man.

The opposers of Messrs. Wesley and Fletcher violently assailed them on this subject. Mr. Southey informs us, in his Life of Wesley, that the Calvinists called the doctrine of free will "a cursed doctrine"—"the most God-dishonoring and soul-destroying doctrine"—"one of the prominent features of the beast"—"the enemy of God"—"the offspring of the wicked one"—"the insolent brat of hell."

But if they had nowhere admitted it, but in all cases strongly denied it, as I suppose you do, still the difficulty would remain; for it grows out of your doctrines inevitably, and is in no sense affected by your admissions or denials. It is to no purpose that you tell me, "God, from eternity, unconditionally and unalterably decreed whatsoever comes to pass, yet so as thereby violence is not offered to the will of the creature," because this again strikes my mind only in the light of a contradiction. It is as though you told me God determined what each distinct volition should necessarily be, yet in such a sense that any volition might have been different from what it is—it is necessarily what it is—it is not necessarily what it is.

But, not to consume your time with what may be considered my own representations of your views upon this point, let me refer to authorities, high in your esteem, and of unquestionable information.

"Neither does God only excite and predetermine the will of men to vicious actions, so far as they are actions, *but he likewise so excites it, that it is not possible but, thus acted upon, it shall act.*" (Witsius.)

"Moreover, as a second cause cannot act, unless acted upon, and previously moved to act, by the predetermining influence of the first, so, in like manner, that influence of the first cause is so efficacious, as that, supposing it, the second cause cannot but act." (Witsius.)

It would certainly be very inexcusable to misunderstand these quotations, so clearly and definitely expressed as they are; and scarcely less inexcusable not to admire the sturdy candor of their learned author in so plainly delivering himself upon such a point.

Second causes, among which he reckons the human will, cannot act, unless, and only as acted upon—when acted upon they must act. This was saying much; but, to let us know that he was fully apprised of the consequences, he goes still further. Not only does God excite the will of men to vicious actions, but, thus excited, it is not possible it shall fail to act—it is under inexorable necessity.

In the Old and New Divinity Compared, I read, "For if God does not possess such absolute control over his creatures, that he can govern them according to his pleasure, how could he have decreed any thing unconditionally concerning them, since it might happen, that, in the exercise of their free agency, they would act contrary to the Divine purpose?"

If this paragraph means any thing, it plainly means that unconditional decrees and free agency are irreconcilable; and as all things are unconditionally decreed, according to the system, there can, of course, be no free agency.

In the trial of Dr. Beecher, Dr. Beecher accuses Dr. Wilson as follows: "Dr. Wilson has made a distinct avowal that free agency and moral obligation to obey law, do not *include any ability of any kind.*" To which Dr. Wilson replied directly in so many words, "With respect to fallen man I do!" "Now," says Dr. Wilson, "let us look at the doctrine of the Confession with this principle in view, that the *state of the man determines the will. The will is always at liberty: choice is an effect always, and not a cause!* It is always produced freely. There is no such thing as bound will. Hence, all do what is good or evil voluntarily, in view of *a motive,* and according to the state of mind in which they are. Take man in a state of innocence. God made him upright; in his own image; his choice is free, and he chooses what is right; but not *from any power in the will.* The will, as I have said, has no power to operate on any thing but the body. His uprightness was in the right state of the affections, and the luminous state of the understanding—in the correct state of the memory, and in his entire moral rectitude in the divine image. *His will was free to do good while no temptation was presented to it.* He had no motive but his accountableness to God, and his love to God. His will operated according to the state of the man. But now look at him in another state—the state of temptation. Motives are now presented to him by the arch tempter, but not to his will at all; they are presented to his understanding and appetites—to his taste for beauty. The fruit is pleasant to the eye; and what was the effect?

The will was not trapped in any other way than this: the temptation addressed to these powers was so strong, that it overcame the dictates of judgment, and the man chose wrong. Volition moves the body: the mind moves the will; and the mind is moved by that without, which is adapted to its constitution." Now who moved that without, and made the constitution?

The foregoing is the language of Dr. Wilson, who, for forty years, occupied the First Presbyterian Church in this city, and during his long life a prominent man in the Church of the west: certainly, for ability and opportunity, inferior to none of his school, and therefore as reliable an exponent as any other. But now observe his honest and candid admission, on an occasion when, of all others, he would be most accurate, and on a point where he would be most critically prepared: "Free agency and moral obligation to obey law, [with respect to fallen man,] do not *include any ability of any kind!*" According to this, free agency, as held by Calvinists, does not include ability of any kind. A man is a free agent, though he have no power at all! He is also responsible to obey law, though he have no ability of *any kind* to do so!

But he more fully unfolds his view, as above, and no one can read the quotation, it seems to me, without sympathizing with the sincere and able author, in the manifest confusion and self-contradictions in which he involves himself. "The will is always at liberty;" yet its choice is always caused by a foreign agent! "When the mind chooses it always chooses freely;" yet it has no kind of ability whatever, but is ruled by the motives in every case! "There is no such thing as bound will;" but it is always an effect, and not a cause! Observe, further, his philosophy of the will, Dr. Wilson carries back beyond or behind the fall. Of man, in innocence, he says, "His will was *free to do good while no temptation was presented to it;*"

but what is implied in this? When temptation came, the will was not free to do good, but bound to do evil, or to yield! This, indeed, he does not leave us to infer, but expressly states that the temptation presented to the first pair was such that it overcame, by its strength, the mind—"the mind moves the will, and was itself moved by that without;" and thus man fell under the force of a temptation, which he had no power to resist. He fell, therefore, when, under the circumstances, he had no power to stand! And yet he was free in doing what he had no power to avoid!

1. The expositor of the Confession, in his notes on the article respecting the will, holds this language: "According to Calvinists, the liberty of a moral agent consists in the power of acting according to his choice; and those actions are free which are performed without external compulsion—physical compulsion—in consequence of the determination of his own mind. The necessity of man's willing and acting, according to his apprehension and disposition, is, in their opinion, fully consistent with the highest liberty which can belong to a rational nature. . . . As nothing can ever come to pass without a cause, the acts of the will are never without necessity—understanding, by necessity, an infallible connection with something foregoing." This I understand to be the doctrine of all Calvinists respecting the will of man, as well before as since the fall; it is often expressed in stronger language.

Now, this view of the will utterly discards this idea of liberty—power to choose either of two alternatives. Here is the real point of difference between us and them: with them liberty is necessity to choose one way according to the motive, but not power to make an opposite choice: with us it is a power to choose either of the various alternatives presented to the mind. Now, upon their doctrine of the will, I base an argument that its decisions are necessitated, and not free; and, hence, that it is absurd for a Calvinist to contend for freedom. Take a man in a state of innocence—for we desire to give the advocates of the system the most favorable opportunity to defend themselves—the question is, Was man capacitated with freedom to stand or fall, in the circumstances? And, according to the Calvinian system, the answer must be, he was not; for he was so constituted that he must yield to the prevailing disposition or strongest motive. He could not avoid this—it was his nature. He had no control of these motives, and when they came upon him he as necessarily was moved by them, as the needle is moved to the pole; it matters not that he chose to move with the influence; for the want of liberty and the fact of necessity were found in the circumstance, that he had no control of his choice: he made his choice necessarily.

Now, I ask Dr. Rice, what does control the choice? He must answer, whatever goes to constitute the prevailing motive. But then I ask, who controls and governs these motives? And he must answer, that all things are arranged and governed by God himself: God controls the motives: the motives control the man. He sins, necessitated by the motive. And, now, where do we find the first cause? Not in the choice; for it was an effect: not in the motives; for they were under the government and control of God. Here, then, we trace the operations of man's will back to God: not as permitted, but procured. If the Calvinists can trace it beyond God, they may free their system from making God the first cause of sin!

Thomas Aquinas, quoted with approval by Witsius, says, "It is essential to the first principle, that it can act without the assistance and influence of a prior agent; so that, if the human will could produce any action, of which God was not author, the human will would have the nature of a first principle. . . . Nor does God only concur with the actions of second causes, when they act, but, also, influences the causes themselves to act."

"Calvinists contend that, as nothing can ever come to pass without a cause, the acts of the will are never contingent, or *without necessity*—understanding, by necessity, a necessity of consequence, or an infallible connection with something foregoing." (Expositor of the Confession.)

This is plain language. The will never acts but as necessitated by a foregoing cause, infallibly producing the act. That foregoing cause was decreed by the divine Being, to produce that precise volition; and it produced it with all the certainty of a necessary effect. That is, the will is free to act in agreement with the irresistible bias of a necessitating cause.

This is the same scheme, if I understand them, taught by Mr. Edwards, and his numerous admirers, in their fruitless effort to reconcile freedom and necessity. "The plain and obvious meaning of the words, freedom and liberty," says Edwards, "is power, opportunity, or advantage, that any one has to do as he pleases." But he also teaches us that the volition is necessary—his will or particular choice, whatever it may be, is necessarily determined by motive, and the motive is fixed by decree; so that, though a man do as he pleases, he is not free, because he cannot please to do otherwise, and by necessity, as stern as the most absolute compulsion, chooses as he does. "This doctrine is identical with fatalism, in its worst form. All that fatalism ever has maintained, or now maintains, is, that men, by a power which they cannot control or resist, are placed in circumstances in which they cannot but pursue the course of conduct which they actually are pursuing. This doctrine never has assumed that in the necessitarian sense men cannot do as they please. All that it maintains is, that they cannot but please to do as they do."

"It is altogether futile, then, to talk about free agency

under such a constitution; the very spring of motion to the whole intellectual machinery, is under the influence of a secret, invincible power; and it must move as that power directs, for it is the hand of Omnipotence that urges it on. He can act as he wills, it is true; but the whole responsibility consists in the volition, and this is the result of God's propelling power. He wills as he is made to will. He chooses as he must choose; for the immutable decree of Jehovah is upon him. And can a man, upon the known principles of responsibility, be accountable for such a volition? It is argued, I know, that man is responsible because he feels that he acts freely, and that he might have done otherwise. To this I reply, that this is a good argument, on our principle, to prove that men are free; but on the Calvinistic ground, it only proves that God hath deceived us. He has made us feel that we might do otherwise, but *he knows* we cannot—he has *determined* we *shall* not; so that, in fact, this argument makes the system more objectionable. While it does not change the fact in the case, it attributes deception to the Almighty. It is logically true, therefore, from this doctrine, that man is not a free agent, and therefore not responsible." "A man chooses what appears to be good," says Mr. Dick, "and he chooses it necessarily, in this sense, that he could not do otherwise. The object of every volition is to please himself; and to suppose a man to have any other object, that is, to will any thing that does not please him in itself, or in its circumstances, is absurd: it is to suppose him to will and not to will, at the same time. He is *perfectly voluntary in his choice; but his willingness is the consequence of the view which his mind takes of the object presented to it, or of his prevailing disposition.*

"Those actions are free which are the effect of volition. In whatever manner the state of mind which gave rise to the volition has been produced, the liberty of the agent is neither greater nor less. It is the will alone which is to be considered, and not the means by which it has been determined. If God foreordained certain actions, and placed men in such circumstances that the actions would certainly take place, agreeably to the laws of the mind, men are, nevertheless, moral agents, because they act voluntarily, and are responsible for the actions which consent has made their own. *Liberty does not consist in the power of acting or not acting,* but in acting from choice. The choice is determined by something in the mind itself, or by something external influencing the mind; but whatever is the cause, the choice makes the action free, and the agent accountable. If this definition of liberty be admitted, you will perceive that it is possible to reconcile the freedom of the will with absolute decrees; but we have not got rid of every difficulty. *By this theory, human actions appear to be as necessary as the motions of matter, according to the laws of gravitation and attraction: and man seems to be a machine, conscious of his movements, and consenting to them, but impelled by something different from himself.*"

This is the deplorable conclusion to which Mr. Dick himself comes. And his only effort to extricate himself is this: "Upon such a subject no man should be ashamed to acknowledge his ignorance." Several things are remarkable in this paragraph. 1. Liberty and necessity are the same thing. 2. Man is accountable for his actions, though he is a machine, and is under a necessity, as that of matter to obey gravitation. The honesty of the reasoner must be admired, while his sophistry is a matter of marvel.

Of the same import is the following, which I quote from an author admired more than any other, perhaps, at the present time—Dr. Chalmers: "Every step of every individual character receives as determinate a character from the hand of God, as every mile of a planet's orbit, or every gust of wind, or every wave of the sea, or every particle of flying dust, or every rivulet of flowing water. This power of God knows no exceptions; it is absolute and unlimited. And while it embraces the vast, it carries its resistless influences to all the minute and unnoticed diversities of existence. It reigns and operates through all the secrecies of the inner man. It *gives birth to every purpose;* it gives impulse to every desire; it gives shape and color to every conception; it wields an entire ascendency over every attribute of the mind: and the will, and the fancy, and the understanding, with all the countless variety of their hidden and fugitive operations, are submitted to it. It gives movement and direction through every point of our pilgrimage. At no moment of time does it abandon us. It follows us to the hour of death, and it carries us to our place, and to our everlasting destiny in the regions beyond it!"

I confess I cannot conceive of a stronger assertion of fatalism, with respect to man and things, than is contained in the foregoing remarkable quotations. All mental and physical processes, from the first link to the end of the chain, are connected together in the relation of cause and effect.

No man can choose differently from what he does; and as he acts from his volitions, he cannot act differently from what he does—it is all fixed by inexorable necessity. Is such a being free? Is this the liberty of man? If this be moderate Calvinism, what must it be in the ultra, high-toned type?

If any thing further should be esteemed necessary upon this point, a few selections from Dr. Emmons, a distinguished divine of New England, and author of an elaborate work on theology, may supply the demand. He says, "Since the Scriptures ascribe all the actions of men to God, as well as to themselves, we may justly conclude that *the Divine agency is as much concerned in their bad as their good actions.* Many are disposed to make a distinction here, and to ascribe only the good actions of men to the Divine agency, while they ascribe their bad ones to the Divine permission. But there appears no ground for this distinction in Scripture or reason. Men are no more capable of acting independently of God, in one instance, than another. If they need any kind or degree of Divine agency in doing good, they need precisely the same kind and degree of Divine agency in doing evil.

"But there was no possible way in which he could dispose them to act right or wrong, but only by producing right or wrong volitions in their hearts. And if he produced their bad as well as good volitions, then his agency was concerned in precisely the same manner in their wrong as in their right actions. His agency in making them act, necessarily connects his agency and theirs together, and lays a solid foundation for ascribing their actions either to him or them, or to both.

"But, since *mind* cannot act any more than *matter* can move, without a Divine agency, it is absurd to suppose that men can be left to the freedom of their own will, to act or not to act, independently of Divine influence. There must, therefore, be the exercise of Divine agency in every human action.

"By this invisible agency upon the minds, he governs all their views, all their thoughts, all their determinations, and all their volitions, just as he pleases, and just according to his *secret* will, which they neither know beforehand, nor can resist, evade, or frustrate."

Thus we prove upon the system both that it makes God the author of sin, and destroys the free agency of man.

These quotations show what Calvinists themselves teach upon the subject in dispute. They are not our deductions, but their own propositions—not our misrepresentations of their views, but their own carefully-studied and well-considered declarations. They are precisely the inferences we should have made from the premise work of their system; but they have saved us the trouble and responsibility, by candidly acknowledging themselves.

And now the argument stands thus: Man can only will as he is moved by Divine agency; and when moved by Divine agency he cannot but will; so, therefore, when man wills it is not a free, but a necessitated act. What a man wills he wills not freely, but he wills because another, by invisible power, irresistibly compels him to will. It is not his own act, but it is an act of which he is made the passive subject, by another operating through him, and a power entirely separate from himself.

He chooses as he does—as necessarily as matter yields to the law of gravitation—and he is no more free in his choice than the earth is in its revolutions. The choice he makes is no more his free act, than the tendency of the needle to the pole is its free act. It makes no difference that choice is supposed in one case and not in the other, because choice is an effect of a cause entirely out of the man, and independent of him, and so, of course, cannot be his act.

Doctor, I wish you would help me here. My difficulty, as you will perceive, is at this point, to know how a man is free in willing, when at the same time his particular exercise of will is an effect of which he is the coerced instrument. Will you tell me how this is?

3. I object to the doctrine, in the third place, because it destroys the accountability of man.

This proposition is so nearly identical with the former, if not entirely so, that it only requires to be stated. Freedom and liberty, I believe all admit, are essential to accountability; and hence the well-grounded apprehension of our Calvinistic brethren, at the imputation, that their doctrine is destructive to freedom of agency.

"To conceive of beings deserving praise or blame," says Dr. Fisk, "for volitions or actions, which occurred under circumstances over which they had no control, and under which no other volitions or actions were possible, and in which these could not but happen, is an absolute impossibility. To conceive them under obligation to have given existence, under such circumstances, to different consequents, is equally impossible. It is to suppose an agent under obligation to perform an absolute and intrinsic impossibility. Let any individual conceive of beings placed by divine Providence in circumstances in which but one act, or series of acts of will, can arise, and these cannot but arise—let him then attempt to conceive of these creatures as under obligations, in the same circumstances over which they have no control, to give existence to different and opposite acts, and as deserving of punishment for not doing so. He will find it impossible to pass such a judgment—human intelligence is incapable of affirming such contradictions."

Thus, by sapping the foundations of free agency, it, at the same time, destroys human accountability, releases man from all obligation, and renders God the only responsible being in the universe.

I would not press illegitimate results upon your system, to give you the trouble of examining, and the unpleasant task of refuting and correcting them; but these, which I present, strike me as so plain and inevitable, and of such force, that you must excuse me for urging them upon your notice. This point—how am I to escape it?

You tell me, that whatever I do, during my whole existence, comes to pass by a decree of God—which decree is the necessitating cause of things. Now, a question here: Am I accountable for doing what, by decree, I am compelled to do? or is the author of the decree accountable? that is, is the agent or instrument responsible? It will not do, Doctor, to tell me, that, though the decree must be complied with, yet that I comply freely, inasmuch as I, of choice, do the thing decreed; because you have told me before, that my choice is, also, wrought in me, directly or indirectly, by the same great Being whose decree binds me—I am not the author of the choice, but the passive instrument of it. Am I accountable when I do nothing but what I am caused to do, by omnipotent agency exerted upon me?

Do I sin against God when I make the very choice which he works in me? when I do the act which that choice dictates? And, when I could not have made another choice, or performed another act, to save the universe, must I be damned for ever, for doing a thing I could not help but do? and must I thus be damned by the very being who made me, and necessitated the act for which he thus destroys me? I desire a plain answer upon these points? You cannot fail to perceive where my difficulties lie, with respect to your system; and you can easily show, either how they do not bear on the system, or how I may escape the inference, or that the inference is not objectionable.

If Dr. Rice denies that God decreed the existence of sin, then he abandons and denies his Confession, which declares that "God, from all eternity, did, by the most wise and holy counsel of his own free will, freely and unchangeably ordain whatsoever comes to pass." If he denies that the decree is the efficient cause of the thing decreed, he antagonizes various authors, quoted in the commencement of this chapter, and particularly Calvin, who says, with Augustine, "The decree of God is the necessity, or necessitating cause, of things;" and, in that case, we hope the Doctor will explain to us what he means by decree—what relation it has to the thing decreed. For the arguments sustaining this objection against the Calvinistic system, I refer Dr. Rice to my preceding remarks, to which I desire him to give a careful consideration, and then, to point out to me wherein they fail to sustain the conclusion. He admits, equally with myself, if the objection is made good, his system is false; for he alledges precisely the same objection against another system as an insuperable difficulty—as an entirely sufficient reason for discarding it as utterly false. Now, either he and I are at fault, in employing the objection against Universalism, or, if sustained against Dr. Rice's system, he is equally bound, with myself, to discard the system so embarrassed; and if not sustained, he will, by so much as he loves truth and deprecates error, point out in what respect it fails.

It will not answer to tell me these things have been often explained, nor yet to deny, or refer to antagonistic professions and disclaimers—the thing we demand, is to have it pointed out how the system can escape the logical consequences we have produced against it. If our logic is good, the system is bad; if the system is good, our logic is bad. It is a plain point—will the Doctor make his election?

Dr. Rice alledges, as an objection to Universalism, that its advocates "are forced to deny the free agency of man, and to maintain that all his actions are necessary." In proof that this is the case, he quotes from Mr. Ballou, "Man is dependent in all his volitions, and moved by necessity." This he esteems a sufficient objection against Universalism, and I agree with him. But I charge Calvinism with including precisely the same doctrine, and refer, for the proof of this charge, to the evidence already adduced. Will Dr. Rice extricate his system?

This same objection he urges against phrenology, in his work upon that subject. He says this system "denies his [man's] free, moral agency, and makes him alike incapable of virtue or vice." This objection is argued at length, and insisted upon as an insuperable difficulty. He is right. But I charge precisely the same difficulty upon his system—

both that it "denies free, moral agency," and destroys the distinction between "vice and virtue." He says of man, in the light of this system, "He is under a physical necessity to act in accordance with the promptings of his cerebral organization, and is incapable of either virtue or vice." Now I charge his system with placing man under a necessity, as stern as that which phrenology teaches; and, consequently, as certainly destroying both his agency and accountability. I have been astonished to find that free agency is a favorite doctrine with Dr. Rice; and I now ask him to reconcile it with his system; and if it cannot be done, admit either that he believes a palpable contradiction, or set aside his system or this doctrine.

4. By destroying the agency and accountability of man, I charge the system further, with destroying the moral character of human acts and volitions—with rendering the terms, vice and virtue, good and bad, as conveying the idea of moral quality—not predicable of man. If the system be true, man is no more a moral being. Do what he may, he is not vicious—he is incapable to be virtuous. He never sins—he cannot; nor the opposite.

This is so plain to my own mind, that I do not see how it can escape your observation. To argue it, would almost be a reflection upon my readers. It would be to attempt to produce conviction, by argument, of a truth, which I firmly believe no human mind can deny, namely, that a person cannot be worthy of praise or blame, for an act over which he has not, and never had, any control whatever. Now, sir, I do not believe that any human intelligence can affirm such a proposition. Morality supposes agency—the system, by inevitable deduction, denies it; and the two fall together. A greater absurdity can scarcely be imagined, than to affirm a man to be virtuous for an act, the choice and performance of which were coerced upon him—the contrary of which he could not have performed, any more than he could usurp the place of the Almighty, and the thing itself he performed only as a passive instrument, operated upon and compelled by Omnipotence. Vice and virtue, which can only be predicated of the free original cause, cannot be affirmed of man; but all vice and all virtue, if there be any such thing, according to the system, have God as their centre, or that fate, which the system, as we shall show in due time, more than intimates, is above Jehovah.

I find, in casting my eye over Dr. Rice's discussion with Mr. Pingree, several things bearing directly on the points to which I have invited his attention.

His fifth article against Universalism is, "That it makes God the author, or cause, of all the sin in the world." He alledges this is a sufficient reason for discarding the system. In this I perfectly agree with him. I also admit that he sustains the objection with unanswerable arguments against Universalism. But now I object precisely the same thing to Dr. Rice's system. I think I have sustained the objection with unanswerable arguments. Will the Doctor show me wherein, if at all, my argument is at fault? And, if not at fault, will he show why he allows the objection to be of sufficient force to set aside one system, and not another equally involved?

The proof he adduces, that Universalism renders God the author of sin, is thus stated: "Universalism maintains that sin proceeds from physical causes, inherent in the human constitution, as it came from the hand of God." This Dr. Rice denounces "a revolting and blasphemous doctrine." But why so? Why revolting and blasphemous? Simply, because it renders God the author of sin; in this sense, that sin proceeds from physical causes, inherent in the human constitution, which constitution God made.

Now, I ask Dr. Rice, does not he maintain that God as

absolutely created or caused sin as the system he discards? That system attributes the authorship of sin to God, by asserting that sin inheres in the nature of man; and God created the nature, and so caused sin.

Dr. Rice maintains that God actually decreed the existence of sin, and that his decree was the cause of its existence; so much so, that it could not but be, being decreed, and could not have been without being decreed.

Dr. Rice says, "One of the clearest truths in mental philosophy is, that man is a free, moral agent, and, therefore, an accountable being. It is a truth to which the consciousness of every individual bears testimony the most unequivocal." With this sentiment I fully accord; but I charge upon Dr. Rice that he has embraced a system which denies this clearest and most important of truths, to which human consiousness bears unequivocal testimony; and my reasons for so charging his system have been heretofore presented, (pages 36–48.) Will he show me how to escape the force of these reasons?

I beg the Doctor to believe me sincere, in asking for light upon these points. I find him discarding two systems of opinions, for the reasons that they make God the author of sin, and that they are inconsistent with the free agency and accountability of man. These he esteems sufficient reason for rejecting; so do I. But now I find that he, after all, embraces a system, which I firmly believe is beset with the same difficulties: my reasons for this belief are already given. If I am right in my view of his system, he is guilty of inexcusable inconsistency; if I am wrong, in error, my reasonings are incorrect. And now I ask the Doctor to set me right.

5. "I object further: if this doctrine be true, at the final judgment the conscience and intelligence of the universe will and must be on the side of the condemned.

"Suppose that, when the conduct of the wicked shall

be revealed in that day, another fact shall stand out with equal conspicuousness, namely, that God himself hath placed these beings where but one course of conduct was possible to them, and that course they could not but pursue; and that, for having pursued this course—the only one possible—they are now to be punished with everlasting destruction, from the presence of God and the glory of his power, must not the intelligence of the universe pronounce such sentence unjust?" Heaven and hell would equally revolt at it, and all rational beings conspire to execrate the almighty monster capable of such a procedure. Convince the universe that such is the character, and will ultimately be the conduct of God, and he can no more be worshiped, but with hypocrisy, or even contemplated, but with dread, detestation, and abhorrence. I appeal to the consciousness of man—to the philosophy of our nature—to all known processes of thought and feeling—if such would not necessarily be the verdict of humanity. They that enter into heaven, and they that depart to hell, from a judgment-seat where such a principle determines destiny, must go bearing the same sentiment—the same feeling of disgust and horror of the gigantic tyranny ruling over them. Hell would be a refuge from the presence of such a being—its woes a respite from the deeper alarms of his hated and dreaded intercourse.

In the name of Christianity, I protest against a principle involving such blasphemy. It is impossible that the ever-blessed God should be remotely liable, by any thing he has done—by any thing discoverable in his works—by any revelations he has made, either of his character or plans, to such an imputation. Thou glorious Ruler of the universe, what blasphemy of thy blessed name can equal this for enormity—to charge that, for the glory of thy sovereignty, and to manifest thy power, thou art now damning millions of helpless creatures in hell for ever, for no cause, but doing precisely what thou didst compel them to do, and what they could not possibly avoid!

6. Nay, more: I charge the doctrine, not only with putting a plea in the sinner's mouth, at the day of judgment, but, also, with furnishing him with a plea, when he is brought before earthly courts, to answer for his crimes. These, indeed—earthly courts—if Calvinism is true, are only lesser parts of the stupendous economy of tyranny. What justice is there in any power on earth—what right, to try, condemn, and punish men, for any of their acts, if they could not, by any possibility, avoid them—if they were impelled thereto by almighty fate? You do not condemn the gun for shooting the man—the avalanche for burying the city—the falling tree for crushing the traveler; but, according to Calvinism, in Mr. Dick's own language, man is as merely passive in the hands of overruling power. Why punish him for murder, for arson, or any grade of crime? He is the author of no choice—the sovereign of no act; he is but the instrument of an invisible agent—moving as moved upon, without power of resistance. He is the original in no movement of his life, from the cradle to the grave. Why, in the name of humanity, punish him?

7. I object to the system further, as involving, by inevitable consequence, a most dreadful aspersion of the character of God. It gives me no pleasure to prefer such a charge as this against a system, many of whose advocates I dearly love and greatly admire; and, I will say, much less does it give me pleasure to find so much evidence that the charge is well founded. But I do so, Doctor, that you may see how other minds view your system, and that you may disabuse them, if in error.

(1.) The system holds, as I think has been clearly shown, that God is the sole, original, voluntary author of sin—that he chose its existence when as yet it did not exist, and decreed it when, but for his decree, it never could have been—thus declaring that he preferred some sin to universal holiness, if, indeed, his own decree was his choice—thus insulting the purity and holiness of God—making him, not, indeed, the most holy, but the only unholy being in the universe—the cause and source of all impurity, as he is the cause of all creatures.

(2.) It asperses the goodness and benevolence of God, and invests him with all the attributes of sheer cruelty and maliciousness; because it holds that he made the universe as it is, and, for his own pleasure and glory, plunged it himself into all the miseries, temporal and eternal, which it endures, or is to endure. It will not do to tell me, that these miseries are the just punishments of sins, for you told me he caused the sins; and if he caused them, and damns the universe for them, it renders the cruelty more revolting.

(3.) It asperses the justice of God; for it tells me, that God will destroy many of his creatures in hell for ever, with unimaginable torments, for not performing absolute impossibilities, and for doing acts which were utterly unavoidable—acts which he himself caused. What would be the difference between consigning innumerable beings into hell for ever, who had never put forth a wrong volition, or performed a wrong action, and making them, by Omnipotent agency, first perpetrate these wrongs, and then, upon this pretense, damn them, as supposed in the former case? Can this be just?

(4.) The system asperses the truthfulness and sincerity of God—making him to pretend to be of one mind, when he is precisely of an opposite—clothing him with all the lothsome proofs of trickery, and hypocrisy, and duplicity, for the purpose of deceiving his hapless creatures as to his own character, and the reasons of his conduct in respect to them. It arrays his secret and his revealed will in unavoidable and open conflict—the one in unmitigated opposition to the other. He commands one thing, and wills precisely another—enjoins upon certain creatures to do those things, which he not only knows they cannot do, but, also, what he does not will they should do—nay, what he wills they should not do. It puts in his mouth the language, "I have no pleasure in the death of him that dieth," when, in fact, they die for his pleasure—makes him to plead and remonstrate with them, as if he would dissuade them from their sin and ruin, when, in fact, he is the very being who urges them irresistibly on to sin and ruin. He commands one thing and decrees precisely the contrary. He commands the sinner to repent, but decrees he shall not. Well, now, when he commands the sinner to repent, either he wills that the sinner should obey and repent, or he does not—if he does not, then he commands the sinner to do what he does not will he should, or he commands him to violate his will; which command, if the sinner were to obey, he would damn him for ever for violating his will, but, if he does not obey, he will damn him for ever for violating his command. But, again: if the command indicates the will of God, so, also, does the decree, or it does not—if it does not, then God has decreed, or purposed, or willed, that that should come to pass, which he did not will should come to pass. But, if his decree is his will, and his command is his will, and these are opposite the one to the other, then God has two opposing wills, or a will in opposition to itself. His will is always done; and why, then, does he punish one and damn another, when both alike and equally accomplished his will? What havoc such a theory makes with the character and government of God!

Is this so? "Is God at war with himself, or is he sporting and trifling with his creatures? A character so suspicious, to say the least of it, ought not, without the most unequivocal evidence, to be attributed to the adorable Jehovah. In his word we are taught that 'he is of one mind'—that 'his ways are equal;' and who can doubt it? We are told, it is true, to relieve the difficulty, that this seeming contradiction is one of the mysteries of God's incomprehensible nature. But it is not a *seeming* contradiction—it is a *real* one; not an insolvable mystery, but a palpable absurdity. God *prohibits the sinful* act—God *procures the sinful act—God wills the* salvation of the *reprobate, whom* he *has,* from *all eternity, irreversibly ordained to eternal death.*" "What does this doctrine make of our heavenly Father? I shudder to follow it out into its legitimate bearings. It seems to me, a belief of it is enough to drive one to infidelity, to madness, and to death." What can be said reproachful of God, of his holiness, of his justice, of his veracity, of his goodness, which this system does not warrant—which does not flow from it as an inevitable consequence? A resort to Atheism, to any thing, would be a deliverance from such dire and deplorable conclusions. I rejoice to know that its advocates do not embrace them; but will they tell us how they do—how we may escape them? Until I am thus relieved, I must hold the system guilty, not only of absurdity, but of enormous blasphemy, in fact, though not of purpose.

8. "God, from all eternity, freely and unchangeably foreordained whatsoever comes to pass." Now look at this: If true, then God foredetermined, purposed, and appointed, when as yet there was nothing, and when nothing ever could be without his decree, all the events, acts, volitions, and things of every kind, that ever have been, from the foundation of the world, or ever will be throughout eternity—all things, great and small, true and false, consistent and absurd, bad and good, pleasant and disgusting. No contradiction, but what he decreed it. He appointed, in a way that the event must answer the decree, and so because decreed, that all the contradictory views extant in the world should be entertained just as they are—that there should

be Atheists, Pantheists, Deists, infidels, Jews, Mohammedans, Pagans, all grades of idolaters and errorists, all varieties of Christians, and sects of philosophy. And these cannot but be, because they were decreed from eternity. One man was to pray, another blaspheme, another lie, another rob, another murder, another steal, another commit arson, incest, adultery—one deceive, another be deceived, and all because it was decreed from eternity. All thoughts, all words, all desires, all purposes, all volitions, all acts, from first to last, were decreed by God, and in such a way that the event must answer the decree. Now, all this is true, or else Calvinism is false; for Calvinism says, "God, from eternity, freely and unchangeably decreed whatsoever comes to pass." Every thing was included in God's plan, and brought about by his decree. Doctor, do you believe this?

9. I charge upon the system further, that, if generally believed, it is calculated to obliterate the sense of obligation, as well as the theory and fact of it, and, hence, to generate recklessness and universal indifference. By removing the idea of the possibility of reformation, or, indeed, of any responsible control over the character and actions, it effectually neutralizes every motive thereto, and causes the man to throw himself rashly upon the bosom of that stream of fate, which he believes to be irresistible in its current and tendencies. Why shall a sinner seek to reform, when he knows he cannot? Why shall he regret his course and conduct, when he knows they were inevitable? Why shall he raise any questions about the future, when he knows that fate has fixed it irrevocably, irrespective of him? Why shall he intermeddle, in any respect, with his state, character, or prospects, when they are no more subject to him than are the revolutions of Saturn? To believe the doctrine, a man must close his eyes, and yield himself up passively, unresistingly, into the hands of

fate, submitting to all that pertains to him as inevitable and right, because procured by the Almighty. Every impulse a man feels toward regret, or reformation, or effort in his own behalf, is a practical denial of the doctrine. It does not relieve the case a particle, to tell the man, that though final destiny is fixed by decree, yet means are decreed, also, as well as destiny—the same difficulty remains. If the means are decreed—or, in other words, the sins to be an occasion of his damnation, or the virtues to be a pretense for his salvation—he knows that he has nothing to do but passively submit. What else can he do? Can he move only as moved upon? Can he fail to move when moved upon? Doctor, can he do any thing, any thing under heaven, but what God makes him do? If so, what? If not, why be careful?

Will you appeal to facts in proof that such is not the tendency of your system? I shall reply, that they are incompetent to meet the case; that, admitting them to be different from what it is alledged the system would make them, this would only prove that it—the system—had not always worked out its legitimate results; that the bad and disastrous influence had, in some instances, been counteracted by the presence of some wholesome element. But the facts, it is believed, so far from contradicting the above reasonings, do amply corroborate them—so far from antagonizing us, do most fully sustain us. Calvinism has produced, and does now produce, the fruits charged against it; it does so, not only in some, but in many, if not in all instances, where it is not neutralized by the presence of more powerful principles of belief, existing coetaneously in the mind. It is innocent only when it is practically disbelieved. Here is a Calvinistic fatalist in theory, but really, and at heart, a man who is conscious of freedom and responsibility: the man may be, notwithstanding his theoretical error, a most exemplary and consistent Christian. The reason is manifest—his practice results, not from his theoretical creed, but from his actual consciousness—it is good in despite of the former, and in accordance with the latter. But once let him yield all to his belief of fatalism—let him silence the voice of his reason and consciousness, and of God, and give himself up to a firm belief of fate, and then you shall see, as you have often seen, all the results ascribed to such a faith.

10. I object further to the system, that it is wholly without support, either from Scripture or reason. This, I am apprised, is saying much, but no more than I conscientiously believe to be true; and I can only be convinced of error, by hearing, from Dr. Rice, such arguments as I have not been able to discover in the writings of the various authors quoted in this volume, and many others not quoted, with which I have been accustomed to commune for years.

I have endeavored to speak plainly, and to make myself understood upon these points; but I beg you to believe that I have felt no unkindness, and have said nothing with the thought of offending. Indeed, I assure you, I have studied to use mildness; and have, therefore, left many things unsaid, which seemed almost necessary, to show you the full extent of the difficulties which I find pressing your system. I have purposely avoided naming many other real objections—contenting myself, for the present, with referring to those which are so palpable, as to meet every mind at the threshold of an inquiry into your system, and so weighty, as to startle the cautious inquirer at the boldness of doctrines involving such conclusions.

CHAPTER III.

ELECTION AND REPROBATION.

We shall now proceed to consider the doctrine of decrees with relation to election and reprobation particularly. And, as in the former case, we shall appeal to the Confession of Faith, and to accredited Calvinistic authors. Our object is to know precisely what our Presbyterian brethren do believe. We appeal, therefore, to their own statements and explanations. From the Confession of Faith, chapter iii, I read:

"Section 3. By the decree of God, for the manifestation of his glory, some men and angels are predestinated unto everlasting life, and others *foreordained unto everlasting death.*

"Section 4. These angels and men, thus predestinated and foreordained, are particularly and unchangeably designed, and their number is so certain and definite, that it cannot be either increased or diminished.

"Section 5. Those of mankind that are predestinated unto life, God, before the foundation of the world was laid, according to his eternal and immutable purpose, and the secret counsel and good pleasure of his will, hath chosen in Christ unto everlasting glory, out of his mere free grace and love, without any foresight of faith or good works, or perseverance in either of them, or any other thing in the creature, as conditions or causes moving him thereto, and all to the praise of his glorious grace.

"Section 6. As God hath appointed the elect unto glory, so hath he, by the eternal and most free purpose of his will, foreordained all the means thereunto. Wherefore they, who are elected, being fallen in Adam, are redeemed by Christ—are effectually called unto faith in Christ by his Spirit working in due season—are justified, adopted, sanctified, and kept by his power through faith unto salvation. *Neither are any other redeemed by Christ,* effectually called, justified, adopted, sanctified, but the elect only.

"Section 7. The rest of mankind, God was pleased, according to the unsearchable counsel of his will, whereby he extendeth or withholdeth mercy as he pleaseth, for the glory of his sovereign power over his creatures, to pass by and to ordain *them to dishonor and wrath* for their sins, to the praise of his glorious justice."

Of effectual calling:

"Section 1. All those whom God hath predestinated unto life, and *these only,* he is pleased, in his appointed and accepted time, effectually to call, by his word and Spirit, out of that state of sin and death, in which they are by nature, to grace and salvation by Jesus Christ, enlightening their minds spiritually and savingly to God, taking their hearts of stone and giving them a heart of flesh, renewing their wills, by his almighty power determining them to that which is good, and effectually drawing them to Jesus Christ, yet so as they come most freely, being made willing by his grace.

"Section 2. This effectual call is of God's free and special grace alone, not from any thing at all foreseen in man, who is altogether passive therein, until, being quickened and renewed by the Holy Spirit, he is thereby enabled to answer this call, and to embrace the grace offered and conveyed in it.

"Section 3. *Elect* infants, dying in infancy, are regenerated and saved by Christ, through the Spirit, who worketh when, and where, and how he pleaseth. So, also, are other elect persons who are incapable of being outwardly called by the ministry of the word.

"Section 4. Others not elected, although they may be called by the ministry of the word, and may have some common operations of the Spirit, yet they never truly come to Christ, and therefore cannot be saved, much less can men, not professing the Christian religion, be saved in any other way whatsoever, be they never so diligent to frame their lives according to the light of nature, and the law of that religion they do possess; and to assert and maintain that they may, is very pernicious, and to be detested."

Of the perseverance of the saints:

"Section 1. They whom God hath accepted in his beloved, effectually called and sanctified by his Spirit, can neither totally nor finally fall away from the state of grace, but shall certainly persevere therein to the end, and be eternally saved.

"Section 2. This *perseverance of the saints depends not upon their own free will, but upon the immutability of the decree of election,* flowing from the free and unchanging love of God the Father, upon the efficacy of the merit and intercession of Jesus Christ, the abiding of the Spirit and of the seed of God within them, and the nature of the covenant of grace; from all which ariseth the certainty and infallibility thereof."

I have quoted thus largely from the Confession of Faith, that my readers may have the benefit of a full view of the whole scheme of unconditional salvation as taught by Calvinists—all that enters into and renders effectual the decree of election and reprobation. I shall now proceed to quote, as corroborative and explanatory of these articles of faith, from various authors, who are supposed to understand the system, and who have proved their friendship for it by giving their lives to its support. But a quotation or two from the Larger Catechism:

"What is effectual calling?

"Effectual calling is the work of God's almighty power and grace, whereby, out of his free and especial love to his elect, and from nothing in them moving him thereunto, he doth, in his accepted time, invite and draw them to Jesus Christ by his word and Spirit, savingly enlightening their minds, renewing and powerfully determining their wills, so as they, although in themselves dead in sin, are hereby made willing and able freely to answer his call, and to accept and embrace the grace offered and conveyed therein."

"Are the elect only effectually called?

"All the elect, and they *only*, are effectually called, although others may be and often are outwardly called by the ministry of the word, and have some common operations of the Spirit, who for their willful neglect and contempt of the grace offered to them, being justly left in their unbelief, do never truly come to Jesus Christ."

"There is no doubt but the preparation of them both—elect and reprobate—doth depend upon the secret counsel of God; otherwise, Paul had said the reprobates give or cast themselves into destruction; but now he giveth to wit, that *before they are born they are addicted to their lot.*" (Calvin.)

I quote further from the exposition:

"The decree of God, with respect to the everlasting state of men and angels, is known by the name of predestination; and this consists of two branches, generally distinguished by the name of *election* and *reprobation.*

"Our Confession teaches that God made choice of and predestinated a certain and definite number of individuals to everlasting life—that he predestinated them to life before the foundation of the world was laid—that, in so doing, he acted according to his sovereign will, and was not influenced by the foresight of their faith or good works, or perseverance in either of them; and that this purpose is immutable, it being impossible that any of the elect should perish. (P. 65.)

"Christ died exclusively for the elect, and purchased

redemption for them alone; in other words, Christ made atonement only for the elect, and in no sense did he die for the rest of the race. Our Confession first asserts positively that the elect are redeemed by Christ, and then negatively that none others are redeemed by Christ but the elect only. If this does not affirm the doctrine of particular redemption, or of a limited atonement, we know not what language could express that doctrine more explicitly. Some who allow of personal and eternal election, deny any such thing as reprobation. But the one unavoidably follows from the other; for the choice of some must unavoidably imply the rejection of others. Election and rejection are correlative terms; and men impose upon themselves, and imagine they conceive what it is impossible to conceive, when they admit election, and deny reprobation." (P. 70.)

From the Larger Catechism:

"What hath God especially decreed concerning angels and men? God, by an eternal and immutable decree, out of his mere love for the praise of his glorious grace, to be manifested in due time, hath elected some angels to glory, and in Christ hath chosen some men to eternal life, and the means thereof; and, also, according to his sovereign power, and the unsearchable counsel of his own will, hath passed by, and foreordained the rest to dishonor and wrath, to be for their sin inflicted, to the praise of the glory of his justice."

"Many, indeed, as if they wished to avert odium from God, admit election in such a way as to deny that any one is reprobated. *But this is puerile and absurd,* because election itself could not exist without being opposed to reprobation. Whom God passes by, therefore, he reprobates; and *from no other cause* than his determination to exclude them from the inheritance which he predestines for his children." (Calvin's Institutes, vol. ii, p. 163.)

"Though it is sufficiently clear that God, in his secret

counsel, freely chooses whom he will, and rejects others, his gratuitous election is but half displayed till we come to particular individuals, to whom God not only offers salvation, but assigns it in such a manner, that the certainty is liable to no suspicion or doubt." (Ib.)

"Predestination we call the eternal decree of God, by which he has determined in himself what he would have to become of every individual of mankind; for they are not all created with a similar destiny, but eternal life is foreordained for some, and eternal damnation for others. Every man, therefore, being created for one or other of these ends, we say he is predestinated either to life or death." (Ib., vol. ii, p. 145.

"The term predestination includes the decree of election and reprobation. Some, indeed, confine it to election, but there seems to be no sufficient reason for not extending it to the one as well as the other, as in both the final condition of man is preappointed or predestinated. When a choice is made, we must conceive that of a number of persons some are taken, others are left. Election is a relative term, and necessarily involves the idea of rejection." (Dick's Theology.)

"There seems to be no reason, therefore, for denying, that what is called reprobation was a positive decree, as well as election." (Ib.)

"But, although the fall is presupposed to their reprobation, it will appear that the former was not the reason of the latter, if we recollect that those who were chosen to salvation were exactly in the same situation. If there was sin in the reprobate, there was sin, also, in the elect; and we must, therefore, resolve their opposite allotments into the will of God, who gives and withholds his favor according to his pleasure." (Ib.)

"A decree, respecting the condition of the human race, includes the history of every individual, the time of his appearing upon earth, the manner of his existence while he is an inhabitant of earth, as it is diversified by the actions which he performs, and the manner of his existence after he leaves the earth; that is, his future happiness or misery. Whence it followeth, that this knowledge—foreknowledge of the elect—dependeth upon the good pleasure of God, because God foreknew nothing, out of himself, touching those he would adopt, but only marked out whom he would elect." (Calvin.)

"Now he doth refer the whole cause unto the election of God, and the same free, and such as doth not depend upon men; that, in the salvation of the godly, nothing might be sought for above the goodness of God, and *in the destruction of the reprobate nothing above his just severity.*" (Ib.)

"Moreover, although the corruption of nature, which is dispersed over all mankind, before it come into action, is available enough unto condemnation, whereby followeth that Esau was worthily rejected, because naturally he was the son of wrath; yet, *lest any doubt should remain, as though, through respect of any fault or sin, his condition was the worse, it was necessary that as well sins as virtues should be excluded!* Surely, true it is, that the next cause of reprobation is, for that we are all accursed in Adam, yet, to the end we might rest in the bare and simple will of God, Paul did lead us aside from the consideration thereof for so long until he had established this doctrine, namely, *that God hath a sufficient, just cause of election and reprobation in his own will or pleasure.*" (Ib.)

"And, therefore, that doctrine is false, and contrary to the word of God, namely, that God doth choose, or *reject*, as he foreseeth every man worthy or unworthy of his grace." (Ib.)

"God hath elected some, and rejected other some, and the cause is nowhere else to be sought for than in his purpose." (Ib.)

"To all those for whom Christ hath purchased redemption, he doth certainly and effectually apply and communicate the same." (Confession of Faith.)

Either Christ applies and communicates redemption to all, and then Universalism is true, or he did not purchase redemption for all, and so the reprobates never were redeemed.

Upon this point the expositor says:

"This section relates to the extent of Christ's death with respect to its objects; and, in opposition to the Arminian tenet, that Christ died for all, it affirms that the purchase and application of redemption are exactly of the same extent. In the fifth section we were taught, that Christ purchased redemption only for 'those whom the Father hath given unto him;' and here it is asserted, that 'to all those for whom Christ hath purchased redemption, he doth certainly and effectually apply and communicate the same.' What language, then, could affirm more explicitly, than that here employed, that the atonement of Christ is specific and limited; that it is neither *universal* nor *indefinite*, but *restricted to the elect?*"

This view of the atonement is sustained with elaborate argumentation by Mr. Shaw, showing how well and thoroughly he had considered the doctrine. As a specimen of his logic in this case, and I regret to say I find such specimens abounding throughout the system, and in the writings of those eminent men who have so strangely enlisted in its advocacy: "*Universal terms* are *sometimes* used in Scripture in reference to the death of Christ; but *reason* and *common sense* demand that *general* phrases be explained and defined by those that are *special!*"

"God chose, of the whole body of mankind, whom he viewed in his eternal decree as involved in guilt and misery, certain persons, who are called the elect, whose names are known to him, and whose number, being unchangeably fixed by his decree, can neither be increased nor diminished; so that the whole extent of the remedy offered in the Gospel, is conceived to have been determined beforehand by the Divine decree. As all the children of Adam were involved in the same guilt and misery, the persons thus chosen had nothing in themselves to render them more worthy of being elected than any others; and therefore the decree of election is called, in the Calvinistic system, absolute, by which word is meant, that it arises entirely from the good pleasure of God, because all the circumstances, which distinguish the elect from others, are the fruits of their election. For the persons thus chosen, God, from the beginning, appointed the means of their being delivered from corruption and guilt, and by these means, effectually applied in due season, he conducts them at length unto everlasting life. From the election of certain persons, it necessarily follows that all the rest of the race of Adam are left in guilt and misery. The exercise of Divine sovereignty, in regard to those who are not elected, is called reprobation; and the condition of all having been originally the same, reprobation is called absolute in the same sense with election." (Hill's Divinity.)

"I say, with Augustine, that the Lord created those who he certainly foreknew would fall into destruction, and that this was actually so, because he willed it." (Calvin's Institutes.)

"Observe, all things being at God's disposal, and the decision of salvation and death belonging to him, he orders all things by his counsel and decree in such a manner, that some men are born devoted, from the womb, to certain death, that his name may be glorified in their destruction." (Ib., vol ii, p. 169.)

"It is an awful decree, I must confess; but no one can deny that God foreknew the future, final fate of man before he created him, and that he did foreknow it, because it was appointed by him, or decreed. Nor should it be thought absurd to affirm that God not only foresaw the fall of the first man, and the ruin of his posterity in him, but also arranged all by the determination of his own will. For as it belongs to his wisdom to foreknow things future, so it belongs to his power to rule and govern all things by his hand." (Ib., vol. ii, p. 170.)

"But I mean that the actions of men are foreseen by God, not as events independent of his will, but as originating in his determination, and as fulfilling his purpose." (Hill's Divinity.)

"Foolish mortals enter into many contentions with God, as though they could arraign him, to plead their accusations. In the first place, they inquire by what right the Lord is angry with his creatures, who have not provoked him by any previous offense; for that to devote to destruction whom he pleases is more like the caprice of a tyrant, than the lawful sentence of a judge; that men have reason, therefore, to expostulate with God, if they are predestinated to eternal death, without any demerit of their own, merely by his sovereign will. If such thoughts ever enter the minds of pious men, they will be sufficiently enabled to break their violence by this one consideration—how exceedingly presumptuous it is only to inquire into the causes of the Divine will; *which is, in fact, and is justly entitled to be, the cause of every thing that exists.* For if it has any cause, then there must be something antecedent, on which it depends, which it is impious to suppose. For the will of God is the highest rule of justice; so that what he wills must be considered just, for this very reason—because he wills it. When it is inquired, therefore, why the Lord did so, the answer must be, because he would." (Calvin's Institutes.)

"He directs his voice to them, but it is that they may become more deaf; he kindles a light, but it is that they may be made more blind; he publishes his doctrine, but it is that they may become more besotted; he applies a remedy, but it is that they may not be healed. . . . Nor can it be disputed, that, to such persons as God determines not to enlighten, he delivers his doctrine in enigmatical obscurity, that its only effect may be to increase their stupidity." (Calvin's Institutes, vol. ii, p. 192.)

"That the reprobates obey not the word of God, when made known to them, is justly imputed to the wickedness and depravity of their hearts; *provided it be, at the same time, stated that they are abandoned to this depravity, because they have been raised up, by a just but inscrutable judgment of God, to display his glory in their condemnation.* So, when it is related of the sons of Eli, that they listened not to his salutary admonitions, 'because the Lord would slay them,' it is not denied that their obstinacy proceeded from their own wickedness, but it is plainly implied, that though the Lord was able to soften their hearts, yet they were left in their obstinacy, because his immutable decree had predestined them to destruction." (Calvin's Institutes, vol. ii, p. 193.)

"Term election most commonly signifies, that eternal, sovereign, unconditional, particular, and immutable act of God, whereby he selected some from all mankind, and of every nation under heaven, to be redeemed and everlastingly saved by Christ. It sometimes, and more rarely, signifies that gracious and almighty act of the divine Spirit, whereby God actually and visibly separates his elect from the world, by effectual calling." (Zanchius, p. 72.)

"Reprobation denotes either God's eternal preterition of some men, when he chose others to glory, and his predestination of them to fill up the measure of their iniquities, and then to receive the just punishment of crimes, even 'destruction from the presence of the Lord, and from the glory of his power.' This is the primary, most obvious, and most frequent sense in which the word is used." (Ib., p. 74.)

Predestination "may be considered as that eternal, most wise, and immutable decree of God, whereby he did, from before all time, determine and ordain to create, dispose of, and direct to some particular end, every person and thing to which he has given, or is yet to give, being; and to make the whole creation subservient to, and declarative of his own glory. Of this decree actual providence is the execution." (Ib., p. 77.)

"Consider predestination as relating to the elect only, and it is that eternal, unconditional, particular, and irreversible act of the Divine will, whereby, in matchless love and adorable sovereignty, God determined within himself, to deliver a certain number of Adam's degenerate offspring out of that sinful and miserable estate into which, by his primitive transgression, they were to fall, and in which sad condition they were equally involved with those who were not chosen; but being pitched upon and singled out by God the Father, to be vessels of grace and salvation, they were, in time, actually redeemed by Christ—are effectually called by his Spirit, justified, adopted, sanctified, and preserved safe to his heavenly kingdom." (Ib., p. 79.)

"We assert, that all men universally are not elected to salvation; so neither are all men universally condemned to condemnation. . . . The Deity, from all eternity, and, consequently, at the very time he gives life and being to a reprobate, certainly foreknew, and knows in consequence of his own decree, that such a one would fall short of salvation. Now, if God foreknew this, he must have predetermined it; because his own will is the foundation of his decrees, and his decrees are the foundation of his prescience; he, therefore, foreknows futurities, because, by his predestination, he hath rendered these futurition certain and inevitable." (Ib., p. 88.)

"All things whatever arise from, and depend upon the Divine appointment, whereby it was preordained who should receive the word of life, and who should disbelieve it—who should be delivered from their sins, and who should be hardened in them." (Ib., p. 89.)

"We assert, that the number of the elect, and also of the reprobate, is so fixed and determinate, that neither can be augmented or diminished." (Ib.)

"As the future faith and good works of the elect were not the cause of their being chosen, so neither were the future sins of the reprobate the cause of their being passed by; but the choice of the former, and the decretive omission of the latter, were owing, merely and entirely, to the sovereign and determining pleasure of God." (Ib., p. 112.)

"Notwithstanding God did, from all eternity, irreversibly choose out and fix upon some to be partakers of salvation by Christ, and rejected the rest, acting in both according to the good pleasure of his own sovereign will, yet he did not herein act an unjust, tyrannical, or cruel part; nor yet show himself a respecter of persons." (Ib., p. 119.)

"Now he [Paul] beginneth to ascend higher, namely, to show the reason of this diversity, which he teacheth doth not consist in any thing else than the election of God; he doth plainly refer the whole cause to the election of God, and the same free, and such as doth not depend upon men; that, in the salvation of the godly, nothing might be sought for above the goodness of God, and in the destruction, nothing above his just severity. The Lord, in this his free election, is at liberty and free from that necessity, that he should indifferently impart the grace unto all, but, rather, whom he will he passeth over, and whom he will he chooseth." (Calvin, Com., Rom. ix, 11.)

"Although the corruption of nature, which is dispersed over all mankind, before it come into action, is available enough unto condemnation, whereby followeth that Esau was worthily rejected, because naturally he was the son of wrath; yet, *lest any doubt should remain, as though, through respect of any fault or sin, his condition was the worse, it was necessary as well sins as virtues should be excluded.* Surely, true it is, that the *next* cause of reprobation is, for that we are all accursed in Adam, yet, to the end we might learn to rest in the bare, simple will of God, Paul did lead us aside from the consideration thereof, for so long until he had established this doctrine, namely, *that God hath a sufficient, just cause of election and reprobation in his own will or pleasure.*" (Ib.)

"God hath elected some, and rejected other some, and the cause is nowhere else to be sought for than in his purpose. For if the difference were grounded on the respect of works, in vain had Paul moved the question of the righteousness of God, whereof there could be no suspicion, if he handled every one according to his desert. . . . Before men are born, every one hath his lot appointed, by the secret counsel of God." (Ib., chap. ix, v. 14.)

"There are vessels prepared for destruction; that is, bequeathed and destinated to destruction: there are also vessels of wrath; that is, *made and formed to this end*, that they might be testimonies of the vengeance and wrath of God." (Ib., chap. ix, v. 22.)

"There is no doubt but the preparation of them both [elect and reprobate] doth depend on the secret counsel of God; otherwise, Paul had said the reprobates give or cast themselves into destruction; but now he giveth to wit, that before they are born they are already addicted to their lot." (Ib., chap. ix, v. 23.)

"God, from all eternity, decreed to leave some of Adam's fallen race in their sins, and to exclude them from the participation of Christ and his benefits." (Toplady on Predestination, p. 105.)

"Some men were, from all eternity, not only negatively excepted from a participation of Christ and salvation, but positively ordained to continue in their natural blindness and hardness of heart.' (Ib., p. 106.)

Such is the doctrine of predestination, with respect to election and reprobation of men, as held by the Presbyterian Church. It would be easy greatly to increase quotations from their authorities upon this point; but the foregoing are sufficient. And from these, together with the former quotations, we deduce the following, as the sum of their faith:

1. God decreed, from eternity, the fall of Adam, and the ruin or fall of his posterity in him.

2. That, regarding man as fallen, he elected some men, whose names and number were designated, unto everlasting life.

3. That those thus predestinated, were so predestinated, unchangeably and unconditionally, without any reference whatever to their works or character

4. That for these, and these only, he provided a Savior, and all the means necessary to procure their salvation, without any conditions on their part.

5. That the persons thus unchangeably designed, cannot possibly perish, do what they may, but will be irresistibly drawn to Christ, and to justification, adoption, and sanctification.

6. With respect to the rest, whose names and number are also definitely fixed, that he passed them by in their sins, and predestinated them unto destruction.

7. That they were thus passed and predestinated from eternity, and so were ordained to destruction before they were born, of the good pleasure of God, and to the glory of his sovereign justice.

8. That for these he never did provide a Savior, and that consequently they could not be saved, do what they might.

9. That those reprobated in no respect differed from those elected, and the one class were elected, and the other

class reprobated, of the mere sovereign pleasure of God, without any respect to any difference in them whatever.

To sum it all up in a few words, we understand the above to teach, that a certain, definite number of the human race are elected, unconditionally and unalterably, without reference to any thing in them, or to be performed by them, and of the mere good pleasure of God, unto everlasting life, so that they cannot perish; that the rest are so predestinated to eternal damnation, that they cannot be saved, no Savior ever having been provided for them.

To the doctrine thus stated I object, generally, all that has been already urged against the doctrine of decrees, and, particularly, much more which I shall now immediately proceed to state.

1. I object to the system, that it makes God the author of man's fall from holiness into sin. This is a point I desire all my readers to give particular attention to, as it has important bearings on subsequent reasonings. The argument upon which this deduction is founded is very brief, and exceedingly plain. It is this:

"God, from all eternity, did, by the most wise and holy counsel of his own will, freely and unchangeably ordain whatsoever comes to pass." (Confession of Faith.)

But man's fall came to pass; therefore, God, from all eternity, did ordain man's fall.

"The decree of God is the necessity of things." (Calvin.)

But man's fall is something; therefore, God's decree is the necessity, or necessitating cause, of man's fall. But I need hardly be at the pains of arguing out a conclusion so palpable that a child could not fail to perceive it, and, withal, a conclusion admitted by the great projector of the system I antagonize.

"I confess, indeed," says Mr. Calvin, "that all the descendants of Adam fell by the Divine will into that miserable condition in which they are now involved; and this is what I asserted from the beginning, that we must always return, at last, to *the sovereign determination of God's will,* the cause of which is hidden in himself." (Institutes.)

Having thus delivered himself, and anticipating objections to his candid statement from his opponents, he thus enters his defense and explanations:

"For we will answer them thus, in the language of Paul: '*O man, who art thou, that repliest against God?*'"

Certainly a most lucid and satisfactory mode of escaping difficulties!

Let it not be pretended that the fall, though ordained, was ordained as foreseen—decreed because it was perceived as an event that would take place—for this would oppose the system to itself, which teaches that things are not decreed because foreknown, but foreknown because decreed, also, it would oppose the system where it teaches that the decree is itself the cause of all things—the cause without which they could not be.

Shall I be told that, though Adam fell, it was freely—by voluntarily eating the inhibited fruit—in the language of the Confession itself, that, "Our first parents being seduced by the subtilty and temptation of Satan, sinned in eating the forbidden fruit. This their sin God was pleased, according to his wise and holy counsel, to permit, having purposed to order it to his own glory."

All this seems plausible enough; but the slightest scrutiny detects a meaning here not discoverable upon the surface. It would seem to represent that man's fall was his own free and unnecessitated act. But that this is not the meaning, will appear in a variety of ways. If you ask, Could he have done otherwise than as he did? they must answer you, No—God had decreed it thus. He could no more avoid taking the forbidden fruit than he could resist the decree of the Almighty—fall he must, for Omnipotence urged him on to the catastrophe. If you ask them, what, then, they mean by man's falling freely, they will answer in the language of the Confession again:

"Man, in his state of innocency, had freedom and power to will and to do that which is good and well-pleasing to God, but yet mutably, so that he might fall from it."

This again is plausible enough, and would seem to teach that our first parents had power to stand or fall; but a more narrow and careful examination shows that this is not their meaning; for they admit that they could not help but fall, or else they believe that they had power to overcome the decree of God—they may select their own alternative. All they mean, when they speak of freedom before or since the fall, is simply the power man has to do as he pleases—to follow his choice. But now observe, they insist that, when man chooses one thing, he has no power to choose its opposite; for his particular choice was fixed by decree. Adam, when he chose to take of the forbidden fruit, could not have chosen to decline taking it any more than he could overcome a decree of God which fixed his choice as it was. He was free, I am told, because he did as he pleased. I answer, he had no power to please otherwise—therein is his want of freedom. His choice, according to the system, was forced upon him, by placing him in circumstances where another choice was impossible. He fell himself, I am told, by his own act, dictated by his own choice. I answer, the act was decreed from eternity; and the choice which dictated the act was also decreed from eternity; and the circumstances which made the choice necessary were also decreed from eternity; and the man was created and placed in the circumstances, that the choice and act, and consequent fall, should necessarily take place. Thus, neither the act, nor the choice, nor the fall, were free, but all necessitated by unavoidable fate, or decree. God's decree was the sole, original cause of man's fall. I may have occasion to say more upon this point to show other revolting aspects of it; but for the present I pass it to the presentation of other consequences and involvements of the system.

2. I object to the system, in the second place, that it teaches that, when man was thus involved in the sin and miseries of the fall, by God's own agency, he elected a part of the race, whose names and number were definitely fixed, unto everlasting life, without any respect whatever either to their character or deeds, and reprobated or predestinated the residue, whose names and number were also definitely fixed from eternity, unto eternal damnation, and this, also, without reference to their character or deeds. The one part were decreed to be saved not for any thing in them—the other part were preappointed to damnation, not as being wicked. But in both cases eternal destiny was fixed, without respect to any thing in the creature. Do not, I pray you, Dr. Rice, turn away from this appalling proposition. Do not say, in your haste, it is slanderous. Hear my reasons for attributing it to your system.

The argument upon which I base this statement is as follows:

"Although God knows whatever may or can come to pass upon all supposed conditions, yet hath he not decreed any thing because he foresaw it as future, or as that which would come to pass upon such supposed conditions." (Confession of Faith.)

This clause, as I understand it, teaches that God's decree, that any event shall come to pass, was entirely without respect to foreknowledge that such would be the case, and, also, without respect to conditions as a cause moving to the decree. If I am correct in this, and I think I am, then, when God decreed the salvation of the elect, it was entirely without foresight of faith or good works in them—this you admit, and your Confession expressly asserts: and so, when he willed the damnation of the rest, it was, also, without foresight or consideration of sin as a cause thereto—this you deny, and no doubt you will esteem it a misrepresentation of your system. But, if I am mistaken here, all I ask is that you will point out the mistake in my reasonings. A disclaimer will do no good, unless you can show that it does not result from your system. First, you tell me that God, from eternity, unconditionally decreed whatsoever comes to pass; but the damnation of the reprobate comes to pass; therefore, the damnation of the reprobate was unconditionally decreed. But if it was unconditionally decreed, then it could not have been decreed because of sin, for that would make sin the condition; and so your doctrine would be found at fault, when it asserts that the decrees are unconditional.

But it is a necessary conclusion, that the decree of reprobation is without respect to sin for another reason. To suppose it to be upon the foresight of sin is to abandon your system, which teaches that the decrees of God do not proceed from foreknowledge, but foreknowledge proceeds from decree; for, if the reprobates are decreed to reprobation, because of foreseen sin, then is foreknowledge the ground of decree. But, not to take up the time of our readers in reasonings here, it may be shown by numerous references to Calvin himself that this was his doctrine—that neither the salvation of the elect, nor damnation of the reprobate, were ascribable to any thing in the creature, but equally and both to the mere will and pleasure of God—the one part elected to life, and the other to death, simply because God willed it. He says, and I give one quotation as a specimen:

"For this he goeth about to bring to pass among us, that concerning the diversity that is between the elect and reprobate, our minds might be content with this, namely, that it hath so pleased God to illuminate some unto salvation, and blind other some unto death, and not seek any cause above his will; for all external things which make to the excecation of the reprobate are the instruments of his wrath; and Satan himself, which inwardly worketh effectually, is so far forth his minister that he worketh not but at his commandment!

"Therefore, that frivolous evasion or refuge, which the schoolmen have of foreknowledge, doth fall down; for Paul doth not say, that the ruin of the wicked is foreseen of the Lord, but is ordained by his counsel and will: as Solomon also teacheth, that the destruction of the wicked was not only foreknown, but *that the wicked ones themselves were purposely created that they might perish!*

"*God hath elected some, and rejected other some, and the cause is nowhere else to be sought for than in his purpose;* for if the difference were grounded upon the respect of works, in vain had Paul moved the question of the unrighteousness of God, whereof there could be no suspicion, if he handled every one according to his desert."

It is manifest that Calvin finds the cause of reprobation, as well as election, in the will of God alone, irrespective of works. The decree of election involves the decree of reprobation. This is clearly and repeatedly admitted by your own authors, and by your Confession itself.

"By the decree of God for the manifestation of his glory, some men and angels are predestinated unto everlasting life, and *others foreordained to everlasting death.* These angels and men thus predestinated and foreordained, are particularly and unchangeably designated; and their number is so certain and definite that it cannot be either increased or diminished." (Confession of Faith.)

I need not reinsert the quotations, full upon this point, given heretofore—it is admitted, and, if not, it is unavoidably involved. There can be no election of a part, without an implied and actual rejection of the other part, not elected. To present the case in the most favorable aspect for

Calvinism, it stands thus: the human race appear before God as a race of miserable sinners, all under sentence of condemnation. God so beholding them, selects a portion, say, less than one-half, without any reference to character, or any thing else in them—for they are all precisely alike: these he determines to save, or elects them, unconditionally, unto life—sets them apart for himself. The others he passes by, and makes no provision for them whatever, but leaves them, by his sovereign disposal, to eternal damnation. Now this election of a part is, to all intents and purposes, a rejection of the other part. I state it in a manner certainly the least objectionable to a Calvinist. And now, I object to it, even in this favorable aspect, as involving the divine Being in the grossest injustice and criminal partiality.

My reasons for this charge shall be given, in a moment. In the meantime, I hear you say, Had not God a right to extend mercy to a part, without bringing him under obligation to extend it to all? he might in justice have passed all by: he did those no harm, therefore, whom he passed by, because they deserved it; and that he saved any was a mere act of grace. I am familiar with your eloquent declamation on this point; but it falls powerless upon my mind for this reason. How came these miserable creatures in their condition of sin and wretchedness? You must answer me, They were put there by the decree of God. First, he put them all in the consequences of the fall, that he might have an occasion to display his grace, in saving some, and to glorify his justice in damning others! He made them sinners, that he might have a pretense to torment them for ever, to the glory of his sovereign justice If you can reconcile this to justice, I should be happy to have the benefit of your assistance here.

Upon this point, Dr. Fisk says, "The doctrine of unconditional election of a part, necessarily implies the unconditional reprobation of the rest. I know some, who hold to the former, seem to deny the latter; for they represent God as reprobating sinners in view of their sins. When all were sinners, they say, God passed by some, and elected others. Hence, they say, the decree of damnation against the reprobate is just, because it is against sinners. But this explanation is virtually giving up the system, inasmuch as it gives up all the principal arguments by which it is supported. In the first place, it makes predestination dependent on foreknowledge; for God first foresees that they will be sinners, and then predestinates them to punishment. Here is one case, then, in which the argument for Calvinian predestination is destroyed by its own supporters. But, again, if God must fix, by his decree, all parts of his plan, in order to prevent disappointment, then he must fix the destiny of the reprobates, and the means that lead to it. But if he did not do this, then the Calvinistic argument in favor of predestination, drawn from the Divine plan, falls to the ground. Once more: this explanation of the decree of reprobation destroys the Scripture arguments, which the Calvinists urge in favor of unconditional election. The passages, for instance, in Romans ix, which are so often quoted in favor of Calvinian election, are connected with others equally strong, in favor of unconditional reprobation. Now, if these relate to personal election to eternal life, they relate also to personal reprobation to eternal death. But if there is any explanation, by which these are shown not to prove unconditional reprobation to eternal death, the same principle of interpretation will and must show that they do not prove Calvinistic election.

But I have not done with this objection yet. Whoever maintains that "God foreordained whatsoever comes to pass," must, also, hold to unconditional reprobation. Does it come to pass that some are lost? Then, this was ordained. Was sin necessary as a pretense to damn them? Then, this was ordained. From these and other views of the subject,

Calvin was led to say, that "election could not stand without reprobation;" and that it was "quite silly and childish" to attempt to separate them. All, therefore, who hold to the unconditional election of a part of mankind to eternal life, must, to be consistent with themselves, take into their creed the "horrible decree of reprobation." They must believe that in the ages of eternity, God determined to create men and angels for the express purpose to damn them eternally!—that he determined to introduce sin, and harden them in it, that they might be fit subjects of his wrath!—that, for doing as they are impelled to do by the irresistible decree of Jehovah, they must lie down for ever under the scalding vials of his vengeance in the pit of hell! To state this doctrine in its true character is enough to chill one's blood; and we are drawn, by all that is rational within us, to turn away from such a God with horror, as from the presence of an almighty Tyrant. And yet, I charge upon Dr. Rice, and all consistent Calvinists, this appalling dogma.

3. I object to the decree of election and reprobation, still further, that it at the same time renders God a partial being, and destroys entirely the foundation for the doctrine of grace. If it be true there is no grace in the salvation of the elect, there is great cruelty in the damnation of the reprobate, and God is a most partial being; and in all these respects the system is opposed to the Scriptures. "To the reprobates there is certainly no grace or mercy extended. Their very existence, connected as it necessarily is with eternal damnation, is an infinite curse. The temporal blessings which they enjoy, the insincere offers which are held out to them, and the Gospel privileges with which they are mocked, if they can be termed grace at all, must be called damning grace; for all this is only fattening them for the slaughter, and fitting them to suffer, to a more aggravated extent, the unavoidable pains and torments that await them.

Hence, Calvin's sentiment, 'that God calls the reprobate that they may be more deaf—kindles a light that they may be more blind—brings his doctrine to them that they may be more ignorant—and applies the remedy to them that they may not be healed,' is an honest avowal of the legitimate principles of the system. Surely no one will pretend that according to this system there is any grace in the reprobate. And perhaps a moment's attention will show that there is little or none for the elect. It is said that God, out of his mere sovereignty, without any thing in the creature to move him thereto, elects sinners to everlasting life. But if there is nothing in the creature to move him thereto, how can it be called mercy or compassion? He did not determine to elect them because they were miserable, but simply because he pleased to elect them. If misery had been the exciting cause, then, as all were equally miserable, he would have elected them all. Is such a decree of election founded in love to the suffering object, or is it not the result of the most absolute and omnipotent selfishness conceivable? It is the exhibition of a character that sports, most sovereignly and arbitrarily, with his almighty power to create, to damn, and to save."

Shall it be insisted that the salvation of miserable, perishing sinners, is an act of grace? then we continue, in the language of Fisk, to ask, "Who made them miserable, perishing sinners? Was not this the effect of God's decree? And is there much mercy displayed in placing men under a constitution which necessarily and unavoidably involves them in sin and suffering, that God may afterward have the sovereign honor of saving them? Surely the tenderest mercies of this system are cruel—its brightest parts are dark—its boasted mercy hardly comes up to sheer justice even to the elect; since they only receive back what God had deprived them of; and for the want of which they had suffered perhaps for years.

And as to the reprobates, the Gospel is unavoidably a source of death unto death. To them Christ came, that they might have death, and have it more abundantly, to the praise of his glorious justice."

In the language of Mr. Wesley, "How is God good or loving, to a reprobate, or one that is not elect? You cannot say he is an object of the love or goodness of God, with regard to his eternal state, whom he created, says Mr. Calvin, plainly and fairly, 'to live a reproach and die everlastingly.' Surely no one can dream that the goodness of God is at all concerned with this man's eternal state, however God is good to him in this world. What! when, by the reason of God's unchangeable decree, it had been good for this man never to have been born? when his very birth was a curse, not a blessing? 'Well, but he now enjoys many of the gifts of God, both gifts of nature and of providence. He has food, and raiment, and comforts of various kinds; and are not all these great blessings?' No, not to him. At the price which he is to pay for them, every one of these is also a curse. Every one of these comforts is, by an eternal decree, to cost him a thousand pangs in hell. For every moment's pleasure which he now enjoys, he is to suffer the torments of more than a thousand years; for the smoke of that pit which is preparing for him, ascendeth up for ever and ever. God knew this would be the fruit of whatever he should enjoy, before the vapor of life fled away. He designed it should. It was his very purpose in giving him those enjoyments; so that, by all these, he is in truth and reality only fattening the ox for the slaughter. 'Nay, but God gives him grace, too.' Yes, but what kind of grace? Saving grace, you own, he has not; and the common grace he has was not given with any design to save his soul; nor with any design to do him any good at all, but only to restrain him from hurting the elect: so far from doing him good, that this grace also necessarily increases his damnation.

"'And God knows this,' you say, 'and designed it should: it was one great end for which he gave it!' Then I desire to know how is God good or loving to this man, either with regard to time or eternity.

"Let us suppose a particular instance: here stands a man who is reprobated from all eternity; or, if you would express it more smoothly, who is not elected—whom God eternally decreed to pass by. Thou hast nothing, therefore, to expect from God after death, but to be cast into the lake of fire, burning with brimstone—God having consigned thy unborn soul to hell by a decree which cannot pass away. And from the time thou wast born under the irrevocable curse of God, thou canst have no peace; for there is no peace to the wicked, such as thou art doomed to continue, even from thy mother's womb. Accordingly, God giveth thee of this world's goods on purpose to enhance thy damnation. He giveth thee more substance or friends in order hereafter to heap the more coals of fire on thy head. He filleth thee with good; he maketh thee fat and well-looking, to make thee a more specious sacrifice to his vengeance. Good-nature, generosity, a good understanding, various knowledge, it may be, or eloquence, are the flowers wherewith he adorneth thee, thou poor victim, before thou art brought to the slaughter. Thou hast grace, too! but what grace? Not saving grace. That is not for thee, but for the elect only. Thine may be termed damning grace; since it is not only such in the event, but in the intention. Thou receivedst it of God for that very end, that thou mightest receive the greater damnation. It was given not to convert thee, but only to convince; not to make thee without sin, but without excuse! not to destroy, but to arm the worm that never dieth, and blow up the fire that shall never be quenched. Now, I beseech you, how is God good or loving to this man? Is not this such love as makes your blood run cold?"

4. I object to the doctrine further, that it not only teaches the unconditional reprobation of a part of mankind, who, in the language of Mr. Calvin, *were created* for destruction, but it also teaches, in harmony with the foregoing, that Christ never died for the lost—never in any sense made salvation possible. This is not only an inference deducted from the decree of election and reprobation—though it is unavoidably inferable from that decree, because it is manifest, if a man is eternally and unconditionally decreed to be damned, he never had a possibility of salvation. But our proposition is not a mere inference—it is an express statement of Calvinists themselves. Two authorities will answer upon this point.

The Confession of Faith shall be my first reference—it is very explicit. Its language is: "Neither are any other redeemed by Christ, but *the elect only.*"

"In this section we are taught," says Mr. Shaw, the expositor of the Confession, in his work revised and published by the Presbyterian board of publication, and received as a true exposition of their doctrines, "that Christ *died exclusively for the elect,* and *purchased redemption for them alone;* in other words, that Christ made atonement only for the elect, *and that in no sense did he die for the rest of the race.* Our Confession first asserts, positively, that the elect are redeemed by Christ; and then negatively that none other are redeemed by Christ but the elect only. If this does not affirm the doctrine of particular redemption, or of a limited atonement, we know not what language could express that doctrine more explicitly."

These authorities are sufficient for my purpose at present, though a large number equally explicit might be adduced, showing that it is the common opinion of Calvinists, and certainly the only opinion at all consistent with their system.

Well, now, in view of this doctrine, I alledge the following objections:

(1.) It renders the conclusion unavoidable, that the sinner is absolutely damned, not only without the possibility of salvation, but without any fault of his whatever.

For, first, it was certain he was involved in guilt, without his consent, by the sin of Adam, thousands of years before he was born. It will not be pretended that he was to blame for this, unless it can be shown that a man is blameworthy for an act which occurred thousands of years before he had an existence.

Well, as he was involved in guilt, without his consent, so no plan was ever devised by which it was possible for him to escape from his guilt. He is therefore shut up to be damned in hell torments for ever on account of guilt which he had no part in procuring to himself, and from which it was never possible for him to escape. Sir, is not this dreadful?

(2.) I object to this doctrine further, because it finds the cause of the sinner's reprobation and damnation in his corruption of nature alone.

The doctrine is, that mankind were viewed as fallen in Adam, and all of them under condemnation, and deserving of death; whereupon, God, out of his mere good pleasure, elected a certain definite number to life, and passed by the other definite part, and left them under sentence of death on account of their sin. Of what sin! why, their sinful estate in Adam. This then was the cause of their reprobation and damnation—Adam's sin, and not their own!

It will be no relief to this to insist that the reprobates are also punished for their actual transgressions; for there stands the fact, first, that the sufficient cause of their reprobation, was their sinful state; and if this was the sufficient cause, they might, they would have been damned, if they had never committed one single actual sin! They were damned before ever they committed a sinful act themselves! Nay, I go a step further, and say that the actual sins of the reprobates forms no juster ground of their damnation than their natural corruption, even if we should admit that their actual sins were taken into account in their reprobation; for they were brought into existence with a corrupt nature, from which it never was possible for them to free themselves, which they had no consent in bringing upon themselves; and with it their actual sins were absolutely unavoidable, and so could no more constitute a just ground of damnation than would their inherited depravity.

(3.) And here again let me ask, why shall Calvinists demur when we charge them with holding to infant damnation? The fact is, they hold to no other kind of damnation! Every reprobate was reprobated for that which he possessed as soon as he came into the world! He was damned in the purpose of God for his natural depravity, before he was born, and his after actual transgressions were only the fruits of his reprobation! I can see no difference between consigning an infant to hell, as soon as born, and actually sentencing it as soon as born for its then state, and permitting it to live a hundred years to commit actual sins, that a pretense may be actually created for rendering its damnation doubly deep—only that the latter seems worse than the former!

(4.) I object to the doctrine that God really preferred the damnation of a part to the salvation of all—he chose it as more agreeable to himself, not to meet the ends of justice or promote good government, but purely for his own gratification, that a part should be lost to the glory of his justice, than that all should have an opportunity to be saved!

This is apparent in the fact that Calvinists admit that there was merit enough in the death of Christ to secure the salvation of all; but God, by a sovereign act, limited it to a part. He could have saved all as well as a part, but he preferred not to do it! It will not do to reply, he must damn some to vindicate his justice, for it is contended that the death of Christ was ample, entirely sufficient, to satisfy the claims of justice for the whole race: but God, by a sovereign prerogative, chose to limit it to a part. He must therefore have preferred the damnation of a part, the reprobates, or he would at least have made their salvation possible. Can Dr. Rice assign any reason for the damnation of the reprobate, but the mere good pleasure of God? He could have saved them, but he chose not to do so. And why did he choose not to do so? Is it answered, on account of their sins? But why on account of their sins? Could he not have saved all, as well as a part, when there was a sufficient ransom, and the application of it depended upon his mere sovereign will? That the application was not made, therefore, can be ascribed to nothing else but the good pleasure of God, or he damns a large part of mankind simply because he had rather damn them than save them! Is not this blasphemous?

5. To the Calvinian doctrine of eternal reprobation I further object, as being inconsistent with the Scriptures:

(1.) To all those passages which teach that "Christ died for *all men*," for "the whole world," &c. This class of Scripture texts is quite numerous, and very unequivocal.

"Behold the Lamb of God, which taketh away the sin of the world." "God so loved the world that he gave his only-begotten Son, that whosoever believeth on him should not perish, but have everlasting life." "This is indeed the

Christ, the Savior of the world." "For the love of Christ constraineth us, because we thus judge, that if one died for all, then were all dead." "That he, by the grace of God, should taste death for every man." "And he is the propitiation for our sins, and not for ours only, but also for the sins of the whole world." "Who is the Savior of all men, especially of those that believe." "Who gave himself a ransom for ali, to be testified in due time."

We give the above as a selection of texts asserting that the death of Christ was for all men, for every man, for the whole world. The list might be greatly extended; but, for the present, these are sufficient.

(2.) The same fact is clearly taught in all those passages where a parallel is run between the death of Christ and the fall of our first parents. "For as in Adam all die, even so in Christ shall all be made alive." "But not as the offense, so also is the free gift. For if, through the offense of one, many be dead, much more the grace of God, and the gift by grace, which is by one man, Jesus Christ, hath abounded unto many. Therefore, as by the offense of one judgment came upon all men unto condemnation, even so by the righteousness of one the free gift came upon all men unto justification of life."

(3.) The idea that Christ died for the elect only is contrary to those Scriptures, which teach that some for whom Christ died may perish. "And through thy knowledge shall thy weak brother perish, for whom Christ died." "False teachers who privily shall bring in damnable heresies, even denying the Lord that bought them, and bring upon themselves swift destruction." "Of how much sorer punishment suppose ye shall he be thought worthy, who has trodden under foot the Son of God, and hath counted the blood of the covenant, wherewith he was sanctified, an unholy thing, and hath done despite unto the spirit of grace." "Destroy not him, with thy meat, for whom Christ died."

(4.) A further argument is deducible from those passages which make the offers of the Gospel to all men, and require all men to repent and believe, condemning them to death for rejecting the offer, and refusing to comply. "He that believeth on the Son hath everlasting life: and he that believeth not the Son, shall not see life; but the wrath of God abideth on him." "But these are written that ye might believe that Jesus is the Christ, the Son of God, and that believing ye might have life through his name." "He that believeth not is condemned already, because he hath not believed in the name of the only-begotten Son of God." "And said unto them, Go ye into all the world, and preach my Gospel to every creature. He that believeth and is baptized, shall be saved; but he that believeth not, shall be damned." "How shall we escape, if we neglect so great salvation?"

(5.) In all those passages in which men's failure to obtain salvation is placed to the account of their own will, this doctrine of limited atonement, of election, and reprobation, is disallowed. "How often would I have gathered thy children together, as a hen gathereth her chickens under her wings, and ye would not." "And ye will not come to me that ye may have life." "Bringing upon themselves swift destruction." "Whosoever will, let him take the waters of life freely."

It is useless to multiply quotations, since the New Testament so constantly exhorts men to come to Christ, reproves them for neglect, and threatens them with the penal consequences of their own folly, thus uniformly placing the bar of their salvation just where Christ places it in his parable of the supper—in the perverseness of those who, having been bidden to the feast, would not come.

Thus the idea that Christ did not die for all men is contrary to all those Scriptures, in which the atonement is represented as universal—in which it is contrasted with the fall—in which it is represented as possible for those for whom Christ died to perish—in which all men are required to believe, and condemned for not believing—in which failure to obtain salvation is charged to the will and folly of the lost—in which invitations are made to sinners, warnings given to saints, as though the former might be saved, the latter lost—in which conditions are expressed, the volition of the creature is addressed, and final destiny is suspended upon their action, with a great variety of classes of Scriptures needless to mention.

6. If Christ only died for a part of mankind, and if only a definite number may come to him and be saved, I ask Dr. Rice, in the name of all reason and consistency, with what propriety can he invite persons, not of the elect, to come to Christ, to turn that they may have life, to seek the favor of God? &c. Why does he make such invitations? He knows they cannot comply; that it is absolutely impossible; that they have no more power to do so than they have to make a world. Is it not mockery, then, to ask them? Are not all such invitations sheer trifling with interests the most awful and tremendous? Invite a sinner to come to Christ when he cannot—when he dare not! In the name of consistency, how is this to be reconciled with human candor, to say nothing of Divine sincerity?

7. But again: if Christ only died for the elect, why are reprobates commanded to believe? What are they required to believe? Are they required to believe in Christ for salvation. If so, they are either able to believe, or they are not. If not able, they are required to perform an absolute impossibility. If they are able, then they may believe; and as salvation is by faith, a reprobate may be saved; and if saved, he will be saved by believing a lie—that Christ was

his Savior, when in fact he was not: he will also be saved without a Savior; but if he believes and is not saved, he will falsify the Scriptures and the Confession, which teach that whosoever believeth shall be saved.

8. But again: why is the unbelief of the reprobate made the ground of his condemnation—of his final destruction? He is damned for not believing on Christ; that is, for not believing a lie. Had he believed on Christ, if the thing were possible, he would have believed a lie; but for not believing a lie, he is damned for ever. Sir, is not this dreadful! Yet these, and many more such consequences, are the unavoidable results of your system.

9. The sinner's damnation is ascribed to his rejection of Christ—to his resistance of proffered mercy—to his willful distance from God. But, according to this system, he does not reject Christ, for Christ never was offered to him; he could not accept him; he did not refuse mercy, for mercy never was held out to his acceptance; his own will did not keep him in sin, for there never was a way of escape.

10. The Scriptures ascribe the sinner's ruin to his own choice—to his own will; but, according to this system, his will has nothing whatever to do with it; for either it was possible for him to will to come to Christ and be saved, or it was not. If it was possible for him to will to come to Christ and be saved, a reprobate might be saved by Christ, who never died for him; if he could not will to come to Christ, and is damned for not willing it, then he is damned for not performing an impossibility. His destruction is not assignable to the perversity of his own will, but to the fact that no possible chance of salvation was ever given to him.

11. Why do Calvinists demur and complain of us when we say, the reprobate must be damned, do what he may or can? Do they not know this is true? He cannot be saved! It is eternally out of the question, and impossible,

for a cause with which he had no consenting or personal connection, any more than Gabriel had.

12. Why do Calvinists complain when we say, the elect must be saved, do what they may or can? Do they not know that this is so? One of the elect cannot be lost—no sin, in his power, will ever peril his salvation. He cannot, though he exert himself to that end, endanger his soul in the slightest degree. And this Dr. Rice will be compelled to admit. I say not, now, that he will not endanger his salvation, but I say he cannot. He is now saved, and never can be lost. The poor reprobate cannot be saved, do what he may. Tell me not that he might if he would; it is sinning to pretend any thing of the kind. If he willed ever so much, he has no Savior! He is damned without any fault of his, and when escape was impossible.

13. Why remonstrate with the reprobate upon the folly of his course, and about destroying himself? Does not God know that the poor wretch cannot help it? He help it! he was damned thousands of years before he was born! He never had any hand in it originally! And if he has had since, it was only in this way: He was given an existence, which he was compelled to employ in sin, that a pretense might be furnished infinite cruelty for doubly damning him! Why will you die? What language to put in the mouth of God concerning the reprobates!

14. Why expostulate with the elect upon the necessity of watchfulness, the use of means, the danger of coming short of life, and such like? There is no danger to the elect; he can do nothing more nor less than was decreed; and if he could do ever so much, his works have nothing to do in regard to his salvation. Is it pretended, that warnings are designed to stimulate to duty? Then, I answer, a deception is attempted to be played off upon the elect, to promote the fruits of the Spirit!

15. I object to the whole system, that it destroys the

moral government of God, and renders his sovereignty a blind, capricious, and tyrannical sovereignty. The idea of moral government is that of dealing with men according to their deeds; but this system excludes such idea entirely. Men are elected unto life without respect to their deeds, and they are also appointed unto damnation without respect to their deeds. Let it not be said that their deeds are taken into the account, in their election and reprobation; for it is previously said, that these—election and reprobation—are unconditional and without foresight, and so can have no respect whatever to character or conduct; and so, according to Calvinism, there is no such thing as dealing with men according to character or conduct—no moral government. But, even if the system admitted conduct and character as questions in the Divine government, it would not help the case in the slightest degree; because these, according to the system, are necessitated, without any agency of the creature whatever. The character and conduct are forced upon him, and then he is held to account for them! All this may be denied, and no doubt will be; but denials are useless, so long as the system is liable to such logical imputation. According to Calvinism, there is no moral government. When some are admitted to heaven, and others are consigned to hell, the sole cause of their different destinies is the decree of God, by which the former were elected, and the latter reprobated; and their respective vice or virtue was the fruit of their previously determined fate, not its cause. They are rewarded not according to their works, but according to the decree of God.

16. The Calvinian doctrine of election and reprobation, in the place of making the atonement a benefit to the reprobates, makes it an infinite curse, not in its avoidable abuse, but in itself necessarily. So that here is a sovereign scheme of God, intended to be a benefit to some chosen persons, by being, in its very nature, an infinite curse to

others. This must appear in one moment. Let it be remembered, that the atonement, with respect to reprobates, does not make their salvation possible—they cannot be saved by it. Let it be further remembered, that, while it does not make it possible for them to be saved, it makes their damnation a hundred-fold worse than if it had never been made—it does them no real good—it brings them infinite mischief, and this entirely without respect to any thing in them that was voluntary; and this their infinitely increased misery is upon a false pretense. They are called to return unto God—to repent—to believe in Christ—to a holy life: no one of which calls could they possibly obey; and yet, for not obeying, every time they refuse, their damnation is increased. Is not this awful—frightful! Could Satanic cruelty display greater malevolence than is here supposed? Every mercy, every call, every seeming good, is so arranged as necessarily to sink the poor, miserable victim deeper into the quenchless flames of eternal damnation. Thou glorious God of the universe, whose very nature is love, what a representation of thy character!—holding out to thy hapless, miserable creatures, an empty semblance of good, which it is *impossible*, in the nature of things, for them to attain, and then increasing their already dreadful miseries for failing to comply; and still repeating the impracticable, heartless offer, every day, every hour, that, by their unavoidable rejection, they may go on sinking deeper and deeper yet into torments, beyond the power of mind to conceive, and of eternal continuance! Dreadful! dreadful! dreadful! Thou great Spirit of the heavens, art thou such a monster as this!

In the language of Mr. Wesley, "This is the blasphemy for which—however I love the persons who assert it—I abhor the doctrine of predestination: a doctrine, upon the supposition of which, if one could possibly suppose it for a moment, one might say to our adversary, the devil, 'Thou

fool, why dost thou roar about any longer? Thy lying in wait for souls is as needless and useless as our preaching. Hearest thou not that God hath taken thy work out of thy hands? and that he doth it more effectually? Thou, with all thy principalities and powers, canst only so assault that we may resist thee. But he can irresistibly destroy both soul and body in hell! Thou canst only entice. But his unchangeable decree, to leave thousands of souls in death, compels them to continue in sin till they drop into everlasting burnings. Thou temptest; he forceth us to be damned, for we cannot resist his will. Thou fool, why goest thou about any longer, seeking whom thou mayest devour? Hearest thou not that God is the devouring lion—the destroyer of souls—the murderer of men? Moloch caused only children to pass through the fire; and that fire was soon quenched, or, the corruptible body being consumed, its torments were at an end. But God, thou art told by his eternal decree, fixed before they had done good or evil causes whom he destroys to pass through the fires of hell—the fire which shall never be quenched; and the body which is cast thereinto, being now incorruptible and immortal, will be ever consuming and never consumed, but the smoke of their torment, because it is *God's* good *pleasure*, ascendeth up for ever and ever.'

"O how would the enemy of God and man rejoice to hear these things were so! How would he cry aloud and spare not! How would he lift up his voice and say, 'To your tents, O Israel!' Flee from the presence of this God, or ye shall utterly perish! But whither will ye flee: into heaven? He is there. Down to hell? He is there also. Ye cannot flee from an omnipresent, almighty tyrant. And whether ye flee or stay, I call heaven, his throne, and the earth, his footstool, to witness against you, ye shall perish; ye shall die eternally. Sing, O hell, and rejoice ye that are under the earth; for God, even the mighty God, hath

spoken, and devoted to death thousands of souls, from the rising of the sun unto the going down thereof. Here, O death, is thy sting! They shall not, cannot escape; for the mouth of the Lord hath spoken it. Here, O grave, is thy victory! Nations yet unborn, or ere they had done good or evil, are doomed never to see the light of life, but thou shalt gnaw upon them for ever and ever. Let all those morning stars sing together who fell with Lucifer, son of the morning. Let all the sons of hell shout for joy! For the decree is past, and who shall disannul it!"

Do you shudder at this? is your whole soul filled with just horror at the blasphemous intimation? Who, let me ask, is guilty of the enormous blasphemy? Who is it that thus charges God foolishly, nay, wickedly? Reflect, ye that hold to *unconditional election and reprobation!* how can you escape? In the sight of heaven and earth, are you not guilty? Have you not aspersed the glorious God, and made wicked men and devils to triumph in your blasphemies? In the spirit of kindness and love we beseech you to consider these things; and may God help you!

17. The doctrine of election and reprobation, if true, renders the condition of mankind far worse than that of devils in hell; for these were, sometime, in a capacity to have stood; they might have kept their happy estate, but would not; whereas, many millions of men, according to this doctrine, are tormented for ever, without ever having had the opportunity to be happy! It renders the fate of human beings worse than the beasts of the field, of whom the master requires no more than they are able to perform; and if they die, death is to them the end of all sorrow; whereas, man is in pain without end, for not doing that which he never was able to do. It puts him in a far worse state than Pharaoh put the Israelites; for though he withheld straw from them, yet they could obtain it by much labor. But this doctrine makes God to withhold from the reprobates

all means of salvation, so that they cannot attain it by all their pains. Yea, it places mankind in that condition which the poets feign of Tantalus, who, oppressed with thirst, stands in water up to the chin, yet can, by no means, reach it with his tongue; and being tormented with hunger, hath fruit hanging at his very lips, yet so as he can never lay hold of it with his teeth; and these things are so near him, not to nourish him, but torment him. So does this doctrine make God deal with mankind. It makes the outward creation, the work of Providence, the smiting of conscience, sufficient to convince the reprobates of sin, but never intended to help them to salvation. It makes the preaching of the Gospel, and the offer of salvation by Christ, sufficient to condemn them, serving to beget a seeming faith and vain hopes; yet, by reason of God's irresistible decree, all these are wholly ineffectual to bring them the least step toward salvation, and do only contribute to make their condemnation the greater, and their torments the more violent and intolerable. Truly, if these things be so, may the man with his one talent in the day of final settlement say to the Judge, "I knew thee that thou art a hard man, reaping where thou hast not sown, and gathering where thou hast not strewed." Such is Calvinism—such are some of the difficulties of this boasted system, which Dr. Rice, after proclaiming his readiness, nay even anxiety, to defend for years past, has not even attempted to remove, and, though pledged, I venture to predict, to my readers, he never will attempt to remove, by a direct refutation. Dr. Rice knows very well it cannot be done: he will not hazard a trial of his powers here. With all his fondness for debate—with his professed conviction that controversy serves the cause of truth, he will never squarely meet these points. But why is this—why will these issues be avoided? Does any one believe that, if they could be triumphantly met, it would not be done? Do Presbyterians believe this? Does

not Dr. Rice understand his own heart sufficiently well tc know, that his present backwardness proceeds from consciousness that he could not make a successful defense? Let him not deceive himself upon this point—let him not suppose he can deceive the public, who are acquainted with the facts in the case—let him not imagine that either silence or evasion will answer under existing circumstances. If the objections alledged can be answered, let him, as a lover of truth and as a teacher of the erring, come to the work. If we are in error, and he can show it with so much ease, he may thereby advance his cherished system, and do good service in the cause of his Redeemer. Will he allow the opportunity to pass? Will he amuse his readers with evasions—invectives? Or will he come to the work as a candid, magnanimous, Christian disputant? All this is for Dr. Rice to determine.

We have expressed a part of the objections we find against decrees in general, and the decree of election and reprobation in particular, as held by Calvinists. We have studied brevity—presented our arguments in the smallest possible limits, even at the hazard, in some instances, of lessening their force; and we have avoided using a great number of additional arguments, because of their seeming severity. The objections we have thus brought against Calvinism, we believe to be legitimate and unavoidable to the system. For the refreshing of our readers, we subjoin a brief recapitulation.

1. We object to the Calvinistic system, that it renders the conclusion unavoidable that God is the responsible author of sin—author in the sense of originator and cause.

2. It is inconsistent with, and destructive of, the free agency of man.

3. It destroys human accountability.

4. It removes moral quality from human actions and volitions—renders man incapable of vice or virtue.

5. In the day of judgment it must place the conscience and judgment of the universe on the side of the condemned, and against God.

6. It puts a justifying plea in the mouth of the sinner for all his crimes while upon earth, and renders all punishments, human and divine, essentially unjust and tyrannical.

7. It asperses the character of God in a most dreadful manner, inevitably involving,

(1.) His holiness, showing him to be the very centre and author of all impurity.

(2.) His benevolence, showing him to be a minister of cruelty.

(3.) His justice, showing him to be the direst tyrant.

(4.) His truthfulness and sincerity, proving him to be an amalgam of duplicity and falsehood.

8. It makes God self-contradictory, and the author of all the absurdities and contradictions, yea, of all things of whatever description in the universe.

9. It is calculated to do away all sense of obligation, and to produce recklessness, crime, and despair.

10. It is wholly without foundation, either in reason or Scripture.

11. It makes God the author of man's fall.

12. It teaches that some are elected to life, and others unto death, wholly without respect to their character or conduct, thus leaving sin and virtue entirely out of the question in regard to human destiny.

13. It renders God a partial being, and at the same time entirely destroys the doctrine of grace.

14. It teaches not only unconditional reprobation, but also that for the reprobates Christ did not die in any sense.

15. It is inconsistent with the Scriptures:

(1.) Which teach a universal atonement.

(2.) Which teach that some, for whom Christ died, may finally perish.

(3.) Which offer salvation to all men.

(4.) In which failure to obtain salvation is ascribed to the perversity of the human will.

(5.) In which warnings and expostulations are used toward sinners, and also toward saints.

16. It is inconsistent with all calls and invitations to sinners by the ministry of the word.

17. It is inconsistent with commands and exhortations to sinners to believe.

18. It is inconsistent with making the unbelief of the sinner the cause of his condemnation.

19. It is inconsistent with ascribing the sinner's damnation to his rejection of Christ.

20. It is inconsistent in making the sinner's own choice the cause of his ruin.

21. It makes it impossible for reprobates to be saved, do what they may or can.

22. It makes it impossible for the elect to be lost, do what they may or can.

23. It renders all remonstrance, exhortation, or entreaty, either to the elect or reprobates, absurd.

24. It makes the atonement, in itself, in its very nature, and necessarily, an infinite curse to millions of human beings.

Such are a part of the objections we bring against this system—all of them unavoidably bearing against it, and any one of them sufficient, as we believe, to render it unworthy of all credit and respect. And the most casual reader must perceive that each one of these objections must necessarily bring, in its train, many others equally revolting. How, I ask, in the name of reason, Scripture, humanity, and religion, can a system, so embarrassed, find advocates among rational beings?

The only attempt at reply is contained in a denial, that they are a true representation of Calvinism in the premises. The argumentation is thus admitted to be sound. No effort has been made to correct the misrepresentations—no authority has been rejected—no specific points named, but simply a blank denial that Calvinists do not believe what is charged against them—no argument sustaining the charges has been refuted—no quotation set aside. What a beautiful defense this! How creditable to men who have vaunted their readiness for controversy! who have ceased not to disturb sister Churches, who were content with peace, and anxious to maintain it! What an intellectual, manly, Christian palladium this, when consequences unavoidable are proved, to meet them with the rational and lucid reply, "We do not believe these things!" But if this is the best defense your system is capable of, we must not complain. You have done the best you could; and as it is not in our creed to hold men accountable for more than they have ability to perform, we must appreciate your effort.

You will excuse us, however, for going on to show how unsound your defense is, and for pointing out your mistake, in charging us with misrepresentation. You believe that we are guilty—that the system is not so *bad* as we made appear; but we shall show you that the mistake is your own—that it is precisely what we declared.

I have charged upon the system that it makes God the author of sin, and destroys the free agency and accountability of man. Dr. Rice replied—for he commenced replying to my letters, and, for reasons doubtless sufficient in his esteem, abruptly ceased—that the objections had been often refuted, and that no Presbyterian author taught the doctrine which I charged upon them. This last statement of the Doctor's I have shown to be an entire mistake, by quoting many authors who unequivocally teach the very things he denies, and for which he says they would be deposed—I suggest to the Doctor that he had better depose them yet, whether living or dead—Calvin, Hill, Dwight, Chalmers, Witsius, Shaw, the Westminster Assembly, Buck, &c.; and now, having proved that these distinguished men did and do teach precisely what I charged, I leave it with my readers to judge who has misrepresented Calvinists, Dr Rice or myself.

But I shall now proceed to show that the former part of his assertion is also without foundation, in which he says these objections have often been answered. This, I assert, is a mistake—they have never been answered. If Dr. Rice, as he affirms, will refer to a single answer upon which he will rely, and it proves conclusive, we will confess ourselves wrong in the charges we have made. But lest the Doctor will find it convenient to be silent just now, I will help my readers to some of the answers about which these vauntings are made—some of the lucid and luminous refutations given; and to prevent the idea that we have selected weak apologies from feeble men, we shall select from the champions, the confessed fathers of the defense.

Take Witsius: how does he answer to these charges? Hear him: "And though it be difficult, *nay, impossible,* for us to reconcile these truths with each other, [namely, how God causes the vicious actions of men, but not the sin itself,] yet we ought not to deny what is manifest, on account of that which is hard to be understood. We will religiously profess both truths, because they are truths, and worthy of God: nor can the one overturn the other; though in this, our state of blindness and ignorance of God, we cannot see the amicable harmony between them." Now, I appeal to my readers, is not this overwhelming refutation—unanswerable argument! How dare any Arminian ever again name the exploded objection!

But if this does not suffice, hear Calvin himself, and see how, at a stroke of his pen, he demolishes all his opposers. After asserting that Adam fell in consequence of the Divine predestination, and supposing the objection introduced, that this makes God the author of sin, he thus replies: "But it follows not, therefore, that God is liable to this reproach. For we will answer them thus, in the language of Paul, 'O man, who art thou that repliest against God? Shall the thing formed say to him that formed it, Why hast thou made me thus?'" Surely this is sufficient to satisfy any Arminian! Can you, my readers, conceive of logic more irresistible! Is it strange that Dr. Rice should say this old objection has been answered a thousand times! Is not either one of the foregoing replies a thousand-fold answer itself!

But hear Mr. Dick, a modern. He says, in answer to the objection that Calvinism makes God the author of sin, "I confess that the statement may be objected to as not complete; that there are still difficulties that press upon us; that perplexing questions may be proposed, and that the answers which have been returned to them by great divines are not satisfactory in every instance, as those imagine who do not think for themselves, and take too much upon trust. The subject is above our comprehension. There are two propositions of the truth of which we are fully assured—that God has foreordained all things which come to pass, and that he is not the author of sin. *There can be no doubt about either of them in the mind of the man who believes the Scriptures.* He may not be able to reconcile them, but this ought not to weaken his conviction of their truth." Was ever argumentation more transparent! Ye Arminians, how can you withstand such reasoning! How dare you open your lips again! Where shall you find an apology for such temerity!

Since writing the foregoing, I find Dr. Rice has favored us with his mode of escaping from the charges I have brought against his system. Hear him: "Are these representations true?" he asks; and replies, "This question might be answered by a *fair statement* of the doctrine, and a comparison of its principles with the word of God. There is, also, *another way of answering the question satisfactorily, namely, by inquiring what have been the fruits of this and kindred doctrines called Calvinistic?*" Then follows a long article to show that the fruits of Calvinism have been good; and, therefore, the inference is drawn, it is not liable to the charges we have preferred against it. Now, I ask my readers, is not this a novel mode of escaping logical consequences? "*The fruits of the system are good; therefore, the logical consequences, deduced from its premises, are not legitimate!*" Verily, this is logic!

But soberly, Doctor, do you not know, that there is not a particle of soundness in this argument? that, if your premises were admitted—which cannot be done without great abatement—the conclusion does not follow? that, in direct terms, it is a sheer evasion, substituted to lay your own apprehensions, and turn away from the real matter in dispute? Why do you not, with candor and confidence, take up the real issues, and show us how they may be escaped? If it can be done, and you say it can—you tell your readers it has been for a thousandth time—why do you waste your strength in such complete evasions, which must unavoidably produce the impression, that your representations are founded in error?

CHAPTER IV.

THE ATONEMENT.

In this chapter we shall take up the Calvinian view of the atonement. What do Calvinists believe on this point? This question shall be answered by their Confession of Faith, and their standard authors.

The Confession of Faith says: "Wherefore, they who are elected, being fallen in Adam, are redeemed by Christ—are effectually called unto faith in Christ, by his Spirit working in due season—are justified, adopted, sanctified, and kept by his power through faith unto salvation. Neither are *any other redeemed by Christ,* effectually called, justified, adopted, sanctified, and saved, but *the elect only.*"

Upon this section, the expositor of the Confession, indorsed by the board of publication, makes the following remarks: "In this section we are taught, that *Christ died exclusively for the elect, and purchased redemption for them alone;* in other words, that Christ made atonement only for the elect; *and that in no sense did he die for the rest of the race.* Our Confession first asserts, positively, that the elect are redeemed by Christ; and then, negatively, that none others are redeemed by Christ, but the elect only. If this does not affirm the doctrine of particular redemption, or of a limited atonement, we know not what language could express that doctrine more explicitly."

Hear the Confession again: "To all those for whom Christ hath purchased redemption, he doth certainly and effectually apply and communicate the same."

Upon this section, the expositor of the Confession remarks: "This section relates to the extent of Christ's death, with respect to its objects, and in opposition to the Arminian tenet, that Christ died for all men—for those who shall finally perish, as well as for those who shall be eventually saved; it affirms that the purchase and application of redemption are of the same extent. In the fifth section, we were taught that Christ purchased redemption only for those whom the Father hath given him, and here it is asserted that, to all those for whom Christ hath purchased redemption, he doth certainly and effectually apply and communicate the same. What language, then, could affirm more explicitly, than that here employed, that the atonement of Christ is specific and limited, that it is *neither universal* nor indefinite, but *restricted to the elect*, who shall be saved from wrath through him?

"The sacrifice of Christ derived infinite value from the divinity of his person; it must, therefore, have been intrinsically sufficient to expiate the sins of the whole human race, *had it been so intended;* but in the design of the Father, and in the intention of Christ himself, *it was limited to a definite number, who shall* ultimately obtain salvation."

The interpretation thus given to the Confession, is sustained by the author quoted, with eleven arguments in support of limited atonement. I think all will admit, that he has fairly and correctly expressed the sense of his Confession, and the doctrine of all consistent Calvinists. His language is explicit; and I embrace his definition, as the best I have seen, of the Calvinian view of the atonement.

"*Christ died exclusively for the elect, and purchased redemption for them alone; in other words, Christ made atonement only for the elect; and in no sense did he die for the rest of the race.*"

Corroborative of this statement, I shall proceed to quote from many other distinguished Calvinists, that there may be no mistake as to the meaning of the system, as understood by its friends.

"We shall now consider the persons for whom, as a priest, Christ offered himself, and so enter on that subject which is so much controverted in this present age, namely, Whether Christ died for all men, or only for the elect, whom he designed hereby to redeem and bring to salvation. And here let it be premised,

"1. That it is generally taken for granted by those who maintain either side of the question, that the saving effects of Christ's death do not redound to all men, or that Christ did not die, in this respect, for all the world, since to assert this would be to argue that all men shall be saved, which every one supposes contrary to the whole tenor of Scripture.

"2. It is allowed, by those who deny the extent of Christ's death to all men, as to what concerns their salvation, that it may truly be said that there are some blessings redounding to the whole world, and more especially to those who sit under the sound of the Gospel, as the consequence of Christ's death; inasmuch as it is owing hereunto, that the day of God's patience is lengthened out, and the preaching of the Gospel continued to those who are favored with it; and that this is attended, in many, with restraining grace, and some instances of external reformation, which has a tendency to prevent a multitude of sins, and a greater degree of condemnation that would otherwise ensue. These may be called the remote or secondary ends of Christ's death, which principally and immediately designed to redeem the elect, and to purchase all saving blessings for them, which shall be applied in his own time and way: nevertheless, others, as a consequence hereof, are made partakers of some blessings of common providence, so far as they are subservient to the salvation of those for whom he gave himself a ransom.

"3. It is allowed on both sides, and especially by all who own the divinity and satisfaction of Christ, that his death was sufficient to redeem the whole world, had God designed that it should be a price for them, which is the result of the infinite value of it; therefore,

"4. The main question before us is, whether God designed the salvation of all mankind by the death of Christ, or whether he accepted it as a price of redemption for all, so that it might be said that he redeemed some who shall not be saved by him? This is affirmed by many who affirm universal redemption, *which we must take leave to deny.* And they further add, as an explanation hereof, that Christ died that he might put all men into a salvable state, or procure a possibility of salvation for them; so that many might obtain it, by a right improvement of his death, who shall fall short of it, and also that it is in their power to frustrate the end thereof, and so render it ineffectual. This we judge not only to be an error, but such as is highly derogatory to the glory of God, which we shall endeavor to make appear, and to establish the contrary doctrine, namely, *that Christ died to purchase salvation for none but those who shall obtain it.*" (Ridgley's Divinity.)

"We therefore conclude," says Witsius, "that the obedience and suffering of Christ, considered in themselves, are, on account of the infinite dignity of the person, of that value, as to have been sufficient for redeeming, not only all and every man in particular, but many myriads besides, had it so pleased God and Christ, that he should have undertaken and satisfied for them.

"The suretyship and satisfaction of Christ, have also been an occasion of much good even to the reprobate; for it is owing to the death of Christ, that the Gospel is preached to every creature—that gross idolatry is abolished in many parts of the world—that wicked impiety is much restrained by the discipline of the word of God—that they obtain at times many and excellent, though not saving gifts of the Holy Spirit—that they have escaped the pollutions of the world, through the knowledge of the Lord and Savior Jesus Christ. And who can, in short, enumerate all those things which they enjoy, not through accident only, and beside the intention of God and Christ, but by the appointment of God? *Not, indeed, with a design and purpose of saving them, according to the testament, but from a view to make known his long-suffering toward the vessels of wrath, that is, those who are to perish, who dwell among those who are to be saved; for nothing falls out by accident with God, every thing being according to his determinate counsel.*

"That the obedience and suffering of Christ are of such worth, that all, without exception, who come to him, may find perfect salvation in him; and it was the will of God that this truth should, without distinction, be proposed both to them that are to be saved, and to them that are to perish, with a charge not to neglect so great salvation, but to repair to Christ with true contrition of soul; and with a *most sincere* declaration that all who come to him shall find salvation in him.

"*That, nevertheless, Christ, according to the will of God the Father, and his own purpose, did neither engage nor satisfy, and consequently in no manner die, but only for all those whom the Father gave him, and who actually are to be saved.*

"*If we search the matter to the bottom, we shall learn that it never was Christ's intention to satisfy for all in general. Certainly he satisfied only for those he engaged for. But he engaged to do the will of his Father. But this is the will of his Father, not that every man should be saved, but those that were given him, that is, the elect out of every nation, who are to receive the gift of faith.*"

"The two sides of this question [Arminian and Calvinian] do not imply any difference of opinion with regard to the sufferings of Christ's death, or with regard to the number and character of those who shall eventually be saved. They who hold the one and the other side of the question agree, that although the sufferings of Christ have a value sufficient to atone for all the sins of all the children of Adam, from the beginning to the end of time, yet those only shall be saved by this atonement who repent and believe. But they differ as to the destination of the death of Christ—whether, in the purpose of the Father and the will of the Son, it respected all mankind, or only those persons to whom the benefit of it is at length to be applied."

After many remarks highly eulogistic of the doctrine of general or universal redemption, the author remarks of his own, the Calvinistic system:

"The Calvinistic system gives a very different view of the application of the remedy; and *the difference may be traced back to its fundamental principle, that Christ did not die for all men, but for those in every nation who, in the end, are to be saved.* Them only he delivers from the curse, and for them only he purchases those influences of the Spirit, by which faith and repentance are produced." (Hill's Divinity.)

"Nor do we hesitate to admit, that all mankind, as well as those who live under the Gospel's light, have been benefited by the Redeemer's death. Blessings have flowed from this precious fountain of mercy to our sinful world, that would, if Christ had not died, been withheld. But when the question is proposed, What is the extent of the Savior's atonement? for whom did he satisfy Divine justice? in whose place did he lay down his precious life? we *answer, for all to whom his atonement shall be applied; for all whom his Father gave him to redeem.*" (Presbyterian Tracts.)

"Not so the advocates of indefinite atonement. *They affirm that Christ died for all and every man. This we cannot believe.*" (Ib.)

"On the extent of Christ's atonement, the two opinions that have long divided the Church are expressed by the terms, definite and indefinite. The former means, that Christ died, satisfied Divine justice, and made atonement, *only* for such as are saved. The latter means, that Christ died, satisfied Divine justice, and made atonement for all mankind, without exception. *The former opinion, or what is called definite atonement, is that which we adopt.* It may be thus stated: *That the Lord Jesus Christ made atonement to God, by his death, only for the sins of those to whom, in the sovereign good pleasure of the Almighty, the benefits of his death shall be finally applied. By this definition, the extent of Christ's atonement is limited to those who ultimately enjoy its fruits; it is restricted to the elect of God, for whom alone we conceive him to have laid down his life.*" (Presbyterian Tracts.)

"Redemption is certainly applied and effectually communicated to all those for whom Christ has purchased it." (Larger Catechism.)

"And here we believe, after all, lies the main point of dispute in regard to the atonement. Among those who agree as to its nature, the chief question in dispute is, What is its design? what was it intended to effect? This question was briefly discussed in the former discourse, and we endeavored to point out some of the consequences which would flow from the belief, that Christ died intentionally to save all mankind. Such a belief must inevitably lead to Socinianism on the one hand, or Universalism on the other." (Great Supper.)

"The advocates of a limited or definite atonement, [Calvinists,] on the other hand, maintain, that the atonement cannot be considered apart from its actual application—that, in strictness of speech, the death of Christ is not an atonement for any until it be applied—that the sufferings of the Lamb of God are truly vicarious, or, in other words, that Christ, in suffering, became a real substitute for his people, was charged with their sins, and bore the punishment of them, and thus was made a full and complete satisfaction to Divine justice, in behalf of all those who shall ever believe on him—that this atonement will eventually be applied to all for whom, in the Divine intention, it was made, or to all whom God, in his sovereignty, has been pleased to decree its application. They believe, however, notwithstanding the atonement is to be considered as exactly commensurate with its intended application, that the Lord Jesus Christ did offer a sacrifice, sufficient in its intrinsic value, to expiate the sins of the whole world, and that if it had been the pleasure of God to apply it to every individual, the whole human race would have been saved by its immeasurable worth. They hold, therefore, that, on the ground of the infinite value of the atonement, the offer of salvation can be consistently made to all who hear the Gospel, assuring them that if they will believe they shall be saved; whereas, if they will reject the overture of mercy, they will increase their guilt, and aggravate their damnation. At the same time, the Scriptures plainly teach, that the will and disposition to comply with this condition depends upon the sovereign gift of God, and that the actual compliance is secured to those only for whom, in the Divine counsels, the atonement was specifically intended." (Buck.)

"It [the Confession of Faith, chap. iii, sec. vi] is diametrically opposed to the system of the Arminians, who hold that Jesus Christ, by his death and sufferings, made an atonement for the sins of all mankind in general, and of every individual in particular. It is not less opposed to the doctrine maintained by many, that though the death of Christ had a special reference to the elect, and, in connection with the Divine purpose, infallibly secures their salvation, yet that it has also a general reference, and made an equal atonement for all men. The celebrated Richard Baxter, who favored general redemption, makes the following remark upon this and another section of our Confession, [chap. iii, sec. vi, and chap. viii, sec. viii,] which speak against universal redemption: 'I understand not of all redemption, and particularly not of the mere bearing the punishment of man's sins, and satisfying God's justice, but of that special redemption proper to the elect, which was accompanied with an intention of actual application of the saving benefits in time. If I may not be allowed this interpretation, I must hence dissent.' The language of the Confession, in my opinion, will not admit of this interpretation; and, what is more, the Bible is silent about this general redemption, or the general reference of the death of Christ." (Expositor of Confession.)

"It was the will of God that Christ, by the blood of the cross, should efficaciously redeem those, and those *only*, who were, from eternity, elected to salvation, and given to him by the Father." (Buck.)

"It was the most free counsel and gracious will and intention of God the Father, that the quickening and saving efficacy of the most precious death of his Son should exert itself in all the elect, to give unto them *only* justifying faith, and by it to conduct them infallibly unto salvation: that is, it was the will of God that Christ, by the blood of the cross, whereby he confirmed the new covenant, should efficaciously redeem those, and those only, who were, from eternity, elected to salvation, and given to him by the Father." (Synod of Dort.)

The foregoing quotations contain what we understand to be the Calvinian view of the *extent* of the atonement. It would be an easy thing greatly to extend the list of authorities, and also the amount of quotation from each; but this is not deemed necessary, as it is presumed there will be no dispute upon the point now in question.

From the authorities cited, we make the following deductions:

1. Calvinists believe that the death of Christ is of sufficient value, intrinsically, to make atonement for all the sins of the whole world, had it been so intended.

2. That resulting from his death are many benefits and blessings to all men—the reprobate in common with the elect.

3. That though his death is thus sufficient to be an atonement for the world, yet it is not an atonement for all, because he did not die for all, but simply and only for the elect.

The limitation of his death to a part, therefore, in their estimation did not proceed from the fact that his death had only value sufficient to atone for a part, *but from the fact that he did not choose to die, and his Father did not choose that he should die for all, but only for the elect.* The death itself was sufficient to satisfy for all to Divine justice; but in the design of the Father and the Son, there were some for whom it was not so intended, for whom it did not in any sense atone, and who, whatever common temporal benefits they receive through the operations of the plan, never did and never could receive salvation; because, though the death of Christ was a sufficient sacrifice, they were sovereignly excluded from having any part therein by the purpose of God, who intended it for the elect alone, and in no sense for the reprobate.

That these deductions are legitimate, is so palpable as to need no further vindication; they are indeed distinctly made in the quotations from Witsius, Ridgley, and Hill, already given. With the first, of course we make no issue; and with the second, only as it stands connected with the third.

It is with the third we shall contend in what follows. And it is presumed that Calvinists will not find fault with our statement of their faith. We certainly have represented it in the least objectionable light; or, rather, we have allowed its friends so to represent it. If any thing is to be gained by expletives and mitigated statements, we have allowed them this advantage—blending the terrible feature of limited atonement, with the benign history of Providence toward those who are so unfortunate as to be sovereignly excluded from any possible interest in it—the fact that Christ's death is restricted in the intention of the Father and Son to a part, with the acknowledgment that it was ample and sufficient for all, in its own value—the fact that if any fail to be saved by Christ, it is not because he had not ability to save them; but simply because, in his infinite and inscrutable *mercy*, he thought best that it should not apply to some—that though these cannot possibly be saved by Christ, but must, necessarily, be damned for ever, and damned a thousand-fold worse than if he had never died, yet, in lieu thereof, he has given them many temporal benefits, and if he had so chosen he could have done more for them; but he did not so choose. May God conduct us into all truth!

Having thus given the Calvinian view of the extent of the atonement—namely, "*That the Lord Jesus Christ made atonement to God, by his death, only for the sins of those to whom, in the sovereign good pleasure of the Almighty, the benefits of his death shall be finally applied. Neither are any other redeemed by Christ but the elect only. Christ died exclusively for the elect, and purchased redemption for them alone; in other words, Christ made atonement only for the elect, and in no sense did he die for the rest of the race*"—having thus presented their view of the atonement, in their own language, we shall now proceed to name some objections to it.

1. And, first, we object to it in general terms—all that has been objected to the decree of election and reprobation in the former chapter; for the doctrines are so kindred, that much that is applicable to the one may also be applied to the other: what supports the one supports the other; and what opposes the one antagonizes the other to a great extent.

2. Particularly I object to the doctrine of a limited atonement, that it has no foundation in Scripture. Not a solitary passage, from Genesis to Revelation, asserts the doctrine, that Christ died for only a part of mankind—no passage implies it—it finds no countenance in any fact or principle of revelation. That it is repeatedly said that Christ died for particular persons and classes is not disputed, but it is nowhere said, it is nowhere implied, that he did not die for others. This, then, is one great objection I bring to bear against this doctrine—*it is nowhere revealed in the word of God.*

3. I object to it, that it is not only nowhere taught in the word of God, but is *directly contrary* to multitudes of express declarations of revelation, and to the whole tenor of Divine teaching.

(1.) It is contrary to those passages which teach that Christ died for all men—for every man—for the whole world.

(2.) It is contrary to those Scriptures which contrast the death of Christ with the fall of Adam.

(3.) It is contrary to those Scriptures which represent those who are lost as purchased by Christ.

(4.) It is contrary to those Scriptures which make offer of the benefits of Christ's death to all men.

(5.) It is contrary to those Scriptures which require all men to believe on and accept Christ.

(6.) It is contrary to those Scriptures which represent the cause of the sinner's damnation as being his rejection of Christ, and unbelief in him.

(7.) It is contrary to those Scriptures which represent that those who are finally lost might have been saved.

(8.) It is contrary to those Scriptures which represent the Lord as not willing the destruction of sinners, but as regretting their folly, and desiring them to turn and live.

(9.) It is contrary to those Scriptures which represent God as a being of universal love.

(10.) It is contrary to those Scriptures which represent him as impartial.

(11.) It is contrary to those Scriptures which represent him as just.

4. I object that not only is not the doctrine of a limited atonement nowhere taught in the Scriptures, and not only is it diametrically contrary to the whole tenor of revelation, and many express passages thereof, but it is also adversative to all our conceptions of the character of God as the universal parent. In the light, or rather in the darkness, of its consequences, we are compelled to change all our views of his character and nature. Shorn of all his glorious perfections of infinite benevolence, and impartiality, and truth, and sincerity, he is presented to us as a hideous compound of cruelty, and caprice, and duplicity, and falsehood. I know these are severe charges; and it is their indisputable truth, as every one, who will be at the pains of a faithful examination, will be compelled to admit, that makes them severe.

Can any man believe, is it in the power of the human mind, that God is a being of infinite love, when he damns millions of souls eternally, with the most excrutiating tortures, for that which they could not avoid, and this, too, when it was in his power to save them, but he chose not to do it? Can this be believed?

Can any man believe God is impartial, when he, by a sovereign act, takes some men to heaven, and consigns others to hell, when there was no difference between them whatever, but some were chosen, and others rejected, for his pleasure alone? No partiality—no caprice here!

Can any man believe in the truth and sincerity of God, when he proclaims himself ready to save all, and not willing any should perish—when he goes to all with invitations, and promises, and exhortations, and yet the truth is, that many of those thus invited he has damned, for his own pleasure, before they had an existence? Is this in your idea of sincerity?

5. I object, further: if it is true that Christ did not die for those who shall finally be lost, then there never was a *possibility* of their salvation. Either this must be admitted, or it must be assumed that a soul might be saved for whom Christ did not die. There is no other alternative; and our Calvinistic brethren may select either horn of the dilemma. If they select the latter, then they will do away with the necessity of the death of Christ, and find some other name or means whereby to be saved. If they admit the former, then they damn the sinner, when it was eternally impossible for him to escape damnation; and this his damnation is for a cause with which he never had any consenting connection.

But if it was eternally impossible for the sinner to escape damnation, then he is in no way to blame; nor can he, in any sense, reflect upon himself for being lost, seeing it was eternally impossible for him to be saved. He cannot blame himself—no man, no angel, not God, can blame him: it is no fault of his that he is damned; for *he could not* be saved. Let it not be said he brought himself into this miserable condition, from which there is no reprieve; *for the truth is, he had nothing whatever to do with it, unless he personally acted before he had an existence; for his damnation was fixed before he had an existence, and the pretended causes were engendered with him in the womb.* Look at the facts, stripped of all mysticism. There stands a man for whom Christ did not die. Now, that man must be lost! But why? Because, when he was conceived, he became a partaker of a corrupt nature, which, if not regenerated, must eventuate in his damnation. But Christ never died for him, and so his nature cannot be regenerated:

and he must, therefore, necessarily, be damned eternally for that which was given to him with his existence. In Calvin's words, ' Yea, and very infants themselves bring their own damnation with them from their mother's womb."

6. Still further, I object: if there are any for whom Christ did not die, such persons not only cannot avoid damnation, and are not therefore to blame for being finally destroyed, but, moreover, they cannot avoid sinning on as long as they live, and without any cessation or mitigation. *They cannot avoid this.* Mark well this proposition! Human nature is depraved, and unless changed by the grace of God, it must sin on—it must sin ever. This is admitted by Calvinists. But there is no grace out of Christ. If there is a man for whom Christ did not die, there is therefore no means whereby he can be changed—he must, therefore, necessarily, continue to sin. It is useless to remonstrate with him, he must sin—it is his nature, and his nature cannot be changed; for the only Being in the universe who could effect the change, has withheld the means. He sins as necessarily as the planet revolves—as water descends to its level—as the stone projected to the heavens must descend to the earth.

But if he must sin, and cannot avoid it—if the thing is absolutely and entirely beyond his power, and all other available power, the man cannot be to blame for it, can he? Let it not be said he brought the disability upon himself. If this were so, it would relieve the case. But this, you know, is not the fact. His disability came with him into the world—it was communicated as a part of his existence—it was his very and essential nature. And now, was he to blame for an existence and nature which were forced upon him—which never, at any period, he consented to, and which he never could avoid? His first parent may be to blame, but surely he cannot be responsible; for he not only did not bring the disability upon himself, but it was imposed on him without the possibility of its removal. Let him sin—no being in the universe can censure him—he is not to blame. It is his nature, unavoidable to his being. You say he ought not to sin. I answer he cannot help it. You say he ought to help it. I ask, ought he to do an impossibility? Can you affirm this? But you say he can help it, if he will. But can he will? If so, by what power? His own? You will not pretend so much. The power of God? But God will not communicate the requisite assistance. But does God require men to avoid sinning? Then Calvinism is false, or God is unjust.

Take a similar case. There is a man of scrofulous habit—the disease is destroying his life, and no remedy can cure it. You find, on inquiry, that the disease has been in his family for a succession of generations—it is transmitted from father to son. Now, is the man to be blamed for being scrofulous—is he responsible? It was communicated in his conception. Is he to blame for remaining under the influence of the disease? He has tried every remedy in vain, and has found none to cure him. He cannot be cured.

But I object, further: if it is impossible for the sinner to avoid sinning, and if this disability of his was not brought upon himself by his own act, then not only is he not to blame for his sins, but he cannot be required to do right—he is under no obligation to do right. No being in the universe can create such an obligation. This must be so, unless it can be shown that a being can be brought under obligation to perform an absolute impossibility. Will any man, in his senses, pretend so much? Suppose God were to command me this moment to annihilate the sun, and yet give me no more power than I now possess—would his unrighteous command create an obligation? Yet, when he commands that sinner, for whom Christ did not die, to do right, he commands as absolute an impossibility as in the former case. Does this command create an obligation?

No mysticism can escape this plain matter-of-fact statement. But does God require men to do right? Then Calvinism is false, or God is a despot! Calvinists may determine which horn to choose. Let not our opponents refer to the condition of fallen angels and lost sinners, as proof that obligation to do right may remain when the ability is gone. The cases are not analogous. In the former case, the sinner is required to perform what it never was possible for him to do; and the inability was communicated with his existence, and he never could have got clear of it.

8. But I object, further: if the sinner cannot avoid doing sin, and has no available power to do right, then not only is he not to blame for his sins, and absolutely under no obligation to do right, but, moreover, he cannot be punished, either in this world or the world to come, for his delinquencies, without the grossest injustice and sheerest tyranny. He is a fool for inflicting upon himself the torture of remorse, the pang of regret, or as he gives himself any sorrow, any uneasiness about his state. The God who made him, and who punishes him, universal intelligence must pronounce a monster of cruelty! Punish him! for what, I pray you? Is not his very being curse enough? Must other tortures be added? And for what? For his sins? He never could avoid them. For not doing right? He never had the power. Damn him in hell torments for ever for this? O, sir, is not this dreadful! Do you believe our heavenly Father is such a being as this! Does not your blood shiver in your veins at the thought! Is not being bad enough! Must he suffer on for ever, the victim of insatiable malevolence! What should be thought of a human tyrant, who, supposing a certain family of his slaves by birth were disqualified for his service, so that it was absolutely impossible, for a cause connected with their conception, for them to do what he required of them; should, nevertheless, appoint them the usual task, and yet, because

they failed to perform it, at the close of every day, strip them and inflict upon their naked persons inhuman tortures, and this because they did not perform absolute impossibilities—what would all men think of such a monster? Would not the mute earth open her dumb mouth and curse him? Would not the heavens execrate the abhorrent wretch? But shall a thousand-fold worse conduct be charged upon the glorious God, and no one resent the indignity? Under the sanctity of religion, shall the revolting slander be made that he will torture, through all eternity, men, for not performing impossibilities, and the representative go unrebuked? It must not be.

9. But I object, further: if Christ did not die for all, then is it inconsistent and insincere to invite all to come to him and be saved. This is so manifest, that I cannot express my astonishment that Calvinists do not perceive it. Look at it. There stands a man for whom Christ did not die—he never died for him that he might live. Now, I ask, in all consistency, how can that man be invited to come to Christ for life? He cannot come; and if he could, Christ has no life for him. Look at the invitation in the light of these facts. Is it not horrible? Can you present Christ in this attitude, without alarm at the blasphemy? What pretense justifies this invitation—this entreaty? What excuse is there for that Calvinistic preacher, who stands and entreats all sinners to come to Christ, when he professes to believe, first, with respect to the persons for whom Christ died, that they must come in the day of God's power, and cannot come until that time—next, with respect to the reprobate, that he never can come, that the thing is impossible—what must be thought of such a preacher? What would you think of a man who should go into a grave-yard, and address himself in the same way to a congregation of tomb-stones?

Is it pretended that all may be invited to come to Christ,

because his death is sufficient for all? What a miserable evasion! Admit that the death of Christ is sufficient for all, yet there stands the fact, it was not made for all. Some men were eternally excluded from it. Here is a table sufficient to accommodate all the citizens of a city; but it is surrounded by an army, who are instructed to admit only the white portion of its citizens, and to prevent all colored persons from approaching, so that it is absolutely impossible for such to reach that table. Now, I ask, with what consistency could these colored persons be invited and entreated to come to the table and eat, by the same authority that placed an army to prevent their approach, under the pretense that there is enough for all? Would not all men pronounce such a procedure miserable duplicity—abominable, shameless hypocrisy? If there be enough, they have no share in it. But do you say, to justify a universal invitation of sinners to Christ, that not only is there a sufficiency in him for all, but, likewise, all who will may come—there is no let or hinderance but in the sinner's will only? There is no army to prevent him. If he will come, he *may;* and if he will not, whose fault is it?

But, now, look at this. The very reason why the sinner will not come is this—he has no power to will to come. *Here is where the army is planted to prevent—an army of irresistible motives, to prevent him from willing.* He cannot will, and the reason is, the will must be given of God, but it can only be given to those for whom Christ died; but for this sinner he did not die, and, hence, it is impossible for him to have the will. So that to say if he will come he may, and make this the ground of the offer, is arrant trifling. He cannot will to come to Christ, and the reason why he cannot will is, that Christ did not die for him, to make the will possible; so that the bar is not in his will, but in the fact that Christ did not die for him; and hence the hypocrisy of inviting him, when the fact is he is prevented from coming; and if he could come, Christ has not the thing for him which he is invited to receive.

10. I object: if Christ died not for all, then unbelief is no sin in them that finally perish, seeing that there is not any thing for those men to believe unto salvation for whom Christ died not. Their unbelief is no sin, for three reasons: First. Their unbelief is true—Christ did not die for them, and they believe the truth when they believe he did not. Second. They cannot believe without Divine aid, and are not, therefore, sinful for not doing what is impossible. Third. They cannot be required to believe a lie; but if they believed on Christ they would believe a lie; therefore, in not believing, they violate no requirement, and so commit no sin.

11. But if Christ did not die for all men, then it would be a sin in those for whom he did not die to believe he did die for them, seeing it would be to believe a lie. But God commands all men to believe—he therefore commands some men to believe a lie! If he wills them to do what he commands, he wills them to believe a lie—if he does not will them to believe, then he commands them to do what he does not wish them to do!

12. If Christ did not die for those who are damned, then they are not damned for unbelief. Otherwise, you say they are damned for not believing a lie!

13. If Christ died not for all, then those who obey Christ, by going and preaching the Gospel to every creature as glad tidings of grace and peace, of great joy to all people, do sin thereby, in that they go to most people with a lie in their mouth; for if Christ did not die for all, the Gospel cannot be glad tidings of great joy to all. To many it must be a message of unmingled terror and grief; for it only announces that they are hopelessly lost, and that the death of Christ itself is, in its very design, an infinite and everlasting curse to them; for it will unavoidably enhance their damnation a thousand-fold.

But not only does it make those to sin, by publishing absolute falsehood, who publish the glad tidings to all, but, also—and what cannot be written without trembling—it represents our Lord Jesus Christ himself, in the language of Mr. Wesley, "as a hypocrite, a deceiver of the people, a man void of common sincerity; for it cannot be denied, that he everywhere speaks as if he was willing that all men should be saved, and as if he had provided the possibility. Therefore, to say he was not willing that all men should be saved—that he had provided no such possibility, is to represent him as a hypocrite and dissembler. It cannot be denied, that the gracious words which came out of his mouth are full of invitations to all sinners. To say, then, he did not intend to save all sinners, upon proffered and possible conditions, is to represent him as a gross deceiver of the people. You cannot deny that he says, 'Come unto me, all ye that are weary and heavy-laden.' If, then, you say he calls those that cannot come—those whom he knows to be unable to come—those whom he can make able to come, but will not, how is it possible to describe greater insincerity? You represent him as mocking his helpless creatures, by offering what he never intends to give. You describe him as saying one thing and meaning another—as pretending a love which he had not. Him, 'in whose mouth was no guile,' you make full of deceit, void of common sincerity: then, especially, when drawing nigh the city, he wept over it, and said, 'O Jerusalem, thou that killest the prophets, and stonest them that are sent unto thee, how often would I have gathered thy children together, and ye would not.' Now, if you say that he would not, you represent him—which who can hear?—as weeping hypocritical tears over the prey which himself, of his own good pleasure, doomed to destruction."

Such blasphemy as this, one might think, might make the ears of a Christian to tingle. But there is yet more behind;

for just as it honors the Son, so it honors the Father. As alledged, it destroys all his attributes at once—it overturns his justice, mercy, and truth. Yea, it represents the most holy God as worse than the devil can be—as more false, more cruel, and unjust. More false, because the devil, liar as he is, hath never said, "He willeth all men to be saved:" more unjust, because the devil cannot, if he would, be guilty of such injustice as you ascribe to God, when you say that God condemns millions of souls to everlasting fire, prepared for the devil and his angels, for continuing in sin, which, for the grace he will not give them, they cannot avoid; and more cruel, because that unhappy spirit seeketh rest and findeth none, so that his own misery is the occasion of his tormenting others. But God resteth in his high and holy place; so that to suppose him, of his own mere motion, of his pure will and pleasure, happy as he is, to doom his creatures, whether they will or no, to endless misery, is to impute such cruelty to him as I know of no warrant to impute to the great enemy of God and man. It is to represent the most high God as more cruel, false, and unjust, than the devil. Who hath ever said worse of the devil—who can say worse of him, than this, that he is a heartless dissembler, ever deceiving with empty pretenses—that he delights in the misery of his wretched victims? but here it is said of God, that he pretends to desire the happiness of his creatures—that he even comes and implores them to live, weeping over them while he entreats, at the same time that he has doomed them to eternal hell torments of his own pleasure, in such a way as that it is absolutely and for ever impossible for them to escape, and this for sins they never could avoid! If this be the God of the Bible, in what does he differ from its devil, only in his larger growth!

14. If Christ did not die for all men, then God is not sincere in requiring all men to repent, nor can he equitably

make the requisition; for what good could this repentance do them? What remission of sins could it procure for those for whom Christ did not die? Manifestly, none. If it were possible for them to comply with the requirement, it could do them no good; but they cannot comply, if it would be a means of their salvation. And hence it follows, as has been well said by Whitby, "that no impenitent person can justly be condemned for dying in his impenitent estate; for, on this supposition, he may fairly plead that, Christ not dying for him, his repentance, had he been ever so careful to perform it, must have been in vain, since it could not procure the remission of his sins. If here you say that it is an impossible supposition that any one, for whom Christ did not die, should repent, you only strengthen this his plea, enabling him to say he is condemned and perisheth for want of that repentance which, from his birth to his dying day, it was utterly impossible for him to perform. Hence, further, it must follow that God could not equitably require of them, for whom Christ died not, obedience to the laws of Christ, since that obedience, could they be ever so willing or industrious to perform it, could not avail for the remission of their sins, it being only the blood of Christ which cleanseth from sin, which blood never was given for them."

If it were possible for those for whom Christ died not to obey every requisition of the Bible, it would not contribute a particle to their salvation; but if it is impossible, then they are finally to be damned for not performing impossibilities. Thus, the Scriptures are made to require impossibilities, and then to damn men for not complying. At the same time, if they did and could comply, it would not, could not bring them the salvation which is promised to all who comply. Is not this creditable to God and the Bible?

15. If Christ did not die for all, then why does he say he is not willing any should perish? Surely, he is willing

that the greater part should perish, or he would have permitted his death to extend to them. Why do any perish, but that it his sovereign will to limit his death to a part? Indeed, if Calvinism be true, the will of God is the only original cause of the sinner's damnation! Not merely is it the will of God that they should be damned as sinners, but it is because of his will that they are sinners, that they might be damned. This charge, fearful as it is—and I confess it is startling—is based upon what has been abundantly and irrefutably proved in a former place, namely, that God willed the fall of Adam—that he willed that reprobates should come into the world with a necessity to sin—and that, indeed, he is the first and only original cause of all things, sin included; and since he could not cause what was contrary to his will, he must therefore will both the sin and damnation of the reprobate. This is also to be argued from the fact that he, according to Calvinism, limited the death of Christ to a part, when he might have extended it to all, and this for his own pleasure. He did not will that all should be saved from sin and hell, or he would not have limited the death of Christ to a part—he must, therefore, have willed, contrary to his own declaration, that many should die.

Look at it. Calvinists believe that all for whom Christ died, must inevitably be saved; they believe, also, that his death was sufficient for the sins of the whole world. Well, now observe, the only reason why this sufficient atonement does not save the whole world is this: God the Father, and God the Son, of their own good pleasure, limited it to a part. It was their good pleasure, therefore, that the residue should be left in their sins, and perish, and his sovereign pleasure is the cause of their damnation! Dreadful! dreadful! dreadful! The atonement was ample to satisfy the demands of justice—here there was no limit: the condition of all the race was precisely the same—here there was no limit; but in the will of God there was a limit; as a sovereign, for his own pleasure, he limited the remedy which was sufficient for all to a part, and left the others to perish! If this be so, and Calvinists say it is so, are we not shut up to the conclusion, that all who are left in sin and damnation, are so left because God preferred this to their holiness and salvation!

16. But Calvinists tell the poor reprobates, as a kind of palliation of their cruel treatment, that, though God has sovereignly excluded them from salvation in Christ, yet he has done a great deal for them. The death of Christ, it is true, has not made it possible for them to escape the vengeance of eternal fire—for they were created for this—to obtain a mansion in heaven, but it has procured them many temporal blessings, such as the ministry of the word, common operations of the Spirit, invitations of the Gospel, and many other great privileges, for which they, as in duty bound, ought to be very grateful. Ought the reprobates to be grateful for these? Are these blessings? Are they blessings in their design—in their result? Or is it not true, on the contrary, in their very nature and design, they are the greatest curse that ever befell the poor miserable victims of Almighty wrath? Did not the honest Calvin himself say they were intended to fatten them for the slaughter—that "God calls them that they may be more deaf—kindles a light that they may be more blind—brings his doctrines that they may be more ignorant—applies the remedy that they may not be healed!" For any one of these blessings they are destined, in the purpose of God, when he bestows them, to suffer the keenest, deepest pangs of hell for ever! They come to them as angels of light, but infix in the inmost soul a thousand arrows of remorse and anguish, which shall never be extracted through eternity. Blessings! designed and destined to eventuate in eternal woe! God of the universe, protect thy hapless creatures from such blessings as

these! Blessings! sent upon the reprobates, that their condition may be rendered more intolerable than that of Sodom and Gomorrah in the day of judgment—that a pretense may be furnished for heightening the horrors of perdition to utmost excess—*all to the praise of his glorious justice!*

17. If Christ did not die for all, and if only those for whom he did die can be saved, then all for whom he did not die come into the world with the necessity of their damnation; because they come into the world under an arrangement by which their damnation is unavoidable, they must necessarily be damned, because there is no salvation out of Christ, and Christ did not die for them. Now, with the question, whether they will be lost or not, they have nothing to do whatever; because it was settled, from eternity, when it was settled that Christ should not die for them. But do you say, the first cause of their destruction was their corruption of nature, and God only passed them by in their sins, leaving them to suffer just punishment? Very well; let us take your explanation. Then it amounts to this: these persons were left to damnation, because of their corrupt nature. But had they any thing whatever to do in making that corrupt nature? If they had, they must have acted before they existed. But if they had not; then they were assigned to eternal damnation for an act with which they had nothing to do whatever. But, again: if they were assigned to damnation for their corruption of nature, then they were damned for a cause existing in their conception—then they were damned, all of them, when they were unborn; so here we have not the damnation of a few children a span long, but of all who finally perish before they have attained that stature. But, to escape these horrible consequences, do you adopt this evasion, that they were only passed by because of their corruption, and left in a state in which, when they should attain to

personality, they would inevitably sin, and then, on account of these actual sins, they would be condemned and punished? Well, let us look at this for a moment. You say, they were only passed by because of their corruption of nature. What do you mean by this? that it was determined Christ should not die for them? Then, I ask, what was their state thus passed by? Could they be saved? If they could, then they could be saved without the death of Christ? If they could not be saved, must they not necessarily be damned? or is there some intermediate state between salvation and damnation, to which they would be assigned? But, leaving this, let us admit that the final damnation of those passed by, for whom Christ did not die, is on account of their actual sins. The charge still stands true, that they brought with them, into the world, the necessity of their damnation, and its final infliction is without any fault of theirs whatever. The facts are precisely these: These unfortunate—for they are not guilty, if Calvinism is true—persons came into the world with a corrupt nature, which was forced upon them with existence. This nature must unavoidably involve them in actual sins; because, being evil, it can only produce evil. From this corruption there is no escape: Christ did not die for them, and his death is the only means of escape from corruption. They are, therefore, born into the world with a necessity to sin; and if they are to be damned for these sins, they are born with a necessity of damnation! Who has nerves sufficient for these things? Who is the man who can indulge such thoughts of the Ruler of the universe, and the moral government thereof, without feelings of unmingled consternation! Who can believe, that a God of infinite love has brought millions of beings into existence, with the unavoidable necessity of eternal damnation, and this necessity ascribable to nothing in the creature, over which he had control, but merely to the good pleasure of God!

18. I must add, finally, upon this point, before passing to others immediately connected therewith, that if it be true that Christ died but for a part, then it is certain, if the devil knows this, he is the greatest fool in the universe, and Christians next in the dimensions of folly. What has the devil to do any more? Why shall he walk through the earth, seeking prey? Why shall he hunt for the souls of men? He already has his portion! They *are counted out, every soul of them!* Their names and numbers are designated! He cannot get one more, though he move heaven and earth—though he employ every emissary in hell. He cannot come short of one—the thing is for ever impossible, for God is pledged—he has given them to the devil in an everlasting covenant—they were created for him—his they must be! He need not watch and diminish his rest, for God will bring them all safe to him, and no being has power to pluck one of them out of his hand! Let the devil rest, and hell hold jubilee, for God has given them a large part of the human race, for his own glory, and of his own sovereign pleasure!

And what shall be said of the folly of Christians? Know you not, that all for whom Christ died must be brought in, in the day of his power? Not one can fail—the Lord will hasten it in its time. Why shall you labor? you cannot make one hair white or black. Why do you take trouble about those whom God has given to the devil? Would you rob him? It is impossible! What folly you are guilty of! Pray, preach, mourn, weep, make yourselves sad—for what? Know you not it is all in vain? None can perish for whom Christ died; none can escape for whom he did not die. Let the devil and Christians quit their foolish warfare, and be at peace—let the world have rest, for God will not defraud the devil of one soul that is his, and he cannot steal one that is Christ's, and

Christians can do nothing by interference! Let the foolish strife come to an everlasting end.

Such are some of the consequences flowing unavoidably from the proposition, that Christ died but for a part of mankind. That they are terrible, I readily admit—so appalling, that I cannot mention them against you, without seeming to pervert and persecute you; because it must ever seem unaccountable to all men, how rational beings can embrace such absurdities—not to say wicked blasphemies. I have found no pleasure in pointing them out—on the contrary, it has given me unmingled pain. God is my witness, I am sincerely sorry for you—I regard you with commiseration, as the victim of a miserable system, whose frightful errors I must suppose you believe, and, by some fatal infatuation, refuse to renounce. As I have waded through the pages of your divines, I have involuntarily regretted that I found myself under the necessity of becoming acquainted with their unaccountable and horrid teachings—much more, that it became my duty to expose them. Would that you had been content to enjoy peace, and left your neighbors to pursue their own vocation, and not, by your unprovoked intermeddling, rendered it necessary to uncover your revolting and shameful deformities to the observation of our common enemies! And now, what may seem almost as paradoxical as many things in your creed, after all that I have said, I must be allowed to cherish love for your Church, in despite of all her blemishes, and for yourself, also, as a professed follower of my Savior. May the Spirit itself lead us into all truth!

In addition to the foregoing objections to a limited atonement are several others, resulting from the Calvinian view of the nature of the atonement, and the method by which those interested therein become partakers of its benefits.

If Calvinists hold to a limited atonement, as has been

seen in the citations already made, they further hold, as growing out of the nature of the atonement itself, that all those particular persons, for whom it was made, must, in consequence thereof, not only infallibly, but necessarily and unconditionally, be saved.

It may be proper to make a few quotations bearing directly on this point:

"To all those for whom Christ hath purchased redemption, he doth certainly and effectually apply and communicate the same." (Confession of Faith.)

This clause, at the same time, necessarily limits the atonement to those who are finally saved, because it says all for whom it was made will be saved; and it asserts that all for whom it was made must infallibly have its application—they must necessarily be saved by it.

"The Lord Jesus, by his perfect obedience and sacrifice of himself, which he, through the eternal Spirit, once offered up unto God, hath fully satisfied the justice of his Father, and purchased not only reconciliation, but an everlasting inheritance in the kingdom of heaven for all those whom the Father hath given unto him." (Confession of Faith.)

"We are further taught, that the atonement shall be effectually applied by the Holy Spirit to all those who were chosen of God, and redeemed by Christ, and that it shall be effectually applied to them alone." (Expositor of Confession.)

"The Father, from all eternity, gave to Christ a people to be his seed, and be by him brought to glory. . . . He was not merely to procure for them a possibility of salvation, but to secure for them a full and final salvation; and none that were given to him shall be lost." (Ib.)

"The intention of Christ, in laying down his life, was not merely to obtain for those for whom he died a possibility of salvation, but actually to save them—to bring them to a real possession and enjoyment of eternal salvation. From this it inevitably follows, that Christ died only for those who shall be saved in him with an everlasting salvation." (Ib.)

"Christ, therefore, is called our surety, because he engaged to God to make satisfaction for us—the elect; which satisfaction consists in this, that Christ, in our room and stead, did, both by doing and suffering, satisfy Divine justice, both the legislatory, the retributive, and the vindictive, in the most perfect manner, fulfilling all the righteousness of the law, which the law otherwise required of us, in *order to impunity, and to our having a right* to eternal life." (Witsius.)

"But we must proceed a step further, and affirm that the obedience of Christ was accomplished by him in *our room*, in order thereby to obtain for us a right to eternal life. The law which God will have secured inviolable admits none to glory but on conditions of perfect obedience, which none was ever possessed of but Christ, who bestows it freely on his own people." (Ib.)

"But, besides, Christ satisfied the vindictive justice of God, not merely for our good, but also in our room, by enduring those most dreadful sufferings, both in soul and body, which we had deserved, and from which he, by undergoing them, did so deliver us that they could not, with the wrath and curse of God, as the proper punishment of our sins, be inflicted on us." (Ib.)

"The Lord Jesus obtained for the elect, by his satisfaction, an immunity from all misery, and a right to eternal life. . . . A right to all the benefits of the covenant of grace is purchased at once to all the elect, by the death of Christ, so far as that, consistently with the truth and justice of God, and with the covenant he entered into with his Son, he *cannot condemn* any of the elect, or *exclude them from partaking in his salvation; nay, on the contrary,* he has declared that satisfaction being now made by his Son, and accepted by himself, there is nothing for the elect either to suffer or to do, in order to acquire either impunity or a right to life, but only that each of them, in their appointed order and time, enjoy the right purchased for them by Christ, and the inheritance arising from it." (Ib.)

"Before actual conversion, the elect are favored with no contemptible privileges above the reprobates in virtue of the right which Christ purchased for them—such as, first, *that they are in a state of reconciliation and justification*, actively considered, Christ having made satisfaction for them," etc. (Ib.)

"For since Christ did, by his engagement, undertake to cancel all the debt of those persons for whom he engaged, as if it was his own, by suffering what was meet, and to fulfill all righteousness in their room, and since he has most fully performed this by his satisfacton, as much as if the sinners themselves had endured all the punishment due to their sins, and had accomplished all righteousness, the consequence is, he has engaged and satisfied for those, and those only, who are actually saved from their sins." (Ib.)

"Whoever makes a purchase of any thing has an unquestionable right to it; and it not only may but actually does become his property, in virtue of his purchase, upon paying down the price. And herein consists our liberty and salvation, that we are no longer our own, nor the property of sin, nor of Satan, but the property of Christ." (Ib.)

"Divines explain themselves differently as to the conditions of the covenant of grace. We, for our part, agree with those who think that the covenant of grace, to speak accurately with respect to us, has no conditions." (Ib.)

"Jesus Christ was ordained of God to be the Savior of those persons, and God gave them to him to be redeemed by his blood, to be called by his Spirit, and finally to be glorified with him. All that Christ did, in the character of mediator, was in consequence of this original appointment of the Father, which has received, from many divines, the name of the covenant of redemption—a phrase which suggests the idea of a mutual stipulation between Christ and the Father, in which Christ undertook all the work which he executed in human nature, and which he continues to execute in heaven, in order to save the elect; and the Father promised that the persons for whom Christ died should be saved by his death. According to the tenor of this covenant of redemption, the merits of Christ are not considered the cause of the decree of election, but as a part of that decree: in other words, God was not moved by the mediation of Christ to choose certain persons out of the great body of mankind to be saved, but, having chosen them, he conveys all the means of salvation through the channel of this mediation." (Hill.)

"Christ engaged to pay the debt of his people, and satisfy for the wrongs and injuries done by them. There is a two-fold debt paid by Christ as a surety of his people—the one is a debt of obedience to the law of God. Another thing which Christ, as a surety, engaged to do, was to bring all the elect safe to glory." (Gill.)

In the sixteenth and seventeenth chapters of the second book of Calvin's Institutes, it is elaborately taught, that Christ has suffered and obeyed for his elect, so that their salvation is positively secured, their debt being paid, and they being entitled to salvation. "If Christ has satisfied for our sins—if he has sustained the punishment due to us—if he has appeased God by his obedience, then salvation has been obtained for us by his righteousness."

"Justification is an act of God's free grace unto sinners, in which he pardoneth all their sins—accepteth and accounteth their persons righteous in his sight; not for any thing wrought in them, or done by them, but only for the perfect obedience and full satisfaction of Christ, by God imputed to them, and received by faith alone." (Larger Catechism.)

"Although Christ, by his obedience and death, did make a proper, real, and full satisfaction to God's justice, in the behalf of them that are justified, yet, inasmuch as God accepteth the satisfaction from a surety, which he might have demanded of them, and did provide this surety, his only Son, imputing his righteousness to them, and requiring nothing of them for their justification but faith, which also is his gift, their justification is to them of free grace." (Ib.)

"Faith justifies a sinner in the sight of God, not because of those other graces which do always accompany it, or of good works that are the fruits of it, nor as if the grace of faith, or any act thereof, were imputed to him for justification, but only as it is an instrument by which he receiveth and applieth Christ and his righteousness." (Ib.)

"The imputation that respects our justification before God, is God's gracious donation of the righteousness of Christ to believers, and his acceptance of their persons as righteous on the account thereof. Their sins being imputed to him, and his obedience being imputed to them, they are, in virtue hereof, both acquitted from guilt, and accepted as righteous before God." (Buck.)

"The Calvinists say, that the faith and good works of the elect are the consequence of their election. God having, from all eternity, chosen a certain number of persons, did, in time, give his Son to become their Savior—he bestows upon them, through him, (unconditionally,) that grace which effectually determines them to repent and believe, and so effectually conducts them, by faith and good works, unto everlasting life. These are—faith and good works not conditions, but—the fruit of election, and they were, from eternity, known to God, because they were, in time, to be produced, by the execution of the Divine decree." (Hill.)

"The atonement was a satisfaction made for the sins of

the elect, which had respect to them personally, and *secures* the pardon of all their iniquities. Christ was substituted for the elect, to obey and suffer in their stead, and was, by imputation, legally guilty, so that the law could demand his death. In the decree of election, the sinners who will be saved were given to Christ to be justified. They were given when ungodly, and not from any foreseen faith and repentance. The ground of pardon is the mystical union with the Lord Jesus Christ." (Ely's Contrast.)

"Christ, being a propitiation for us, does also imply, that God did also accept of the passive obedience of Christ, together with his action, as sufficient satisfaction to the demands of justice. So that the imputation of the obedience of Christ does fully and perfectly acquit the believer from the guilt of sin, the empire of Satan, the curses of the law, and the damnation of hell. God has received satisfaction from the surety, and, therefore, will demand no more from the principal debtor." (Dickinson.)

"Those whom God effectually calleth, he also freely justifieth; not by infusing righteousness into them, but by pardoning their sins, and by accounting and accepting their persons as righteous; not for any thing wrought in them, or done by them, but for Christ's *sake alone;* not by imputing faith—itself the act of believing—or any other evangelical obedience to them, as their righteousness, *but* by *imputing the obedience and satisfaction* of Christ *unto them,* they receiving and resting on him and his righteousness by faith; which faith they have not themselves—it is the gift of God. . . . Christ, by his obedience and death, did fully discharge the debt of all those that are thus justified, and did make a proper, real, and full satisfaction to his Father's justice in their behalf." (Confession of Faith.)

"Those who maintain that Christ obeyed the law, and suffered its penalty in our stead, and thereby made a true and proper satisfaction to Divine justice, believe that his obedience and suffering, constituting what is usually styled his righteousness, are imputed to the believer for his justification, Christ's righteousness being received by faith, as its instrument. Accordingly, justification consists, not only in the pardon of sin, or, in other words, in the release of the believing sinner from punishment, but also in the acceptance of his person as righteous, in the eyes of the law, through the obedience of Christ, reckoned or imputed to him, by which he has a title to eternal life." (Old and New Theology, p. 133.)

"They whose sins he bore in his own body on the tree—whose sins he suffered for, cannot, with the most palpable violation of all right, and law, and justice, be themselves constrained to suffer for the same sins. Therefore, the atonement, the satisfaction rendered to Divine justice, is as extensive as the sheep of Christ's flock, and *no more*—the atonement is as long and as broad as the salvation of God; or, in other words, they whose sins are washed out in the blood of Calvary must be saved, and none others can be. In other words, they, and all they for whom Christ died, for whom he paid the ransom or price of redemption, will be saved, and none other." (Junkins on Justification, p. 220.)

"As God doth not will that each individual of mankind should be saved, so neither did he will that Christ should properly and immediately die for each individual of mankind: whence it follows, that though the blood of Christ, from its own intrinsic dignity, was sufficient for the redemption of all men, yet, in consequence of his Father's appointment, he shed it intentionally, and, therefore, effectually and immediately, for the elect *only*." (Toplady et Zanchius, p. 37.)

"The absolute will of God is the original spring and efficient cause of his people's salvation. I say the original and efficient; for, *sensu complexo*, there are other intermediate causes of their salvation, which, however, all result from, and are subservient to this primary one—the will of God. Such are his everlasting choice of them to eternal life; the eternal covenant of grace entered into by the Trinity; the incarnation, obedience, death, and intercession of Christ for them: all of which are so many links in the great chain of causes." (Ib., p. 43.)

"Since this absolute will of God is both immutable and omnipotent, we infer, that the salvation of every one of the elect is most infallibly certain, and can by no means be prevented. This necessarily follows, from what we have already asserted and proved concerning the Divine will, which, as it cannot be disappointed or made void, must undoubtedly secure the salvation of all whom God wills should be saved." (Ib., p. 48.)

"By the purpose or decree of God, we mean his determinate counsel, whereby he did, from all eternity, preordain whatsoever he should do, or permit to be done, in time. In particular, it signifies his everlasting appointment of some men to life, and of others to death, which appointment flows entirely from his own free and sovereign will." (Ib., p. 47.)

"Nor could the justice of God stand, if he were to condemn the elect, for whose sins he has received ample satisfaction at the hand of Christ; or if he were to save the reprobate, who are not interested in Christ." (Ib., p. 92.)

"Those who are ordained to eternal life, were not so ordained on account of any worthiness foreseen in them, or of any good works to be wrought by them, nor yet for their future faith; but solely of free, sovereign grace, and according to the mere pleasure of God. This is evident, among other considerations, from this: that faith, repentance, and holiness, are no less the free gift of God than eternal life itself." (Ib., p. 94.)

"Not one of the elect can perish; but they must all, necessarily, be saved. The reason is this: because God simply and unchangeably wills that all and every one of those whom he hath appointed unto life should be eternally glorified. . . . Now, that is said to be necessary, *quod nequit aliter esse,* which cannot be otherwise than it is." (Ib., p. 98.)

"Of those whom God hath predestined, none can perish, inasmuch as they are all his own elect. They are the elect who are predestinated, foreknown, and called according to purpose. Now, could any of these be lost, God would be disappointed; therefore, they can never perish." (Ib., p. 99.)

"Our blessed Redeemer has not only procured for believers the pardon of their sins and reconciliation unto God, but he has also purchased for them a title to God's favor here, and eternal happiness hereafter. Now, if Christ has purchased this inheritance for the believer, and made over the title to him in his justification, who shall deprive him of his own estate, procured for him at such an infinite price?" (Dickinson's Five Points, p. 268.)

Now, from these quotations I make the following deductions, as further setting forth the Calvinian view of the atonement:

1. All those for whom Christ died must necessarily be saved, and cannot by any means perish.

2. Their salvation is thus certain, because his death actually paid their debt to Divine justice, and procured them a right to eternal life, by suffering and obeying in their stead, which suffering and obedience is made theirs by imputation.

That we do no injustice to our Calvinistic brethren, when we charge them with teaching that all for whom Christ died—the elect—must infallibly be saved, we presume no one of their number will deny, as it would be a denial of all their written, and, so far as I know, of their oral teaching. Upon this point, indeed, they are peculiarly eloquent and harmonious. Their whole system is shaped to accommodate it. And if I do at all understand the quotations already made, and the general tone of Calvinistic theology, the ground of the certainty of the salvation of the elect is this: 1. They are the elect, or they are the persons chosen of God, with an unchangeable purpose, from eternity, to be saved, and they must, therefore, be saved. 2. But, second, as God ordained these some to glory, so he appointed the means of infallibly bringing them to glory, which were that Christ should become their surety, and both obey and suffer for them, and so purchase a title for them to everlasting life. In other words, Calvinists believe that the elect will necessarily be saved, because Christ has suffered the penalty due for all their sins, and that they cannot therefore be held to suffer—their sins are indeed no longer theirs, having been imputed to Christ, and he has already suffered their penalty; and, further, he, by his holy and spotless life, has fulfilled all righteousness; and this, his obedience and righteousness, is accounted or imputed to the elect—those for whom he died—so that their righteousness is henceforth complete in Christ; and thus, by virtue of his death and obedience, which have perfectly satisfied the law for them, they must be saved.

Am I correct in this apprehension of Calvinism? Will any Calvinist say I am not? Do they not all teach that Christ has entirely paid the debt of his people?—that he has perfectly satisfied for their sins?—that nothing is wanting, on their part, to render the atonement, thus made for them, complete? Do they not also teach that Christ has fully obeyed all righteousness for his people, and that this—his obedience—is imputed to them, and thus becomes their own? that is, it is just the same as though they had themselves perfectly obeyed.

And this transfer of their sins to Christ, and of his

righteousness to them, is entirely without conditions on their part. Now, mark well this point. They are not required to do any thing by which this atonement, in either branch of it, becomes theirs. It is so independently of them! *Whatever they are expected to do, as the elect, is not a means whereby this satisfaction becomes theirs, but it is because this satisfaction is theirs.* I ask my readers to look critically into these points, as my object is here to show some of the labyrinthian intricacies of this system, and expose some of its most dangerous errors. Here is one of the points where, for purposes of convenience, it is wont to assume an Arminian garb, and bewilder with its equivocations. Calvinists talk about conditions—Dr. Rice is wont to use this language—as though they believed it depended upon something which the elect should do, whether the atonement should be applied to them or not—they talk about salvation by faith and repentance, as though these were conditional to salvation! Now, the common idea attached to the term condition is this: that it is something upon which the occurrence of another thing depends. When we speak of conditions of salvation, we mean something by which salvation is brought about. When we speak of the condition, as performed by man, we mean something which he may or may not perform, according as he wills, and upon which his salvation depends. But Calvinists do not mean this when they use the term condition—they do not mean that the question, whether the atonement shall apply to the elect, depends upon any conditions which he may or may not perform. On the contrary, they believe that it is his, and is applied without any condition—that whatever the sinner does in his salvation, is because the atonement is already irresistibly applied to him, and not that he may procure its application. He is regenerated irresistibly, because he is atoned for; and then, because he is regenerated, he must produce all the fruits of faith, repentance, &c.; and now, to talk about these as conditions of salvation, is sheer nonsense—it is to talk about conditions of the existence of a thing, which depend upon its existence, and are consequent thereto.

To the doctrine contained in the above statement,

1. I object, first, that, making the salvation of those for whom Christ died both infallible and unconditional, it is a doctrine nowhere taught in the Scriptures. It is utterly without foundation in the Bible. It is spurious ore, reprobate silver, taken from some other mine besides Divine revelation.

2. It is expressly contrary to all those Scriptures which teach a conditional salvation;

3. To those which teach that some for whom Christ died may come short of life;

And to all the classes of Scriptures already enumerated against this doctrine of limited atonement.

4. I object: it renders it unnecessary, nay, impossible, for the elect to do any thing in order to their salvation, and as it is unnecessary and impossible for them to do any thing conditional to salvation, so it does not require them to do any thing. Whatever they shall find themselves able to do, and whatever they are required to do, is the fruit of their being already saved without their consent. Is this the doctrine of the Bible? Let it not be said, that Calvinists teach that faith is a condition of salvation, implying a free exercise of the creature. This is what they teach: that certain persons are elected unto life—that for these Christ makes satisfaction, or, in other words, saves them—that this salvation includes the spiritual life, from its beginning to its eternal completion in heaven—and that this is developed, 1. In irresistible regeneration, or the new birth, without the action of the man. 2. That this irresistible regeneration develops, as a cause, the fruits of faith and a holy life. 3. That these are crowned with glory; but the

man, in the whole process, has only passively experienced an unconditional salvation, commenced and perfected by irresistible agency. This, then, is my objection, that it renders it unnecessary and impossible for the elect to do any thing in order to their salvation.

5. But I further object, that, if true, then the persons for whom Christ died are not only not required to do any thing in order to their salvation, but, also, that they cannot avoid being saved—the thing is utterly and eternally out of the question, if Calvinism is true—they cannot prevent themselves from going to heaven. My proposition is not that they will not, but *they cannot*—nothing in the range of their power—they may sin to their utmost ability, and they will not suffer the least inconvenience from it, so far as their eternal salvation is concerned. But now look at this. There stands a man that never can get to heaven—the thing is impossible, and eternally has been so. Poor creature! he must suffer the torments of an ever-burning hell—he must lie down with devils, and weep, and wail, and sorrow, without relief, while the spark of immortality glows in his undying soul—he cannot help it—and this for no avoidable fault of his—he was created to howl amid these flames. There stands another man—by nature he is precisely such as the former—but this man cannot possibly miss of heaven. Nothing that he can do can keep him out of its blessedness. He may sin until his enormities would make a devil pale, if it were possible; but this cannot even endanger his salvation; his price has been paid, and saved he must be; he is deprived of the ability to keep himself from salvation! And now the question arises, why this difference? And you are told it is the good pleasure of God! Hold, I beseech you! Does not your whole nature rise up against such a sentiment? Is there not an involuntary shudder at the bare idea? Does not your reason, and all that is human in you, revolt at it?

But is not this sentiment calculated, inevitably, to produce licentiousness, recklessness, and despair? What else can be its legitimate fruits? It comes to all men, elect and non-elect, with the first lesson: You are impotent—you cannot do any thing toward achieving salvation, until you are regenerated—you cannot even put forth a virtuous desire, until this work is accomplished. This being so, the sinner must wait for regeneration; for he cannot stir till he is regenerated. But then follows the second lesson: If you are not of the elect, you cannot be regenerated; for Christ has died for none but the elect, and no man can be regenerated for whom Christ did not die; but if you are of the elect, you cannot avoid being regenerated, because all for whom Christ died must be regenerated, or effectually called; and this by irresistible, unsolicited grace. At this point, the sinner perceives that the whole matter is infallibly fixed—that his agency is entirely excluded: if elect, the work must be done: if not elect, it is impossible; and now ensues, as a necessary consequence, hopeless inaction or reckless licentiousness. With these truths in his mind, what can be said to a sinner as an inducement to attend to his salvation? or, rather, is it not all sheer folly to address him at all on that subject?

Do you exhort him to forsake sin? He says, "I cannot." To repent? "I cannot, until regenerated. This is God's work, and not mine." Do you warn him of danger, and exhort him to flee? He smiles at your childish folly, and answers you, "It is all fixed without my agency." Thus the whole man is neutralized, and hopeless recklessness superinduced.

6. But what has now been objected had respect alone to this aspect of the subject: that the salvation of those for whom Christ made atonement, is infallibly certain and unconditional on their part. I now object, further, to the ground upon which salvation is declared. It has two parts:

1. Christ has absolutely paid the debt of his people, and released them from the obligation. In other words, he took their sins upon himself, and suffered their penalty in such a way that they cannot be required to suffer themselves; so that they can commit no sin but what Christ has fully satisfied for it. If this be true, of course the elect must unconditionally escape punishment, because their punishment has already been inflicted upon their substitute, and Divine justice is fully and entirely satisfied. 2. As the elect are thus brought into the enjoyment of unconditional salvation, so far as deliverance from punishment is concerned, so, in the second place, they are, by a similar process, made completely righteous; namely, as Christ suffered for them, so, also, he obeyed for them, and his perfect righteousness is imputed to them. He obeyed perfectly, and fulfilled all righteousness, and this is imputed to them, or it is accounted precisely the same as though they had obeyed themselves; and, therefore, they are accounted worthy of life, as being righteous in Christ. Thus the elect are brought into the enjoyment of unconditional salvation, by having their sins imputed to Christ, and his righteousness imputed to them.

But will it be said, that this imputation does not savingly take place without faith, and, therefore, that faith is a condition of salvation—a condition without which the elect are not saved—it is only when they believe that Christ's righteousness is imputed to them? But look, for a moment, at this sheer sophistry and deception—for the language certainly does mislead.

The doctrine is, that the salvation of these persons—the elect—is first determined in the immutable decree of God; then Christ, to secure it, satisfies and obeys for them, which gives them an unconditional title to life; and then *he irresistibly regenerates them, and this regeneration necessarily produces faith.* And now shall it be pretended that this faith, which is itself a necessary effect of irresistible regeneration, is a condition of salvation! It must, at least, be admitted, that, if it is a condition, the elect is entirely passive in complying with it; and so his salvation, dependent as it is upon this condition, is not dependent upon him, in any sense—upon any thing he can do, or refuse to do; and so, of course, he has nothing to do but to submit as a passive subject throughout; and this he cannot help but do. To talk about conditions of salvation in such an arrangement—about salvation depending upon faith, must, in all candor, seem like a nonsensical abuse of language. Much more so, to appeal to the sinner to believe, in order that he may be saved, warning him that, if he does not, he must be damned, thus seeming to imply that he has power to perform a condition by which he may be saved, when faith is no more in his power than is the annihilation of the universe!

But, further, if Christ has absolutely paid the debt for his people, so that nothing more is necessary to acquit them from punishment—if the punishment has been inflicted, and justice satisfied, without any thing further, then it is manifest nothing more can be requisite to free them from punishment; and so their sins cannot be punished, and they cannot, therefore, be in any peril when they sin.

7. But if this be true, then it is certain that no motive can be drawn from eternity to enforce virtue, or restrain from vice. None can be drawn for the reprobate; for his destiny is fixed; damned he must be, and his sins cannot make it any more certain. None to the elect; for their destiny is also fixed, and no sin, possible to them, can unsettle it. Well, say that I do not know which I am, elect or reprobate; or I do know, it is all the same. Eternity, as it respects destiny, can bring no motive to bear on my conduct, because conduct cannot affect my

unconditional salvation or damnation. If Christ died for me, no sin I can commit can keep me out of heaven. If he did not die for me, nothing that I can do can get me in; and hence, in either case, my conduct is entirely unimportant. Will this doctrine do to preach? Is this the doctrine of the Bible? Is it consistent with our views of moral government? What would be thought of a man who should preach it? Yet such are the unavoidable consequences of Calvinism!

8. If this be true, then particularly is it impossible for the elect, after they have once received the gift of faith, ever to become guilty; and yet Calvinists believe that even the elect, after regeneration, and pardon, and adoption, may fall into grievous sins, nay, must continue to sin as long as they live. But now observe the consequence I charge here: if it is true that faith secures the imputation of both Christ's suffering and obedience to the believing soul, and if this imputation is consequent upon faith—and all this Calvinists believe—then I insist that any sin, committed by the believer, cannot either involve him in guilt or condemnation. Not condemnation, for the satisfaction of Christ is imputed: not guilt, for the imputation of Christ's perfect righteousness makes him completely righteous, and he cannot, therefore, have any guilt: so that whatever sin the elect commit, after they have been regenerated and united to Christ by faith, does not involve them in guilt, because, by virtue of their faith, their sins have all been taken from them, and imputed to Christ, and his righteousness has been imputed to them, so that they cannot be less than complete in his righteousness. Whether they sin, therefore, or be holy, it is all one—whether they fall away into grievous delinquencies, such as would shame even the reprobates, as Calvinists believe they may, or continue faithful, it is no difference—the question of their final salvation is neither rendered doubtful thereby, nor is the fact of their perfect

righteousness; for both are infallibly secured by virtue of their union with Christ.

9. Finally: I object to the whole Calvinian view of the atonement as dishonorable to that transaction, and its author. It renders it a mere commercial transaction—a thing of bargain and sale—so many souls given for so much blood—so many sins remitted at so much price. The Father agrees to give the Son so many souls at so much price. The Son agrees to suffer such a quantum for the forgiveness of so many sinners. In the language of another: "This hypothesis measures the atonement, not only by the number of the elect, but by the intensity and degree of the suffering to be endured for their sin. It adjusts the dimensions of the atonement to a nice mathematical point, and poises its infinite weight of glory even to the small dust of a balance. I need not say that the hand which stretches such lines, and holds such scales, must be a bold one. Such a calculation represents the Son of God as giving so much suffering for so much value received in the souls given to him; and represents the Father as dispensing so many favors and blessings for so much value received in obedience and sufferings. This is the commercial atonement, which sums up the worth of a stupendous moral transaction by arithmetic, and, with its little span, limits what is infinite." Upon this view of the atonement, it was once wittily and truthfully remarked: "God must have loved the devil much more than his Son, for he gave him the larger portion of the human race without any price, charging his Son full price for the meagre share he allotted to him."

Further: if this be true, I cannot see any mercy or grace in the Father; and, *certainly*, there is no such thing as forgiveness. The punishment is fully inflicted, not a particle abated, not, indeed, upon the culprit himself, but upon his substitute. But where, then, is forgiveness? How are the elect pardoned? Has not their debt been paid to the utmost farthing? What remains to be pardoned? Is there any great clemency in relinquishing a claim when it has been fully liquidated—paid to the utmost farthing? Is such the mercy of our Lord? The atonement, regarded in this light, can be nothing short of a stupendous slander of the character of God. So it seems to me.

Such are a part of the objections we bring against the Calvinian view of the atonement. It may be proper, briefly, to recapitulate here. The views of the atonement objected to are: First. That it is limited to part of the race. Second. All for whom it was made must be infallibly saved. Third. It consists in actually suffering and obeying for those for whom it was designed. To these views we have objected.

1. The doctrine of a limited atonement has no foundation in the Scriptures.

2. It is directly contrary to the Scriptures, which teach:

(1.) That Christ died for all.

(2.) Which contrast the extent of the benefits of Christ's death with the extent of the evils of Adam's sin.

(3.) Which represent those who are lost as purchased by Christ.

(4.) Which offer the benefits of Christ's death to all.

(5.) Which require all men to believe in and receive Christ.

(6.) Which make the sinner's damnation a result of his rejection of Christ.

(7.) Which teach that those who are finally lost might have been saved.

(8.) Which represent God as a being of universal love.

(9.) As willing the salvation of those who may come short.

(10.) As impartial, etc. It will be perceived in a moment, how all such Scriptures bear against a limited atonement.

3. It is adverse to all our conceptions of God, converting him rather into a monster of cruelty, than the parent of all.

4. It renders it impossible that a large part of the human race ever could be saved.

5. It renders it equally impossible for a large part of our race to avoid sin.

6. It destroys the obligation to do right, and subverts the obligation to virtue.

7. It renders all punishments for sin unjust and tyrannical.

8. It renders all general invitations to all men to come to Christ, insincere and hypocritical.

9. It renders unbelief, on the part of the reprobates, no sin.

10. It would make belief, on their part, a sin.

11. It renders the damnation of reprobates a damnation for not believing a lie.

12. It commissions all ministers to preach a lie, and makes God the Father and the Son party to it.

13. It renders the requisition upon all men to repent useless and insincere.

14. It makes the damnation of men of the will of God, falsifying his own word.

15. It renders the atonement, in its nature, an eternal curse.

16. It renders it certain that many men were created with an absolute necessity of damnation.

17. It renders the strife between the devil and Christ a stupendous folly.

18. It is liable to all the objections, additionally, that were brought against election and reprobation.

19. It renders it unnecessary and impossible for the elect to do any thing in order to their salvation.

20. It makes it impossible for them to peril their salvation. They cannot avoid salvation.

21. It imputes the obedience and suffering of Christ to believers in a manner unknown in the Scriptures.

22. It destroys all the motives, drawn from eternal destiny, to influence human conduct.

23. It renders it impossible for the elect ever to become guilty, after regeneration.

24. It dishonors and degrades the atonement into a mere commercial transaction—a thing of barter and sale.

To this list of objections many more might be added, any one of which is sufficient alone to damn the system embarrassed with it and its consequences, to unspeakable and irreparable infamy.

And, now, may we again appeal to our Calvinistic friends to examine the grounds, and be not angry with us because of our plainness of speech? We have no contention but for the truth. Let us look well to it, that we be not found, in our pride, clinging to prejudice, and rejecting truth, and the God of truth. That we have objected many things against you which you do not believe, we know perfectly well; but we show you that these consequences flow from your premises. Now, what will you do? You know the consequences cannot be escaped. Can they? How? Will you, then, embrace consequences and all? How can you do this? But if not, will you discard the premises? One you must do, or, in the eyes of all reasonable men, of God himself, be found guilty of gross, may I not say? criminal inconsistency. Why cling to errors so unlovely as those of Calvinism? What in your nature, in reason, in religion, in God, does not turn away from the horrid compound with lothing, with disgust?

CHAPTER V.

EFFECTUAL CALLING.

In harmony with the doctrine of election and reprobation, and of a limited atonement, and the unconditional salvation of all those for whom the atonement was made, is the doctrine of effectual calling and its cognates, which we shall now proceed to notice. Upon this point Calvinists deliver themselves with unusual freedom and plenitude. A selection from them will set the matter in a proper light.

"All those whom God hath predestinated unto life, and those *only*, he is pleased, in his appointed and accepted time, effectually to call, by his word and Spirit, out of that state of sin and death in which they are by nature, to grace and salvation by Jesus Christ; enlightening their minds, spiritually and savingly, to understand the things of God; taking away their heart of stone, and giving unto them a heart of flesh; renewing their wills, and, by his almighty power, determining them to that which is good, and effectually drawing them to Jesus Christ; yet so as they come most freely, being made willing by this grace. This effectual call is of God's free and special grace *alone*, not from any thing at all foreseen in man, *who is altogether passive therein*, until being quickened and renewed by the Holy Spirit, he is thereby enabled to answer this call, and to embrace the grace offered and conveyed in it." (Confession of Faith, chap. x, sec. i and ii.)

"What is effectual calling?

"Effectual calling is the work of God's almighty power and grace, whereby, out of his free and especial love to his elect, and from nothing in them moving him thereunto, he doth, in his accepted time, invite and draw them unto Jesus Christ by his word and Spirit, savingly enlightening their minds, renewing and powerfully determining their wills, so as they, although in themselves dead in sin, are hereby made willing and able freely to answer this call, and to accept and embrace the grace offered and conveyed therein.

"Are the elect only effectually called?

"All the elect, and they *only*, are effectually called, although others may be, and often are, outwardly called by the ministry of the word, and have common operations of the Spirit, who, for their willful neglect and contempt of the grace offered to them, being justly left in their unbelief, do never truly come to Jesus Christ." (Larger Catechism, ques. 67 and 68.)

The expositor of the Confession, in his comments upon the sections above, remarks, "That in this calling the operations of the Holy Spirit are irrevocable." We admit that there are common operations of the Spirit, which do not issue in the conversion of the sinner; but we maintain that the special operations of the Spirit overcome all opposition, and effectually determine the sinner to embrace Jesus Christ as he is offered in the Gospel. If the special operations of the Spirit were not invincible, but might be effectually resisted, then it would be uncertain whether any would believe or not, and consequently possible, that all which Christ had done and suffered in the work of redemption might have been done and suffered in vain.

"That in this calling the sinner is altogether passive, until he is quickened and renewed by the Holy Ghost." (P. 143.)

"We are made partakers of the benefits which Christ hath procured, by the application of them to us, which is the work especially of God the Holy Ghost."

"Redemption is certainly applied, and effectually communicated, to all those for whom Christ hath purchased it." (Larger Catechism, ques. 58 and 59.)

"In regeneration we are *passive*, and receive from

God: it is an irresistible, or, rather, an invincible work." (Buck.)

"The power of God, exerted in regeneration and conversion of sinners, is invincible. Those who speak of irresistible grace, mean that it cannot finally be resisted; that it will overcome all the efforts of corrupt nature to counteract its design; and that it will ultimately render sinners obedient to the faith. Man must submit in the end to the power of God; and this will be more evident if we consider that his power is not only sufficient to compel the most refractory to yield, although with the greatest reluctance, but that it can take away the spirit of opposition, and so influence the hearts of men, that this submission shall be voluntary. *Were we to say that the grace of God is not invincible, we should be under the necessity of adopting the opinion, which we have already proved to be unscriptural, that there is in man a power to comply or not to comply with the call of the Gospel.* We should take the work of conversion out of the hand of God, and commit it to man himself. After God had done all that he could do for our salvation, it would depend upon ourselves whether the intended effect should follow." (Dick.)

"According to the Scriptures, regeneration is a change, effected by Divine grace, in the state of the soul—the supernatural renovation of its faculties—the infusion of a principle of spiritual life. It is evident that if this is a just definition, the sinner is passive." (Ib.)

"In opposition to all the modifications of error upon this point, we affirm that conversion is effected by the almighty grace of God; that, although man does not concur in it, he is, in the first instance, passive, and his concurrence is the consequence of supernatural power communicated to him; and that he does not come to God till he is effectually called, by the operation of the Holy Spirit in his soul." (Ib.)

"The first immediate fruit of eternal election, and the principal act of God, by which appointed salvation is applied, is effectual calling. And this calling is that act by which those who are chosen by God, and redeemed by Christ, are sweetly invited and effectually brought from a state of sin to a state of communion with God in Christ, both externally and internally." (Witsius, book iii, chap. v, sec. i.)

"But this call is given partly externally, by a persuasive power called moral suasion; partly internally, by a real, supernatural efficacy, which changes the heart. The external call is, in some measure, published by the word of nature; but more fully by that of supernatural revelation, without which every word of nature would be insufficient and ineffectual. The internal comes from the power of the Holy Spirit, working inwardly on the heart; and without this, every external, revealed word, though objectively very sufficient, as it clearly discovers every thing to be known, believed, and done, yet is subjectively ineffectual, nor will ever bring any person to the communion of Christ." (Ib., sec. vii.)

"By that same word, whereby the elect are called to communion with God and his Christ, they are also regenerated to a far more excellent life." (Ib., chap. iv, sec. i.)

"Regeneration is that supernatural act of God whereby a new and divine life is infused into the elect person spiritually dead, and that from the incorruptible seed of the word of God, made fruitful by the infinite power of the Spirit." (Ib., sec. iv.)

"If we consider this first principle of life, there is not the least doubt but regeneration is accomplished in a moment; for there is no delay in the transition from death to life. No person can be regenerated so long as he is in the state of spiritual death; but in the instant he is, he begins to live—he is born again. Wherefore, no intermediate state between the regenerate and unregenerate can be imagined, so much as in thought." (Ib., sec. viii.)

"Hence, it appears, there are no preparations antecedent to the first beginning of regeneration; because, previous to that, nothing but mere death, in the highest degree, is to be found in the person to be regenerated. And, indeed, the Scripture represents man's conversion by such similitudes as show that all preparations are entirely excluded." (Ib., chap. vi, sec. ix.)

"You will say, then, are there no preparatory dispositions to the first regeneration? I confessedly answer, there are none—agree with Fulgentius. With respect to the birth of a child, the work of God is previous to any will of the person that comes into the world; so in the spiritual birth, whereby we begin to put off the old man." (Ib., sec. xiii.)

"And this is that regeneration which is so much declared in the Scriptures—a new creation—a resurrection from the dead—a giving of life, which God, *without us*, worketh in us. And this is by no means effected by the doctrine alone sounding without, by moral suasion, or by *such a mode of working, that, after the operation of God, it should remain in the power of man to be regenerated or not regenerated, converted or not converted,* but is manifestly an operation supernatural, at the same time most powerful, and most sweet, wonderful, secret, and infallible in its power, according to the Scriptures, not less than or inferior to creation or the resurrection of the dead; so that all those, in whose hearts God works in this admirable manner, are certainly, infallibly, and efficaciously regenerated, and, in fact, believe. And thus their will, being now renewed, is not only influenced and moved by God, but, being acted on by God, itself acts and moves." (Synod of Dort, chap. iii, sec. xii.)

"The power of God exerted in regeneration is invincible.

We do not deny that the grace of God may be resisted, not only by the finally impenitent, but by those who ultimately yield to it; but, in the end, man must yield to the power of divine grace; because his power is sufficient to subdue the most stubborn will, to remove all opposition, and to influence the hearts of men, that they, at last, yield voluntary submission, without compulsion or force exerted upon their minds. In regeneration, in the moment of the act, the soul is passive." (Helffenstein.)

"As the child is passive in generation, so is the child of God in regeneration." (Bosten.)

"Regeneration is an irresistible, or, rather, an invincible work of grace." (Buck's Theological Dictionary—Regeneration.)

"In regeneration we are passive, and receive from God." (Ib.)

Without multiplying authorities, for the above are sufficient for all our purposes, we shall now proceed to deduce a statement of doctrine, and then set forth our objections.

And, from the above, we derive as the faith of Calvinists upon the subjects of effectual calling, irresistible grace, and regeneration—(these subjects were blended, because, in the Calvinian system, they constitute essentially but one branch of doctrine, as the above quotations abundantly show. Whatever may be their shades of difference and divers ramifications, they spring from one identical principle and its cognates—to all intents and purposes they are the same:)

1. That, up to the moment of effectual calling—regeneration—a man cannot cease from sin; he has not the power to do so.

2. None but the elect ever are effectually called—regenerated.

3. When the elect are effectually called, they cannot help but yield; they have no power to resist.

4. This effectual call is sent upon the elect without any conditions or preparation on their part.

Now, to the doctrine thus summed up—and no Calvinist dare dispute any point included in it—I shall proceed to alledge a number of objections; and it will be with the good sense and candor of my readers, to decide whether they constitute sufficient reasons for discarding the doctrine.

1. I object to this doctrine, that it is anti-scriptural, nowhere taught in the word of God, and contradictory to much that is therein taught: as that salvation is conditional—that all may seek and find—that they are criminal who do not seek—that many are lost who might have been saved—that the Spirit may be resisted—that repentance and faith precede regeneration—indeed, the doctrine is in palpable conflict with the whole tenor of revelation. This is one objection.

2. But, further, I object, that if regeneration is the work of irresistible grace, wrought without previous conditions, then they who are not regenerated, are not to be condemned for remaining unregenerate. It is attributable to no fault in them, and so cannot render them blameworthy, because it is a matter with which they have nothing whatever to do. It is God's work, and not theirs in any sense; they are passive entirely, from beginning to end; and so, if there be any wrong in their remaining unregenerate, the wrong is not in them, because it is not by their consent.

But if it be said the wrong is not in their remaining unregenerate, but in their being so in the first instance, then, I reply, neither are they to blame for this, because it, also, was entirely without their consent. They were born corrupt, and so cannot be guilty for this; they cannot escape from corruption, and so are not guilty for remaining in it; and, therefore, they have no guilt whatever because of their corruption. From this reasoning there is no escape, but an assumption that men are absolutely and damnably guilty for that over which they have not now, and never did have, any control. Believe this who can! but let my tongue cleave to the roof of my mouth before I can so calumniate the adorable Jehovah!

3. If the doctrine be true, men are not to be condemned for actual sin, unless they are condemnable for not avoiding that which they never had power to avoid. For they were brought into the world with a corrupt nature, without any consent of theirs, unless they consented before they had an existence; and being thus born, they never could cease from sin without regeneration; and they never had power to promote or secure regeneration, and so are not to be condemned for the sins they commit prior to regeneration, unless they are to be condemned for an absolute impossibility.

4. If this doctrine be true, then they who are not regenerate not only are not to be condemned for not being regenerate, and for actual sins committed prior to regeneration, but, also, they cannot be required to be holy in heart or in life, unless it is assumed that men may justly be required to do what they never had, and have not, the power to do. If they do not do right, they violate no requirement, but a requirement to perform an impossibility, which is the requirement of an abhorrent despot, and not of the glorious Jehovah.

5. If this doctrine be true, there can be no punishment for either depravity or sin, unless men are punishable for not performing impossibilities. If men are finally punished with eternal torments, then they are punished without any cause on their part, but simply that they did not do what it was eternally impossible for them to do. They are punished for impenitence and unbelief; but impenitence and unbelief are the unavoidable fruit of a corrupt nature; from this corruption there is no deliverance but by regeneration; man has no power to regenerate himself, and he can do

nothing to induce God to regenerate him: he is, therefore, damned in hell for ever, for that over which he had no more control than the angel Gabriel. Think of hell! then think of such a fate! Can God be chargeable with such a government and conduct as this?

6. If the doctrine be true, then men cannot be required to do any thing to promote their salvation; for their salvation is not susceptible of being promoted, as it is unconditional. In salvation man is not a co-agent, but a mere passive subject. Until the work is commenced by irresistible regeneration, he can do nothing but sin. When regeneration takes place, all the rest follows as a necessary effect or unavoidable fruit.

7. They cannot, with any propriety, be invited or exhorted to repent and seek God; for the thing is impossible; and to invite or exhort men to perform an impossibility, is trifling—is nonsense. A Calvinistic minister, who believes that up to the moment of regeneration a man cannot repent and turn to God—and who, also, believes that regeneration is a gift of God without conditions, and, also, that when regeneration is given, men must repent—and yet urges, and invites, and implores men to repent and turn to God, must be accounted guilty of the strangest inconsistency, to say the least of it.

8. They cannot, with any propriety, be required to do one thing rather than another, before regeneration, only as one sin is preferable to another; for whatever they do must be sinful. Nothing that a man can do before regeneration is good; it is all sin. If he prays for the forgiveness of his sins, it only increases them. If he observes the Sabbath, if he reads the Scriptures, if he goes to the house of God, if he fasts, and mourns, and humbles himself before God, it is all sin. But, it is said, a man cannot do these things until regenerated: but that is precisely my proposition; he can

do nothing but sin, and cannot turn away from it any more than he can create a universe—cannot even try. Why, then, ask him or labor with him upon the subject?

9. If this be true, then it must be that God prefers that the elect should commit a great deal of sin before they are regenerated. For their regeneration is his work; he can do it one time as well as another; for it is by irresistible grace, and against the sinner's disposition, whenever it is done; and that he leaves them unregenerate a long term of years, must be because, on the whole, he prefers that during this period they should be unregenerate and sinful, rather than regenerate and holy.

10. Yea, more: if this doctrine be true, God must prefer all the impenitence, and unbelief, and sin, that is in the world. For if regeneration is his work alone, independent of all conditions, and if regeneration would produce holiness, then the reason why the world remains unregenerate and unholy must be, that, on the whole, God prefers it. He prefers that it should be as it is, or he would make it otherwise. There is no other reason but his preference; for a sufficient atonement has been made to remove all impediments out of the way, so far as Divine justice is concerned; and in the creature there is nothing but what might be overcome by irresistible grace. That such grace is not exerted, is of the good pleasure of God alone; and this good pleasure must arise from the fact, that, in view of all things, God prefers the final impenitence and unholiness of some persons to their holiness, and their eternal destruction to their everlasting salvation.

11. If this doctrine be true, man is not a free agent in consenting to salvation, nor yet in refusing to consent; because in the former case the will is irresistibly coerced to its choice; in the latter it has no ability to make a contrary election. In both cases it acts under an irresistible agency. For if the soul, under the influence of the effectual call,

retains its freedom, it has power to resist; but then the call would not be irresistible; but if it has no power to resist, but must necessarily choose, then it is not free. And if without the effectual call it might choose life, then without the effectual call it might be saved; but if it has not the power, then it is not free.

12. I object to this doctrine, because it antagonizes the doctrine of salvation by faith, and makes faith an involuntary exercise—these both. Is not regeneration salvation from depravity? and is it not the work of salvation commenced in the soul? If so, and if regeneration precedes faith, is it not inevitable that faith is not a condition to salvation to this extent? And if faith is a necessary effect of regeneration, can it be a voluntary exercise? And if it is not a voluntary exercise, can it, with any propriety, be called a condition of any thing which follows after it? And, particularly, can men be exhorted to its exercise, as though it were a condition to which they are competent?

Can a regenerate person be lost? If not, regeneration itself infallibly secures salvation, with all that is included therein. And if it does secure salvation, how can any thing which comes after it be called a condition of salvation? Must not every thing following after rather be said to be included in salvation?

13. I object to this doctrine, further, that it not only makes salvation an involuntary and unconditional work, but it also does away with repentance entirely. Look at it soberly, and see if it is not a shocking misrepresentation, not only of the particular teachings and general tone of the Bible, but, also, of all experience. There is a man who, up to this moment, is a sinner; and now, without any conviction or turning of heart to God, or any use of means—while his heart is proud, and stubborn, and sinful as ever, he is in one instant, by irresistible grace, born of God; in the same instant he is justified; but preceding his justification

and succeeding his regeneration, he exercises faith and repentance! Now, I ask, in the name of reason and religion, is this so? Will the world furnish one solitary witness to an experience of this kind?

14. According to this doctrine, a Christian is no more to be esteemed for his virtues, than a sinner for his sins; and the latter is no more to be censured than the former; because they are both passive, and only passive, with respect alike to their sins and virtues: the only difference between them is produced by irresistible fate. Indeed, the whole system of Calvinism, in its peculiar tenets, inevitably destroys both the accountability of man, and the distinctions between vice and virtue. If one man is irresistibly and invincibly drawn to a holy life, and another man is equally irresistibly drawn to an unholy and sinful conduct, and this without any thing under their control, it must be manifest, that, though there is a difference, it may be both in the character and conduct of the individuals; yet they are neither commendable nor censurable, or, indeed, in any sense responsible for the difference.

Yea, further, does not Calvinism also teach, not only that men are entirely passive in their states and actions, but that, in their sins as much as in their most holy exercises, they actually perform the will of God. The will of God, according to their teaching, cannot in any thing be frustrated. Nothing comes to pass but that he willed it. The devil does his will as much as the archangel. Where is the difference? In what is the one more approvable or censurable than the other? Is this one to be damned? Why? Did he not do the will of God? Did he do any thing, more or less, than, in the will of God, was purposed before the foundation of the world? Is he damned for doing the will of God! He is damned for sinning; but that very sin was the will of God? God willed him to do; he but complied—accomplished what his Maker wished him to do—what it was not only impossible he should avoid, but what, if he had avoided, would have been a breach of his Maker's will—the damnable sin! O, sir, what dreadful work this kind of *stuff* makes with the character and reputation of God! Do you find no difficulties upon these points? Then must you be blind indeed! Consult your own experience—interrogate your consciousness; it will teach you better. You will find, beyond any power to convince you to the contrary, that you believe that a change in your character and life was not wrought without your consent—that your consent was not produced by irresistible power. You will find that your recollection of repentance is, that you repented long and deeply, with tears and sorrow, before you found forgiveness—that this repentance was attended with a distressing sense of both unpurged corruption and unremoved condemnation. If any man had asked you, then, whether your vile nature was changed—regenerated—or not, what would have been your answer? That you were not only unpardoned, but vile! A change indeed had been wrought—but not the change of nature—making you a child of God. Such is the testimony of your experience: every step is fresh in your memory; you can never forget it. By some instrument, it matters not what, where, or when, your mind was arrested: truth flashed upon your guilty conscience; you saw and admitted it. A simple conviction of your utter sinfulness was the result. You pondered what to do. A struggle, and you determined to seek for life. What next? You now began seriously to reflect—you betook yourself to the Bible, or to some religious friend—you prayed. Your sense of guilt and wretchedness increased. How bitter now was the mingled cup of your sorrow! You repented before God, did you not? You struggled on, through doubts and fears, now ready to lay hold by faith, then sinking into deep despair! At last, in the utmost extremity, forgetting all, by a mighty exertion, you embraced the atoning sacrifice—you believed. Do you not recollect it? Was it not so? Then came rest! Your nature was changed. You saw it—you felt it—you realized it; no earthly power could convince you to the contrary; believing you were a new man in Christ Jesus, and had now no condemnation. I appeal to every Christian, was it not so? Your experience, then, as well as God's word, and the voice of reason, are against the dogma we here oppose.

Much more might be said, to show the danger of the error under examination—how it destroys all sense of obligation—how it contents the sinner in his sins—how it neutralizes all effort—how it shields the conscience from all appeals and exhortations; but all this must be present to the reflecting and considerate reader. In view of them, let him hesitate; nay, let him promptly throw from him an unsupported dogma, fraught with such deadly influences. Let no cherished prejudices—no long attachments, cause him to deal compassionately with the dangerous delusion. It deserves no mercy; let it find none. Let the mind always contemplate it naked; its deformities will make it sufficiently detestable. It is only when it is cloaked and masked that it has attractions; when seen in its native and real character, with its consorts and relatives, it will be sufficiently hideous; no mind will admit it. It will stand, without, with its kindred errors, equally execrated by reason and religion, by the voice of God, and the instinct of mankind. Dear reader, may we be guided by the infinite Spirit into all truth!

CHAPTER VI.

PERSEVERANCE.

In this chapter we shall treat of the perseverance of the saints—a subject of scarcely inferior importance to those already considered. It falls in at this point naturally, and forms an indispensable part of this most wonderful system; for, certainly, whatever else may be said of Calvinism, it must be admitted that it is a complete system. Starting out with the radical principle, that all events are fixed by eternal decree, it infers that those who will be finally saved must be so decreed to salvation—then the means must be fixed—then they must operate infallibly—then they must accomplish the end; the elect must be kept to the end.

"They whom God hath accepted in his Beloved, effectually called, and sanctified by his Spirit, can neither totally nor finally fall away from the state of grace, but shall certainly persevere therein to the end, and be eternally saved.

"This perseverance of the saints depends not upon their own free will, but upon the immutability of the decree of election, flowing from the free and unchangeable love of God the Father, upon the efficacy of the merits and intercession of Jesus Christ, the abiding of the Spirit and of the seed of God within them, and the nature of the covenant of grace; from all which ariseth, also, the certainty and infallibility thereof.

"Nevertheless, they may, through the temptation of Satan and the world, the prevalency of corruption remaining in them, and the neglect of the means of their preservation, fall into grievous sins, and for a time continue therein; whereby they incur God's displeasure, and grieve his Holy Spirit, and come to be deprived of some measure of their graces and comforts, have their hearts hardened, and their consciences wounded, hurt and scandalize others, and bring temporal judgments upon themselves." (Confession of Faith, chap. xvii, sec. i–iii.)

"The perseverance of the saints is one of the articles by which the creed of the followers of Calvin is distinguished from that of the followers of Arminius. The latter hold, that true believers may fall into sins inconsistent with a state of grace, and may continue in apostasy to the end of life; and, consequently, may finally fall into perdition. In opposition to this tenet, our Confession affirms, that true believers can neither totally nor finally fall away from a state of grace, but shall certainly persevere therein to the end, and be eternally saved. We affirm, that the total apostasy of believers is impossible, not in the nature of things, but by the Divine constitution; and, consequently, that no man, who has been once received into the Divine favor, can be ultimately deprived of salvation." (Expositor of the Confession, p. 198.)

"As the grace of God, which is conceived to derive its efficacy from his power of fulfilling his purpose in those for whom it is destined, overcomes all the opposition with which it is at first received, so it continues to be exerted amidst all the frailty and corruption which adhere to human nature in a present state. It is not exerted to such a degree as to preserve any man from every kind of sin; *for God is pleased to teach Christians* humility, by keeping up the remembrance of that state out of which they were delivered, and to quicken their aspirations after higher degrees of goodness, by leaving them to struggle with temptation, and to feel manifold infirmities. But, although no man is enabled, in this life, to attain to perfection, the grace of God preserves those to whom it is given from drawing back to perdition. The doctrine of the perseverance of the saints flows necessarily from that decree by which they were, from eternity, chosen to salvation, and from the manner in which, according to the Calvinistic system, the decree was executed; and all the principles of the system must be renounced, before we can believe that any of those for whom Christ died, and who, consequently, became partakers of his grace, can fall from that grace, either finally—by which is meant, they shall not, in the end, be saved—or totally—by which is meant, that they shall, at any period of their lives, commit sins so heinous and presumptuous, and persist in them so obstinately, as, at that period, to forfeit entirely the Divine favor." (Hill, p. 540.)

"Upon this subject professed Christians are divided in sentiment, as, indeed, they are upon every article of faith. The doctrine of our Church, in which I believe all the reformed Churches concurred, is expressed in the following words: 'They whom God hath accepted in the Beloved, effectually called, and sanctified by his Spirit, can neither totally nor finally fall away from the state of grace, but shall certainly persevere therein to the end, and be eternally saved.'" (Dick, vol. ii, p. 283.)

"We assert, then, that true believers cannot fall totally or finally from grace. It may seem that the use of both these words is unnecessary; because, if they cannot fall totally, it follows that they cannot fall finally; but they are intended to oppose the doctrine of Arminians, who affirm, that although a saint may fall totally from grace, he may be restored by repentance; but, since this is uncertain, and does not always take place, he may, also, fall finally, and die in his sins. Now we affirm, that the total apostasy of believers is impossible, not in the nature of things, but by the Divine constitution; and, consequently, that no man, who has been once received into the Divine favor, can be ultimately deprived of salvation." (Ib., vol. ii, p. 284.)

"God doth continue to forgive the sins of those who are

justified; and, although they can never fall from the state of justification, yet they may, by their sins, fall under God's fatherly displeasure, and not have the light of his countenance restored unto them until they humble themselves, confess their sins, beg pardon, and renew their faith and repentance." (Confession of Faith, chap. xii, sec. 5.)

"As justification is an act completed at once, so those who are justified cannot come into condemnation. The sins which they afterward commit, cannot revoke the pardon which God has graciously given them; but they may subject them to his fatherly displeasure and temporary chastisement. Here we must revert to the well-known distinction between judicial and fatherly forgiveness. Though God, in the capacity of a judge, pardons all the sins of believers in the most free and unconditional manner, in the day of their justification, yet that forgiveness, which, as a father, he bestows upon his justified and adopted children, is not in general vouchsafed, without suitable preparation on their part for receiving and improving the privilege [!!]" (Expositor of the Confession, p. 158.)

"May not true believers, by reason of their imperfections, and the many temptations and sins they are overtaken with, fall away from the state of grace?

"True believers, by reason of the unchangeable love of God, and his decree and covenant to give them perseverance, their inseparable union with Christ, his continual intercession for them, and the Spirit and seed of God abiding in them, can neither totally nor finally fall away from the state of grace, but are kept by the power of God through faith unto salvation." (Larger Catechism, ques. 79.)

If it should be objected to this statement, that, although Calvinists believe in the necessity of the salvation of those for whom Christ died, yet they believe it is conditional, or is made to depend upon the faith of the believer, I reply, it is admitted that Calvinists teach that faith is a condition of salvation; but now observe, they teach that it is irresistibly communicated—if it is a condition, it is not a condition dependent, in any sense, upon the believer himself, but is an effect wrought in him without his consent.

"The covenant of redemption secures the continuance and growth of the principle of grace, until the believer shall be perfected in heaven. In this life he never utterly falls for one moment from grace." (Ely's Contrast, p. 274.)

"The holiness of the Christian continues to the end." (Dwight.) Upon this proposition, Dr. Dwight delivers one of his most labored sermons, to prove the necessary final perseverance of the saints.

Upon this point it will scarcely be necessary for me to adduce a larger number of quotations. Those already given are full and authoritative. This, indeed, is a point where less reference to authority is required than almost any other of the Calvinian creed; here they all harmonize. The final perseverance of the saints, with them, is a frankly-avowed and cherished sentiment. To rob them of this, would be to rob them of one of their gods. If their view of election is true, this is consequentially true; if their doctrine of the atonement is true, this cannot be false; if their doctrine of effectual grace is true, this must follow. So that they are, at least, consistent with themselves in believing and teaching it; they could not do otherwise. It is an integral part of the same great system of fatalism and irresponsibility, which has been examined in this book.

The doctrine, as taught in the above quotations, may thus be stated:

1. Persons once regenerated may fall into grievous sins, and continue therein for a time indefinite.

2. They cannot totally fall away, but, however sinful they may become, will continue to be children of God.

3. They cannot finally perish, but must necessarily come to eternal life.

Such is the doctrine of the Presbyterian Church, as taught by their Confession of Faith and standard authors. To it we find many and, to us, insuperable objections. Read and judge for yourselves.

1. And first, we object, the doctrine is without warrant from the word of God. It is admitted that passages are found in the Scriptures, which, *disconnected from their relations, might allow of a construction partly favorable to a doctrine resembling the above.* But no passage clearly teaches it; none necessarily infers it; no principle of revelation sanctions it; if it could be true, its truth never can be derived from the Bible. This, then, is our first ground of objection, and to a Christian it is sufficient; he need go no further; here he will be content to put an end to his inquiries. It is not of the Bible, it cannot, therefore, be received, will be his reasoning.

2. But second, I object further, and as growing out of the foregoing, not only is this doctrine not taught in the Bible, but, what is more fatal to it, the Bible teaches that it is false, by teaching that precisely what it denies is the truth. It is to be discarded not alone because the Bible does not teach it, but because the Bible asserts its falsehood. Revelation is not *silent* upon the point, but it is expressly, fully, unmistakably *against* the assumption. The doctrine itself is false, or the Bible. I cannot better express this objection than in the following language of Mr. Wesley, in his tract on Perseverance. He thus presents the Scripture argument:

"For thus saith the Lord: 'When the righteous turneth away from his righteousness, and committeth iniquity, in his trespass that he hath trespassed, and in his sin that he hath sinned, in them shall he die.' (Ezek. xviii, 24.)

"That this is to be understood of eternal death appears from the twenty-sixth verse: 'When a righteous man turneth away from his righteousness and committeth iniquity, and dieth in them, [here is temporal death,] for his iniquity that he hath done he shall die.' [Here is death eternal.]

"It appears, farther, from the whole scope of the chapter, which is to prove, 'the soul that sinneth, it shall die.' (V. 4.)

"If you say, 'The soul here means the body,' I answer, that will die whether you sin or no.

"Again, thus saith the Lord: 'When I shall say to the righteous, that he shall surely live, if he trust to his own righteousness, [yea, or to that promise as absolute and unconditional,] and commit iniquity, all his righteousness shall not be remembered; but for the iniquity that he hath committed shall he die.' (Chap. xxxiii, 13.)

"Again: 'When the righteous turneth from his righteousness, and committeth iniquity, he shall even die thereby.' (V. 18.)

"Therefore, one who is holy and righteous in the judgment of God himself, may yet so fall as to perish everlastingly.

"But how is this consistent with what God declared elsewhere? 'If his children forsake my law, and walk not in my judgments, I will visit their offenses with the rod, and their sin with scourges. Nevertheless, my loving kindness will I not utterly take from him, nor suffer my truth to fail. My covenant will I not break, nor alter the thing that is gone out of my lips. I have sworn once by my holiness, that I will not fail David.' (Psalm lxxxix, 30–35.)

"I answer, there is no manner of inconsistency between one declaration and the other. The prophet declares the just judgment of God against every righteous man who falls from his righteousness. The Psalmist declares the old loving kindnesses which God sware unto David in his truth. 'I have found,' saith he, 'David, my servant; with my holy oil have I anointed him. My hand shall hold him fast, and my arm shall strengthen him. His seed, also, will I make to endure for ever, and his throne as the days of heaven.' (V. 20, 21, 29.) It follows: 'But if his children forsake my law, and walk not in my judgments, nevertheless, my loving kindness will I not utterly take from him, nor suffer my truth to fail. My covenant will I not break. I will not fail David. His seed shall endure for ever, and his throne as the sun before me.' (V. 30, &c.)

"May not every man see, that the covenant here spoken of relates wholly to David and his seed or children? Where, then, is the inconsistency, between the most absolute promise made to a particular family, and that solemn account, which God has here given, of his way of dealing with all mankind?

"Beside, the very covenant mentioned in these words, is not absolute, but conditional. The condition of repentance, in case of forsaking God's law, was implied, though not expressed; and so strongly implied, that, this condition failing—not being performed, God did also fail David. He did 'alter the thing that had gone out of his lips,' and yet without any impeachment of his truth. He 'abhorred and forsook his anointed,' (v. 38,) the seed of David, whose throne, if they had repented, should have been 'as the days of heaven.' He did 'break the covenant of his servant, and cast his crown to the ground.' (V. 39.) So vainly are these words of the Psalmist brought to contradict the plain, full testimony of the prophet!

"Nor is there any contradiction between this testimony of God by Ezekiel, and those words which he spake by Jeremiah: 'I have loved thee with an everlasting love; therefore, with loving kindness have I drawn thee.' For do these words assert, that no righteous man ever turns from his righteousness? No such thing. They do not touch the question, but simply declare God's love to the Jewish Church. To see this in the clearest light, you need only read over the whole sentence: 'At the same time, saith the Lord, I will be the God of all the families of Israel, and they shall be my people. Thus saith the Lord, The people which were left of the sword found grace in the wilderness; even Israel, when I caused him to rest. The Lord hath appeared of old unto me,' saith the prophet, speaking in the person of Israel, 'saying, I have loved thee with an everlasting love; therefore, with loving kindness have I drawn thee. Again I will build thee, and thou shalt be built, O virgin of Israel.' (Chap. xxxi, 1–4.)

"Suffer me here to observe, once for all, a fallacy which is constantly used by almost all writers on this point. They perpetually beg the question, by applying to particular persons assertions or prophecies which relate only to the Church in general, and some of them only to the Jewish Church and nation, as distinguished from all other people.

"If you say, 'But it was particularly revealed to me, that God had loved me with an everlasting love,' I answer, suppose it was—which might bear a dispute—it proves no more, at the most, than that you, in particular, shall persevere; but does not affect the general question, whether others shall, or shall not.

"Secondly. One who is endued with the faith that purifies the heart—that produces a good conscience, may, nevertheless, so fall from God as to perish everlastingly.

"For thus saith the inspired apostle: 'War a good warfare; holding faith and a good conscience; which some having put away, concerning faith have made shipwreck.' (1 Tim. i, 18, 19.)

"Observe, 1. These men [such as Hymeneus and Alexander] had once the faith that purifies the heart—that produces a good conscience; which they once had, or they could not have 'put it away.'

"Observe, 2. They 'made shipwreck' of the faith; which necessarily implies the total and final loss of it; for a vessel once wrecked can never be recovered; it is totally and finally lost.

"And the Apostle himself, in his second Epistle to Timothy, mentions one of these two as irrecoverably lost. 'Alexander,' says he, 'did me much evil: the Lord shall reward him according to his works.' (2 Tim. iv, 14.) Therefore, one who is endued with the faith that purifies the heart—that produces a good conscience, may, nevertheless, so fall from God as to perish everlastingly.

"'But how can this be reconciled with the words of our Lord, "He that believeth shall be saved?"'

"Do you think these words mean, 'He that believes,' at this moment, 'shall' certainly and inevitably 'be saved?'

"If this interpretation be good, then, by all the rules of speech, the other part of the sentence must mean, 'He' that does 'not believe,' at this moment, 'shall' certainly and inevitably 'be damned.'

"Therefore, that interpretation cannot be good. The plain meaning, then, of the whole sentence is, 'He that believeth,' if he continue in faith, 'shall be saved; he that believeth not,' if he continue in unbelief, 'shall be damned.'

"'But does not Christ say elsewhere, "He that believeth hath everlasting life?" (John iii, 36,) and, "He that believeth on Him that sent me hath everlasting life, and shall not come into condemnation; but is passed from death unto life?"' (John v, 24.)

"I answer, 1. The love of God is everlasting life. It is, in substance, the life of heaven. Now, every one that believes, loves God, and, therefore, 'hath everlasting life.'

"2. Every one that believes, 'is,' therefore, 'passed from death'—spiritual death—'unto life,' and,

"3. 'Shall not come into condemnation,' if he endureth in the faith unto the end; according to our Lord's own words, 'He that endureth to the end shall be saved;' and,

'Verily, I say unto you, If a man keep my saying, he shall never see death.' (John viii, 51.)

"Thirdly. Those who are grafted into the good olive tree, the spiritual, invisible Church, may, nevertheless, so fall from God as to perish everlastingly.

"For thus saith the apostle: 'Some of the branches are broken off, and thou art grafted in among them, and with them partakest of the root and fatness of the olive tree. Be not high-minded, but fear: if God spared not the natural branches, take heed lest he spare not thee. Behold the goodness and severity of God! On them which fell severity; but toward thee, goodness, if thou continue in his goodness; otherwise thou shalt be cut off.' (Rom. xi, 17, 20–22.)

"We may observe here, 1. The persons spoken to were actually grafted into the olive tree.

"2. This olive tree is not barely the outward, visible Church, but the invisible, consisting of holy believers. So the text: 'If the first fruit be holy, the lump is holy; and if the root be holy, so are the branches.' (V. 16.) And, 'Because of unbelief, they were broken off, and thou standest by faith.'

"3. These holy believers were still liable to be cut off from the invisible Church, into which they were then grafted.

"4. Here is not the least intimation of those who were so cut off being ever grafted in again.

"Therefore, those who are grafted into the good olive tree, the spiritual, invisible Church, may, nevertheless, so fall from God as to perish everlastingly.

"'But how does this agree with the 29th verse, "The gifts and calling of God are without repentance?"'

"The preceding verse shows: 'As touching the election, [the unconditional election of the Jewish nation,] they are beloved for the fathers' sake:' for the sake of their forefathers. It follows, [in proof of this, that 'they are beloved for their fathers' sake,' that God has still blessing in store for the Jewish nation:] 'For the gifts and calling of God are without repentance;' for God doth not repent of any blessings he hath given them, or any privileges he hath called them to. The words here referred to were originally spoken with a peculiar regard to these national blessings. 'God is not a man, that he should lie; neither the son of man, that he should repent.' (Num. xxiii, 19.)

"'But do you not hereby make God changeable? Whereas, "with him is no variableness, neither shadow of turning."' (James i, 17.) By no means. God is unchangeably holy; therefore, he always 'loveth righteousness and hateth iniquity.' He is unchangeably good; therefore, he pardoneth all that 'repent and believe the Gospel.' And he is unchangeably just; therefore, he 'rewardeth every man according to his works.' But all this hinders not his resisting, when they are proud, those to whom he gave grace when they were humble. Nay, his unchangeableness itself requires, that, if they grow high-minded, God should cut them off—that there should be a proportionable change in all the Divine dispensations toward them.

"'But how then is God faithful?' I answer, in fulfilling every promise which he hath made, to all to whom it is made—all who fulfill the condition of that promise. More particularly, 1. 'God is faithful' in that 'he will not suffer you to be tempted above that you are able to bear.' (1 Cor. x, 13.) 2. 'The Lord is faithful, to establish and keep you from evil'—if you put your trust in him—from all the evil which you might otherwise suffer, through 'unreasonable and wicked men.' (2 Thess. iii, 2, 3.) 3. 'Quench not the Spirit; hold fast that which is good; abstain from all appearance of evil; and your whole spirit, soul, and body, shall be preserved blameless unto the coming of our Lord Jesus Christ. Faithful is he that calleth you, who also will do it.' (1 Thess. v, 19, &c.) 4. Be not disobedient unto the heavenly calling; and 'God is faithful, by whom ye were called, to confirm you unto the end, that ye may be blameless in the day of our Lord Jesus Christ.' (1 Cor. i, 8, 9.) Yet, notwithstanding all this, unless you fulfill the condition, you cannot attain the promise.

" 'Nay, but are not "all the promises, yea and amen?" ' They are firm as the pillars of heaven. Perform the condition, and the promise is sure. Believe, and thou shalt be saved.

" 'But many promises are absolute and unconditional.' In many, the condition is not expressed. But this does not prove there is none implied. No promises can be expressed in a more absolute form, than those above cited from the eighty-ninth Psalm. And yet we have seen a condition was implied even there, though none was expressed.

" 'But there is no condition, either expressed or implied, in those words of St. Paul: "I am persuaded that neither death, nor life, nor height, nor depth, nor any other creature, shall be able to separate us from the love of God, which is in Christ Jesus our Lord." ' (Rom. viii, 38, 39.)

"Suppose there is not—which will bear a dispute—yet what will this prove? Just thus much: that the apostle was, at that time, fully persuaded of his own perseverance. And I doubt not but many believers, at this day, have the very same persuasion, termed in Scripture, 'the full assurance of hope.' But this does not prove that every believer shall persevere, any more than that every believer is thus fully persuaded of his own perseverance.

"Those who are branches of the true vine, of whom Christ says, 'I am the vine, ye are the branches,' may, nevertheless, so fall from God as to perish everlastingly.

"For thus saith our blessed Lord himself, 'I am the

true vine, and my Father is the husbandman. Every branch in me that beareth not fruit, he taketh it away. I am the vine; ye are the branches. If a man abide not in me, he is cast forth as a branch, and is withered; and men gather them, and cast them into the fire, and they are burned.' (John xv, 1–6.)

"Here we may observe, 1. The persons spoken of were, in Christ, branches of the true vine. 2. Some of these branches abide not in Christ, but the Father taketh them away. 3. The branches which abide not are cast forth—cast out from Christ and his Church. 4. They are not only cast forth, but withered; consequently, never grafted in again. Nay, 5. They are not only cast forth and withered, but also cast into the fire. And, 6. They are burned. It is not possible for words more strongly to declare, that even those who are now branches in the true vine, may yet so fall as to perish everlastingly.

"By this clear, indisputable declaration of our Lord, we may interpret those which might be otherwise liable to dispute; wherein it is certain, whatever he meant beside, he did not mean to contradict himself. For example: 'This is the Father's will, that of all which he hath given me, I should lose nothing.' Most sure; all that God hath given him, or, as it is expressed in the next verse, 'every one which believeth on him,' namely, to the end, he 'will raise up at the last day,' to reign with him for ever.

"Again: 'I am the living bread: if any man eat of this bread [by faith] he shall live for ever.' (John vi, 51.) True; if he continue to eat thereof. And who can doubt of it?

"Again: 'My sheep hear my voice, and I know them, and they follow me. And I give unto them eternal life; and they shall never perish, neither shall any pluck them out of my hand.' (John x, 27, 28.)

"In the preceding text the condition is only implied; in this, it is plainly expressed. They are my sheep that hear my voice, that follow me in all holiness. And 'if ye do those things, ye shall never fall.' None shall 'pluck you out of my hands.'

"Again: 'Having loved his own which were in the world, he loved them unto the end.' (John xiii, 1.) 'Having loved his own,' namely, the apostles—as the very next words, 'which were in the world,' evidently show—'he loved them unto the end' of his life, and manifested that love to the last.

"Once more: 'Holy Father, keep through thine own name those whom thou hast given me, that they may be one, as we are one.' (John xvii, 11.)

"Great stress has been laid upon this text, and it has been hence inferred, that all those whom the Father had given him—a phrase frequently occurring in this chapter—must infallibly persevere to the end.

"And yet, in the very next verse, our Lord himself declares, that one of those whom the Father had given him, did not persevere unto the end, but perished everlastingly.

"His own words are, 'Those that thou gavest me I have kept, and none of them is lost, but the son of perdition.' (John xvii, 12.)

"So one even of these was finally lost!—a demonstration that the phrase, 'those whom thou hast given me,' signifies here, if not in most other places, too, the twelve apostles, and them only.

"On this occasion, I cannot but observe another common instance of begging the question—of taking for granted what ought to be proved. It is usually laid down as an indisputable truth, that whatever our Lord speaks to or of his apostles, is to be applied to all believers. But this cannot be allowed by any who impartially search the Scriptures. They cannot allow, without clear and particular proof, that any one of those texts which related primarily to the apostles, as all men grant, belong to any but them.

"Those who so effectually know Christ, as by that knowledge to have escaped the pollutions of the world, may yet fall back into those pollutions, and perish everlastingly.

"For thus saith the apostle Peter, 'If after they have escaped the pollutions of the world, through the knowledge of the Lord and Savior Jesus Christ, [the only possible way of escaping them,] they are again entangled therein and overcome, the latter end is worse with them than the beginning. For it had been better for them not to have known the way of righteousness, than, after they have known it, to turn from the holy commandment delivered unto them.' (2 Peter ii, 20, 21.)

"That the knowledge of the way of righteousness, which they had attained, was an inward, experimental knowledge, is evident from that other expression—they had 'escaped the pollutions of the world;' an expression parallel to that in the preceding chapter, verse 4, 'Having escaped the corruption which is in the world.' And in both chapters, this effect is ascribed to the same cause; termed in the first, 'the knowledge of Him who hath called us to glory and virtue;' in the second, more explicitly, 'the knowledge of the Lord and Savior Jesus Christ.'

"And yet they lost that experimental knowledge of Christ and the way of righteousness; they fell back into the same pollutions they had escaped, and were 'again entangled therein and overcome.' They 'turned from the holy commandment delivered to them,' so that their 'latter end was worse than their beginning.'

"Therefore, those who so effectually know Christ, as by that knowledge to have escaped the pollutions of the world, may yet fall back into those pollutions, and perish everlastingly.

"And this is perfectly consistent with St. Peter's words, in the first chapter of his former epistle: 'Who are kept by the power of God through faith unto salvation.'

Undoubtedly, so are all they who ever attain eternal salvation. It is the power of God only, and not our own, by which we are kept one day or one hour.

"Those who see the light of the glory of God in the face of Jesus Christ, and who have been made partakers of the Holy Ghost, of the witness, and the fruits of the Spirit, may, nevertheless, so fall from God as to perish everlastingly.

"For thus saith the inspired writer to the Hebrews: 'It is impossible for those who were once enlightened, and have tasted of the heavenly gift, and were made partakers of the Holy Ghost, if they fall away, to renew them again to repentance; seeing they crucify to themselves the Son of God afresh, and put him to an open shame.' (Hebrews vi, 4, 6.)

"Must not every unprejudiced person see, the expressions here used are so strong and clear, that they cannot, without gross and palpable wresting, be understood of any but true believers?

"They 'were once enlightened;' an expression familiar with the apostle, and never by him applied to any but believers. So: 'The God of our Lord Jesus Christ give unto you the spirit of wisdom and revelation: the eyes of your understanding being enlightened, that ye may know what is the hope of his calling, and what is the exceeding greatness of his power, to us-ward that believe.' (Ephesians i, 17–19.) So again: 'God, who commanded the light to shine out of darkness, hath shined into our hearts, to give the light of the knowledge of the glory of God in the face of Jesus Christ.' (2 Corinthians iv, 6.) This is the light which no unbelievers have. They are utter strangers to such enlightening. 'The God of this world hath blinded the minds of them which believe not, lest the light of the glorious Gospel of Christ should shine unto them.' (V. 4.)

"'They had tasted of the heavenly gift, [emphatically so called,] and were made partakers of the Holy Ghost.' So St. Peter likewise couples them together: 'Be baptized for the remission of sins, and ye shall receive the gift of the Holy Ghost,' (Acts ii, 38,) whereby the love of God was shed abroad in their hearts, with all the other fruits of the Spirit. Yea, it is remarkable that our Lord himself, in his grand commission to St. Paul, to which the apostle probably alludes in these words, comprises all these three particulars. 'I send thee to open their eyes, and to turn them from darkness to light, and from the power of Satan unto God, [here contracted into that one expression, 'they were enlightened,'] that they may receive forgiveness of sins, ['the heavenly gift,'] and an inheritance among them which are sanctified,' (Acts xxvi, 18,) which are made 'partakers of the Holy Ghost,' of all the sanctifying influences of the Spirit.

"The expression, 'They tasted of the heavenly gift,' is taken from the Psalmist, 'Taste and see that the Lord is good.' (Psalm xxxiv, 8.) As if he had said, Be ye as assured of his love, as of any thing you see with your eyes. And let the assurance thereof be sweet to your soul, as honey is to your tongue.

"And yet those who had been thus 'enlightened,' had 'tasted' this 'gift,' and been thus 'partakers of the Holy Ghost,' so 'fell away' that it was 'impossible to renew them again to repentance.'

"'But the apostle makes only a supposition: "If they should fall away."'

"I answer: the apostle makes no supposition at all. There is no *if* in the original. The words are, Ἀδύνατον τοὺς απαξ φωτισθέντας, καὶ παραπεσόντας, that is, in plain English, 'It is impossible to renew again unto repentance those who were once enlightened and have fallen away;' therefore, they must perish everlastingly.

"'But if so, then farewell all my comfort.'

"Then your comfort depends on a poor foundation. My comfort stands not on any opinion, either that a believer can or cannot fall away—not on the remembrance of any thing wrought in me yesterday, but on what is to-day—on my present knowledge of God in Christ, reconciling me to himself—on my now beholding the light of the glory of God in the face of Jesus Christ, walking in the light as he is in the light, and having fellowship with the Father and with the Son. My comfort is, that through grace I now believe in the Lord Jesus Christ, and that his Spirit doth bear witness with my spirit that I am a child of God. I take comfort in this, and this only, that I see Jesus at the right hand of God—that I personally for myself, and not for another, have a hope full of immortality—that I feel the love of God shed abroad in my heart, being crucified to the world, and the world crucified to me. My rejoicing is this, the testimony of my conscience, that in simplicity and godly sincerity, not with fleshly wisdom, but by the grace of God, I have my conversation in the world.

"Go and find, if you can, a more solid joy, a more blissful comfort, on this side heaven. But this comfort is not shaken, be that opinion true or false, whether the saints in general can or cannot fall.

"If you take up with any comfort short of this, you lean on the staff of a broken reed, which not only will not bear your weight, but will enter into your hand and pierce you.

"Those who live by faith, may yet fall from God, and perish everlastingly.

"For thus saith the same inspired writer, 'The just shall live by faith; but if any man draw back, my soul shall have no pleasure in him.' (Hebrews x, 38.) 'The just [the justified person] shall live by faith;' even now shall he live the life which is hid with Christ in God; and if he endure unto the end, he shall live for ever. 'But if any man draw back,' saith the Lord, 'my soul shall have no pleasure in him;' that is, I will utterly cast him off; and, accordingly, the drawing back here spoken of is termed, in the verse immediately following, 'drawing back to perdition.'

"'But the person supposed to draw back, is not the same with him that is said to live by faith.'

"I answer, 1. Who is it, then? Can any man draw back from faith who never came to it? But,

"2. Had the text been fairly translated, there had been no pretense for this objection. For the original runs thus: Ὁ δίκαιος ἐκ πίστεως ζήσεται· καὶ ἐὰν ὑποστείληται. If ὁ δίκαιος, 'the just man that lives by faith [so the expression necessarily implies, there being no other nominative of the verb] draws back, my soul shall have no pleasure in him.'

"'But the apostle adds: "We are not of them who draw back unto perdition."' And what will you infer from thence? This is so far from contradicting what has been observed before, that it manifestly confirms it. It is a farther proof that there are those 'who draw back unto perdition,' although the apostle was not of that number. Therefore, those who live by faith, may yet fall from God and perish everlastingly.

"'But does not God say to every one that lives by faith, "I will never leave thee nor forsake thee?"'

"The whole sentence runs thus: 'Let your conversation be without covetousness, and be content with such things as ye have; for He hath said, I will never leave thee nor forsake thee.' True, provided 'your conversation be without covetousness,' and ye 'be content with such things as ye have.' Then you may 'boldly say, the Lord is my helper, and I will not fear what man shall do unto me.'

"Do you not see, 1. That this promise, as here recited,

relates wholly to temporal things? 2. That, even thus taken, it is not absolute, but conditional? And, 3. That the condition is expressly mentioned in the very same sentence?

"Those who are sanctified by the blood of the covenant, may so fall from God as to perish everlastingly.

"For thus again saith the apostle: 'If we sin willfully, after we have received the knowledge of the truth, there remaineth no more sacrifice for sin, but a certain fearful looking for of judgment and fiery indignation, which shall devour the adversaries. He that despised Moses' law, died without mercy under two or three witnesses. Of how much sorer punishment shall he be thought worthy, who hath trodden under foot the Son of God, and hath counted the blood of the covenant, wherewith he was sanctified, an unholy thing!' (Hebrews x, 26-29.)

"It is undeniably plain, 1. That the person mentioned here, was once sanctified by the blood of the covenant. 2. That he afterward, by known, willful sin, trod under foot the Son of God. And, 3. That he hereby incurred a sorer punishment than death, namely, death everlasting.

"Therefore, those who are sanctified by the blood of the covenant, may yet so fall as to perish everlastingly.

"'What! Can the blood of Christ burn in hell? or can the purchase of the blood of Christ go thither?'

"I answer, 1. The blood of Christ cannot burn in hell, no more than it can be spilled on the earth. The heavens must contain both his flesh and blood until the restitution of all things. But,

"2. If the oracles of God are true, one who was purchased by the blood of Christ, may go thither. For he that was sanctified by the blood of Christ, was purchased by the blood of Christ. But one who was sanctified by the blood of Christ, may, nevertheless, go to hell; may fall under that fiery indignation which shall for ever devour the adversaries.

"'Can a child of God, then, go to hell? or can a man

be a child of God to-day, and a child of the devil to-morrow? If God is our Father once, is he not our Father always?'

"I answer, 1. A child of God, that is, a true believer—for he that believeth is born of God—while he continues a true believer, cannot go to hell. But, 2. If a believer make shipwreck of the faith, he is no longer a child of God; and then he may go to hell, yea, and certainly will, if he continues in unbelief. 3. If a believer may make shipwreck of the faith, then a man that believes now, may be an unbeliever some time hence; yea, very possibly, to-morrow; but, if so, he who is a child of God to-day, may be a child of the devil to-morrow. For, 4. God is the Father of them that believe, so long as they believe. But the devil is the father of them that believe not, whether they did once believe or no.

"The sum of all this is: if the Scriptures are true, those who are holy or righteous in the judgment of God himself—those who are endued with the faith that purifies the heart, that produces a good conscience—those who are grafted into the good olive tree, the spiritual, invisible Church—those who are branches of the true vine, of whom Christ says, 'I am the vine, ye are the branches'—those who so effectually know Christ, as by that knowledge to have escaped the pollutions of the world—those who see the light of the glory of God in the face of Jesus Christ, and who have been made partakers of the Holy Ghost, of the witness, and of the fruits of the Spirit—those who live by faith in the Son of God—those who are sanctified by the blood of the covenant, may, nevertheless, so fall from God as to perish everlastingly.

"Therefore, let him that standeth take heed lest he fall."

I have thus at length presented the argument of Mr. Wesley on this point, because of its Scriptural weight and importance. It is sufficient. No candid, unprejudiced reader, it seems to me, can arise from its study without conviction of its truth. But though sufficient, I must ask attention to one or two additional considerations, bearing against the doctrine under examination. Logical consequences are fatal to it; among many instances we select the following:

1. If the doctrine be true, after conversion a man is no longer a free agent. In this, as in all respects with the fate and absurdity of the system, he is brought under a necessity which he has no power to avoid. He cannot fall away from salvation. It will not do for Calvinists to modify the doctrine by saying he will not; its distinct assumption is, he cannot; he has no sufficient power. Let us look closely at this. Either a man, after conversion, can fall into vicious practices and sins, or he cannot. If he cannot, he is not a free agent in a state of trial. If he can, then he may be lost—finally perish; or if he does not finally perish, he must either be saved in his sins, or he must be saved from his sins. The former alternative no one embraces; but if he must be saved from his sins—and this depends upon repentance and faith—the man is not a free agent in these exercises, because he is under an absolute necessity, his salvation being unavoidable; whatever is necessary thereto is, also, unavoidable; and being so, the man is no longer free, unless a man may, at the same time, be free not to do, and yet under an unavoidable necessity to do, a given thing. Thus it appears that the doctrine of fate or absolute necessity legitimately results.

2. I object, it renders the condition of saints in this life more secure than that of the angels in heaven, and of our first parents in paradise. They, notwithstanding their purity and the favor of an approving Creator, had power to fall and perish. Can it be presumed that frail mortals in this state of trial may not? or, if so, why not? Is the faithfulness and immutability of God plead? In what sense do

these secure believers more infallibly than the angels of heaven—than Adam in a state of innocence.

3. If this doctrine is true, it is no difference what a man does after conversion; he cannot peril his soul—cannot even render his salvation doubtful. Thus it inculcates recklessness and licenses crime. Taken in connection with the doctrine of pre-irresistible regeneration, it must unsettle all ideas of responsibility, and do away with every motive to a holy life. For, first, the man cannot avoid being regenerated; it is operated upon him, or in him, by irresistible power, and then, being regenerated, he may become during life a devil in sin, but he cannot miss of heaven. Now, what sheer licentiousness is here! what more is requisite to induce unlimited and incurable recklessness? The man is in no danger—it is all one; let him indulge to the utmost excess; he is safe, and cannot be less so. Is this Christianity? Is this iniquitous teaching to be palmed upon the world as God's truth?

4. I object, further, if the doctrine of final perseverance be true, then sin is not so abhorrent in a Christian as it is in a sinner—is not attended with the same consequences. The sins into which a believer may fall are accounted sufficient to damn a sinner, but are not sufficient to make a whit uncertain the salvation of the believer, if committed by him. What strange theology! Is it not a principle, and a true one, that where much is given much will be required? the greater the obligation, the greater the guilt of delinquency? But in this case the principle is reversed. A man, because he has been made the subject of distinguishing grace, may now sin most aggravatedly, but he will only be loved the more; the greater his crimes, the greater the love manifested in his continual pardon. Is not this teaching that we may sin that grace may abound?

5. The doctrine is not analogous to, or resultant from, or in harmony with, the doctrine of Christianity. This has

been shown abundantly in the refutation of cognate errors. The grounds upon which it is based are false, and the superstructure stands upon emptiness. As conclusions drawn from false premises are worthless and void, so this doctrine vanishes with its foundations, which have been demonstrated to be false. The idea of perseverance, is dependent upon the doctrines of election, commercial atonement, sovereign and irresistible grace. No one can think of it separate and apart from these. These being destroyed, therefore, to dream of this is equivalent with supposing a cause without an effect, or a sequence without a premise.

6. It is contrary to the known conviction and consciousness of, I venture to say, all Christians. There may be a sense of security in the minds of believers, greater in some than in others; but it is believed that honest and careful scrutiny into the subject, will show that believers universally feel, whatever may be their attainments in grace, that there is a possibility of their coming short of salvation—that they yet have the fearful power to keep themselves out of eternal life. Is not this so? I appeal to the consciousness of every one who may chance to read these pages. Do you not feel the certainty of such a power and possibility? Nay, is there not an undefined uneasiness lest you may come short; and if not this, a sense of the necessity of much diligence, that you may at last enter into life? Does not God, in his own word, appeal to such a possibility, to stimulate his children to constant and needful exertion? Is this consciousness false? Is our heavenly Father trifling with us, in his admonitions, exhortations, and expostulations, addressed to us in view of such imminent liability?

7. I object, that it is contrary to probability, if not certainty, with respect to individuals whose history is given in the Scriptures, who at one time were recognized as children of God, and whose final damnation is unquestionable. It is, also, contrary to probability with respect to many persons

known in every age of the Church; some of whom, I doubt not, will be readily called up to the recollection of my readers—persons who, at one time, gave most indubitable evidence of genuine repentance and conversion, and who for many years brought forth all the fruits of a real Christian life, such as it is admitted could not exist without the influence of grace, yet, after all, fell into the most dreadful sins, and died in the very midst of their iniquities, gloating in their shame, and who must have finally perished or entered into life with their sins, or have been made holy after death!

Such are some of the objections we urge against the doctrine under examination. It is without warrant from the Bible. It is contrary to the explicit statements of the Bible. It is opposed to its facts, principles, and implications. It is inharmonious and discordant with its doctrines. Its logical consequences are antagonistic to the reason and nature of man, to the genius of religion, and to the consciousness of our species. It is a dangerous doctrine, productive of recklessness, licentiousness, and crime, as its legitimate offspring. All this is objectionable to it, without a single redeeming or apologetic circumstance. To embrace it, is to act in advance of, if not to abandon, common sense; and to be influenced by it, is to endanger all the interests of sound virtue and true religion, theoretical and practical, so far as these are under the guardianship of Christianity.

CHAPTER VII.

THE HEATHEN WORLD.

THE Calvinistic view of the heathen world, as it is peculiar in itself, and most appalling in its consequences, deserves a brief separate notice. It is thus stated in the Confession of Faith:

"Others not elected, although they may be called by the ministry of the word, and may have some common operations of the Spirit, yet they never truly come to Christ, and, therefore, cannot be saved. *Much less can men, not professing the Christian religion, be saved in any other way whatsoever, be they never so diligent to frame their lives according to the light of nature, and the law of that religion they do profess; and to assert and maintain that they may, is very pernicious and to be detested.*" (Chap. x, sec. 4.)

"Those cannot be saved who are totally destitute of revelation. Though the invitation which nature gives to seek God, be sufficient to render those without excuse who do not comply with it, yet it is not sufficient, even objectively, for salvation; for it does not afford that lively hope which maketh not ashamed, for this is only revealed by the Gospel; whence the Gentiles are said to have been without hope in the world. It does not show the true way to the enjoyment of God, which is no other than faith in Christ. It does not sufficiently instruct us about the manner in which we ought to worship and please God, and do what is acceptable to him. In short, this call by nature never did, nor is it even possible that it ever can, bring any to the saving knowledge of God; the Gospel alone is the power of God unto salvation to every one that believeth. We are persuaded there is no salvation without Christ; no communion of adult persons with Christ, but by faith in him; no faith in Christ without the knowledge of him; no knowledge but by the preaching of the Gospel; no preaching of the Gospel in the works of nature." (Expositor of the Confession, p. 145.)

From this quotation I learn that the Presbyterian Church believes in the reprobation, and inevitable damnation, of the whole heathen world. This they have, as above quoted, made an article of their creed. It is not to be wondered at, that this horrible dogma has been kept as much as possible out of view—only introduced as necessity required It is, however, sufficiently avowed, to inextricably convict the system. Dr. Rice, I find, has committed himself to its support. He says, "Vast multitudes have lived and died in Pagan darkness. Now, of what avail is it to say, that Christ designed, by his atonement, to save all men, when the truth is, that to vast multitudes he has not given the means of availing themselves of the provisions?" This quotation, if its meaning is at all discernible, teaches that Christ did not die with a design to save all men, and that the heathen world were among the number of those to be excluded from the provisions of his atonement. They were first excluded from the death of Christ; and then, in proof thereof, they were denied the means of making it available. Thus they were reprobated to death, and the means were appointed to secure the end. I suppose there will be no need that additional authorities be referred to, or quotations increased. These are sufficient, and it remains simply that we offer our objections; if, indeed, the doctrine is not so horrible in itself, as to need no formal statement of its consequences, to render it detestable to all.

I object to it, in general, that it is revolting to every sensibility of the soul—to every feeling of humanity—to all that is generous in religion and reason. Together with other elements of the Calvinistic faith, it dishonors, it demonizes the God of the universe! Look at it. The whole heathen world inevitably, necessarily damned! Have you pondered this fearful proposition? What a wholesale destruction is here! Two-thirds of the human race damned every thirty years, without the possibility of salvation, not including the vast array of reprobates in Christian countries! Not less than seven hundred millions of souls damned every generation! All reprobates! Behold that dreadful column marching forward to the unavoidable doom! Twenty-one hundred millions—twice the whole population of the globe every hundred years—damned!—consigned to the vengeance of eternal fire, to endure the woes of hell for ever! Behold them, as that column sinks away into the mouth of the burning pit—but ever supplied with new recruits at the further end, and thus moving on from age to age—filling the insatiable jaws of the yawning gulf! And, as you see that column move, and hear the roar of the devouring abyss, into whose flaming jaws they plunge, ask the question, why are all these damned? And you shall be answered by the Calvinist of the nineteenth century—by Dr. Rice, whom you may imagine as standing upon the verge of the devouring crater—it is the good pleasure of God—they are reprobates! They are damned, not because they are heathen—this is their misfortune, not their crime—but they are reprobates! If they are damned at all, there never was a time, since God passed his eternal decree, when they might have been saved; for then their doom was fixed, according to the good pleasure of God! Do you ask for a reason for this appalling opinion? you are met with the satisfactory reply, "*Who art thou that repliest against God?*"

Add to this melancholy, dreadful procession, all the descendants of Abraham, and all the reprobates in nominally Christian countries. Stay, until your vision takes in the utmost of the slowly-moving column of souls. Behold the cataract of immortal spirits, dashing on perpetually down the steeps of the ever-yawning and insatiable abyss!

Lo! that river, as it stretches away through ages and generations—a river of immortal beings swallowed up in hell! And now, pause and consider again, who are these? what is that hell into which they plunge? and why are they so damned? These are God's creatures, made and fashioned by himself! That abyss into which they are cast, is the place of eternal torment! Stop—take in the thought, *eternal*. Eternal! No end! A million years are gone—they suffer on! As many millions of ages as there are grains of sand in the solid globe have passed—they suffer still! And still, as many myriads more as atoms in the universe, multiplied by every second that had passed before—and now, their woe is just begun! Not a second, compared with their eternal years, is passed! And now, behold their woe—their death of deaths! To them there is no hope! No light will ever dawn upon their dungeon—no mercy will ever speak peace to their troubled spirits! Stay yet a moment—let us alight on yonder burning crag! And now, I ask, why these woes—why all these lost? I hear the answer; it comes from the Calvinists of the nineteenth century—it comes from Dr. Rice—they are reprobates—they were made for these flames! There never was a time when they had power to escape them! They dwell amid these waves of eternal wrath, not for any avoidable fault of theirs, but to the praise of God's glorious power! My spirit alternately shivers and burns at the horrid imputation! What has God done, that his rational creatures should so foully slander his adorable character? Pardon me; every power of my soul mutinies at the blasphemy.

Presbyterians, do you believe this? It is in your Confession, but is it in your hearts? Do you believe that God is such a being as this? Such a sentiment, if it were true, it seems to me, is sufficient to shroud the universe in endless mourning, and pervade all intelligences with consternation and dread. To state it, is to execrate it. Reason, humanity, religion, turn from it with disgust and detestation.

1. But, particularly, I object to this doctrine; it is nowhere taught in the Scriptures. Nct a single passage can be found, warranting even its inference, upon correct principles of interpretation. This, taken in connection with its horrid import, renders its belief, if not a crime against God, a reproach alike to humanity and Christianity.

2. I object to this doctrine, that it is absolutely contrary to express revelation—to its principles, and its direct teaching.

(1.) It is contrary to the principle that is laid down in the parable of the talents, "Where no law is, there is no transgression." (Rom. iv, 15.) "Sin is not imputed where there is no law." (Rom. v, 13.)

(2.) To express teaching. "For as many as have sinned without law, shall, also, perish without law," &c. (Rom. ii, 8.)

3. I object to the doctrine: if the whole heathen world are inevitably and necessarily damned, then they are damned without any fault of their own, or they are punished unavoidably—they are placed in circumstances where such damnation is the consequence of that over which they have not, and never did have, any control.

Are they damned for being heathen? But they are not responsible for this. They certainly had no part in electing whether they would be heathen or not. Is a man to be damned because he has the misfortune to be born in one region of the earth—not in another? Is such the law by which men are finally to be judged—such the principle upon which the momentous question of eternal destiny is to be fixed?

Are they to be damned because they have never been favored with the light of revelation? Are they responsible for this? Is it a sufficient reason for casting a man into hell, that he never heard of the existence of a Bible? Is this the ground upon which the God worshiped by Christians determines the fate of his creatures?

Are they to be damned because they have not exercised faith in the Son of God? Could they exercise faith in a being of whom they never heard? Had they power to believe on one they never knew? Is it sin in a man not to believe in Jesus, if he never heard of any such being—did not, and could not, know any thing respecting him?

If for none of these, for what are the heathen all necessarily damned? Because they did not live up to the light they had? But can this be shown, that no heathen ever acted according to his best light? But when the condemnation of the heathen is placed upon the ground that they willfully transgressed the law they have, it abandons the whole Calvinian assumption of their unavoidable damnation; for, if they willfully transgressed, they might have obeyed; then they would have been saved, and so their damnation is not unavoidable.

Is not the reason of their damnation, according to Calvinism, simply this—they are reprobates? Before they were born, they were assigned their fate: not, indeed, from any foresight of any thing in them; but because it was the sovereign pleasure of God that they should be damned! For some cause, sufficient to infinite Wisdom, but which he has not thought necessary to reveal to the human race, he saw that it would be best that they should be damned, and he, therefore, made them to this end. But, that he might seem to have an excuse for such monstrous cruelty, he first caused the parents of these reprobates to become depraved, and then, for this depravity, consigned them to destruction; but left them in the world long enough for them to manifest their depravity, and then, for this outward manifestation, executes upon them the vengeance of eternal fire.

And, that the outward manifestation might be infallibly secured, and so the excuse be certain, and the corresponding punishment inflicted, he consigned them to heathenism—a state, in which the Christian virtues were impossible, but in which they might, nay, certainly would, work all manner of uncleanness with greediness, and indulge in the utmost excess of vice; and so heathenism would be the means to justify damnation, as the end purposed of God from eternity. What admirable machinery is this! How infinite Malevolence arranged and contrived all, to the accomplishment of the appalling aim and end! Eternal damnation of an immortal and unoffending intelligence, the supreme, ultimate object! To secure this, as a next step, the fall of the first man, and so the corruption of his race. Then, all being corrupt, the reprobation of a large number on account thereof. Then, to justify the sentence of reprobation upon these, their consignment to heathenism, that they might, unavoidably, become personally vicious and sinful, that the universe might suppose their damnation to be on account of their sins, and so God escape the odium of cruelty, at the same time that it was all fixed and executed according to his will. Horrid! horrid! Heathenism, in order to previously appointed damnation!

4. If this doctrine be true, there is neither justice nor goodness in God. We assert this awful consequence without qualification—without timidity. With us, no proposition can be more certainly true than this. We must learn to believe black is white, and white is black, when we can believe that God is a just being, at the same time consigning millions of beings to the flames of hell, for that over which they never had, and never could have, any control—for that which was absolutely unavoidable. When I can believe that a God of goodness is capable of such conduct, I shall be prepared to embrace any absurdity—any contradiction, however revolting. No language can express my horror—

my detestation of such a sentiment. Yet such is the inevitable consequences of the Calvinistic theory—a consequence, like a horrid ghost, haunting it at every turn. It flows from reprobation—from limited atonement—from the sinner's inability—from the unavoidable damnation of the heathen world. With each, with all of them, the justice and goodness of God is in eternal conflict, if it is unjust and unmerciful to damn a being for ever, for not performing impossibilities; which, who, that has the feelings of humanity, not to say the benevolence of a Christian, can doubt? If this doctrine be true, why, then, shall I doubt the damnation of idiots and infants? Is the one more repulsive than the other? If a heathen may justly be damned for not having faith in Christ, of whom he never heard, why may not my innocent, unconscious babe be damned, by the same Moloch, for a similar reason; the injustice, the fiendish cruelty, in the one case would be no greater than in the other.

5. I object to this doctrine, that it claims our belief, not only against evidence the most convincing—evidence derived from the word and principles of revelation, as well as from the reason and common sense of mankind—but, also, without a shadow of proof to support it, derived from any quarter. It ought not to be believed if there were no evidence to the contrary, because there is none in its support; but to ask for it the credence of reasonable and Christian men, under these circumstances, when reason and Christianity equally and absolutely condemn it, and nothing supports it, can be little short of madness; it is preposterous in the extreme. If there was conflicting evidence—if any thing could be said in its favor—if any solitary reason could be urged in its support—but to ask of men to believe one of the most revolting and blasphemous dogmas that falsehood and fanaticism ever invented, without any reason, and in opposition to the spontaneous judgment of the race, and to the word of God,

and to the nature and fitness of things, is a species of boldness which scarcely knows a parallel.

6. If this doctrine is true, involving, as it does, the justice and goodness of God, and clothing him in the opposite and dreaded character of cruelty and maliciousness, it must unsettle the confidence of the universe in him, and cause him only to be hated and lothed by every rational being. Let such a sentiment once prevail—let the idea obtain that the Almighty sways such a government, and is actuated by such attributes, and heaven and hell will differ but in name. Dismay and despair, mingled with rage and detestation, will be the universal and only consciousness. Angels will join their curses with devils, and mute nature, if possible, would reverberate the merited anathema from sphere to sphere. Such a conviction must whelm creation in anarchy; for it removes the only basis of order—confidence in the great Parent and Sovereign of all, and persuasion that his government is established in justice and truth. Let this be removed, and what remains but curses and death? Who could reverence and love—who could adore and worship such a God? None but devils and fiends, who should recognize, in his hated and baleful character, their own abhorred attributes infinitely surpassed. Thus, the doctrine would unavoidably anarchize and subvert the whole government of God. The fact itself would be entirely competent to such a result, but, much more so, the principles upon which it is founded, or from which it emanated. Let any one be at the pains to study the philosophy of his own nature—of his own mind—and he will not fail to come to the same conclusion. He will see that such a result is legitimate to such a cause with respect to himself, and so with respect to all other beings similarly constituted.

But why shall I add reasons upon this point? Is it possible that humanity can be so perverted as to require it? Is it not so manifestly detestable, that, at its bare mention all nature spontaneously rises up to curse it? Where, in the universe, will it find an argument—an advocate? Let it be stripped naked, and stand forth in its own true character—without meretricious drapery—without mask or vail of any kind. And who shall come from heaven, or earth, or hell, to plead its cause? Who but the father of lies, who lives to blaspheme, and who might dare to assert even this, as the very climax of his infernal blasphemies? But, Presbyterians, you do not believe this. It is in your creed, but you have abandoned it. I charge not the dreadful blasphemy upon you; if any of you still cling to it, it is without understanding consequences. What I charge you with is, inconsistency in holding on to and supporting such a creed, and so propagating such sentiments. Be careful how you do this; you see—you cannot but see—the appalling consequences. I have named them in candor, with all plainness, but in love. Do consider them in the same spirit; do not take offense at their frightful and dreadful import; but simply ask, are they true? and then decide accordingly. And will the Lord help you, and finally bring us where truth will shine as the day, and error disappear for ever!

Infant Damnation.—It is deemed proper, in connection with the foregoing, to say something on the subject of infant damnation. This horrible doctrine has, from time immemorial, been charged upon Calvinists, and, certainly, not without abundant evidence. But it is now so universally disclaimed, that, we suppose, a reformation has been wrought upon this point. This much good has come of the manner in which our fathers exposed the horrors of the system; and, as we delight to see error renounced, we congratulate our friends on so much evidence of their conversion. All dying infants belong to the elect! This is what I suppose them now to believe. But I cannot, to save me, tell how, or why, they believe this; unless it be to escape the odium of avowing an opposite sentiment.

But, now, what I want to bring out distinctly is this, that, in renouncing the doctrine of infant damnation, they have not relieved the system a particle. It still labors under an odium, as horrid and detestable, as though it professed the old dogma. Though it now believes that no infants are damned, it still believes in what is precisely the same! Nay, it believes what is transcendently worse and more horrible! Its difficulties are not diminished, they still press it with unabated force.

They believe that those who shall finally perish, were reprobated, from eternity, to destruction—that they were passed by in the decree of election, and, as a consequence, consigned to eternal damnation. Now, mark: this reprobation took place long ages before they were born. It excluded them from heaven; it consigned them to hell—irrevocably, unchangeably! This, millions of years before they had an existence. As soon as they were conceived, they were damned; when born, they were under irreversible sentence—they were virtually destroyed!

And, now, observe, further: the cause of this reprobation and consequent damnation, was their simple, inherited corruption. It was what belonged to them in their conception—what was engendered in the womb—what was given to them when being was given to them. They were not reprobated for what they would be and do, as foreseen of God; but he passed them by, or reprobated them, for their inherited corruption alone, or what he saw them to be in Adam. Thus they were reprobated without any actual personal sin. That is, they were consigned to damnation when they were not a *span long*—unborn infants—and for what belonged to them as such, without reference to what they would be. Is not this infant damnation? Does it not show that every reprobate was damned, in the purpose of God, and inevitably, when, as yet, he was an unborn infant, and for what he was at that period? What else is infant damnation? Can any one tell me? In what does this differ from actually casting an infant, gasping its first breath, into the eternal gulf? But this, as abundantly shown, all Calvinists are bound to believe; they cannot escape it.

But I have said this is worse, in connection with other points of the system, than simple infant damnation. I repeat it. A moment's attention will show you the correctness of the position. The doctrine is, that certain persons were reprobated to certain and unavoidable damnation when they were born—before it. Well, now, observe, further: they believe that every actual sin will increase the torments of the damned—that for every abuse of *mercies* enjoyed, blessings offered, their punishment will be enhanced and increased. Look, for a moment, if you have the moral nerve, at the compound horrors of the system, in the light of these points. Every sin will magnify the torments of the damned. Now, why were they permitted to live to commit personal sins, and thus increase their torments? Why? Not that they might repent—not that they might turn and live. This was eternally impossible. Why, then, were they permitted to live? For this—read it with dismay—that they might have an opportunity to increase their damnation a million-fold—that they might prepare for themselves a deeper, hotter, more awful hell! It would have been a mercy in God to have sent them to hell when they breathed their first sweet breath upon a mother's bosom! Monster of cruelty that he was, why did he not then send them out of life to a mitigated perdition? Why did he offer them mercies, when he knew they could not accept them? Why did he strive with them early and late? Why did he invite them to life, when he knew it was absolutely impossible for them to comply, and when he also knew that for every such offer rejected their damnation would be greatly magnified? Why this? Was it not cruel in the extreme? Would it not have been an act of transcendent generosity, Godlike compassion, to have actually, as he did in his purpose, sent them all to hell in their infancy? Thus it appears, that the doctrine of actual infant damnation would greatly relieve, instead of increase the horrors of Calvinism. Is there any possible escape from this conclusion? If there is, I cannot see it. I wish I could. Dear reader, do not turn in anger away from this fearful imputation. Ponder it; see if it is not true. I know it is most dreadful and terrific. I tremble to write it. When I reflect what it makes of the character of God, I shudder! Ye angels, who dwell in light, and see with open vision, is the God of your rapturous worship such a being as this? Nay, would not such an imputation cover your heavens with dismay, and fill your seraphic bosoms with consternation and dread? Does not the universe, from the seraphim to the worm, pronounce it false and blasphemous?

Sovereignty of God.—This subject, though of sufficient importance to claim a separate and distinct notice, must, for the present, be disposed of by a brief notice, in connection with the foregoing.

In Calvinism, all things are resolved into sovereignty. No difficulty so great, but the sovereignty of God explains it. No absurdity, or contradiction, or blasphemy so appalling, but here is its defense: "Even so, Father, for so it seemeth good in thy sight." "Who art thou that repliest against God?" "Shall the thing formed say to him that formed it, why hast thou made me thus?"

That God is sovereign, no one disputes. That he has a right to rule, and does rule in heaven and earth, is not even questioned. But we protest, in the name of reason and religion, and for the honor of God, against appealing to his sovereignty for the purpose of propagating slanders against his character—against so understanding and construing it, as to bring it in conflict with his justice and other attributes of his nature. He has no rights inconsistent with his own glorious nature—he has no sovereignty that can act adversely to his glorious perfections. He is a sovereign. But he is a sovereign God, not a sovereign devil. His is not an irresponsible, blind, capricious sovereignty. His rights and his rule are not resolvable into mere arbitrary acts of will. He rules in righteousness, and wisdom, and truth. And what conflicts with these, God claims no right to—he has no right to; to say to the contrary would be to dishonor him. The sovereignty of God, therefore, never should be quoted in support of, or excuse for, what is manifestly contrary to these. He has no such sovereignty. When any thing is charged to him which requires such a supposition, it is false and slanderous to God. Here is where Calvinism commits one of its greatest practical blunders—a misapprehension of the nature of sovereignty! It assumes that such and such things are so—revealed in the Bible; and, it matters not how horrible the assumption, it holds itself under no obligation to consider the consequences, however glaringly false, and inconsistent, and dreadful. It is all referred to God's sovereignty. It is all answered in a breath: "Even so, Father!" Shame on s ch trifling and profanation of holy things! Suppose ye that the God of the universe feels himself honored with such sacrifice? Does he esteem such a defense—a defense which demonizes his character to illustrate his sovereignty? No, no, it is a mistake! God's sovereignty explains no principle that is manifestly wrong—sanctions no fact that is inconsistent with justice. "The Judge of the whole earth will do right;" he cannot do wrong. His sovereignty gives him no such power.

CHAPTER VIII.

THE WILL.

In the present chapter we call attention more particularly to the Calvinian view of the will. This subject has been involved in former chapters, but it is of such importance as to demand separate and distinct treatment.

What, then—it immediately becomes an important question—is the Calvinistic view of the will, and of agency? This will be better understood by reference to their acknowledged standards.

"God hath endued the will of man with that natural liberty, that it is neither forced, nor, by any absolute necessity of nature, determined to good or evil.

"Man, in his state of innocency, had freedom and power to will and to do that which is good and well-pleasing to God; but yet, mutably, so that he might fall from it.

"Man, by his fall into a state of sin, hath wholly lost *all* ability of will to any spiritual good accompanying salvation; so as a natural man, being altogether averse from that good, and dead in sin, is not able, by his own strength, to convert himself, or to prepare himself thereto." (Confession, chap. ix, sec. i, ii, iii.)

This chapter gives a very inadequate account of the Calvinistic doctrine upon the point in question until its terms are explained, and the views of authors are consulted. It will be perfectly understood by the following explanations.

In the Old and New Divinity Compared I read, "For if God does not possess such absolute control over his creatures, that he can govern them according to his pleasure, how could he have decreed any thing unconditionally concerning them, since it might happen, that, in the exercise of their free agency, they would act contrary to the Divine purpose?"

If this paragraph means any thing, it plainly means that unconditional decrees and free agency are irreconcilable; and, as all things are unconditionally decreed, according to the system there can, of course, be no free agency.

Thomas Aquinas, quoted with approval by Witsius, says, "It is essential to the first principle, that it can act without the assistance and influence of a prior agent; so that, if the human will could produce any action, of which God was not author, the human will would have the nature of a first principle."

"Nor does God only concur with the actions of second causes, when they act, but, also, influences the causes themselves to act. . . . Calvinists contend that, as nothing can ever come to pass without a cause, the acts of the will are never contingent, or *without necessity*—understanding by necessity, a necessity of consequence, or an infallible connection with something foregoing." (Expositor of Confession.)

"Calvinists contend, that a power in the will to determine its own determinations, is either unmeaning, or supposes, contrary to the first principles of philosophy, something to arise without a cause; that the idea of the soul exerting an act of choice, or preference, while, at the same time, the will is in a perfect equilibrium, or state of indifference, is full of absurdity and self-contradiction; and that, as nothing can ever come to pass without a cause, the acts of the will are never contingent, or *without necessity*—understanding, by necessity, a necessity of consequences, or an infallible connection with something foregoing. *According to Calvinists, the liberty of a moral agent consists in the power of acting according to his choice;* and those actions are free which are performed without any *external* compulsion or restraint, in consequence of the determinations of his own mind. The *necessity* of a man's willing and acting in conformity to his apprehensions and dispositions, is, in their opinion, fully consistent with all the liberty which can belong to a rational nature. The infinite Being *necessarily* wills and acts according to the absolute perfection of his nature, yet with the highest liberty. Angels *necessarily* will according to the perfection of their nature, yet with full liberty; for this sort of necessity is so far from interfering with liberty of will, that *the perfection of the will's liberty lies in such a necessity.*" (Expositor of Confession, p. 136.)

"Neither does God only excite and predetermine the will of men to vicious actions, so far as they are actions, *but he likewise so excites it, that it is not possible but, thus acted upon, it shall act.*" (Witsius.)

"Moreover, as a second cause cannot act, unless acted upon, and previously moved to act, by the predetermining influence of the first, so, in like manner, that influence of the first cause is so efficacious, as, that supposing it, the second cause cannot but act." (Ib.)

"Every step of every individual character, receives as determinate a character from the hand of God, as every mile of a planet's orbit, or every gust of wind, or every wave of the sea, or every particle of flying dust, or every rivulet of flowing water. This power of God knows no exceptions: it is absolute and unlimited. And, while it embraces the vast, it carries its resistless influences to all the minute and unnoticed diversities of existence. It reigns and operates through all the secrecies of the inner man. It *gives birth to every purpose;* it gives impulse to every desire; it gives shape and color to every conception; it wields an entire ascendency over every attribute of the mind: and the will, and the fancy, and the understanding, with all the countless variety of their hidden and fugitive operations, are submitted to it. It gives movement and direction through every one point of our pilgrimage. At no moment of time does it abandon us. It follows us to the hour of death, and it carries us to our place, and to our everlasting destiny in the regions beyond it." (Dr. Chalmers.)

"A man chooses what appears to be good," says Mr. Dick, "and he chooses it necessarily, in this sense, that he could not do otherwise. The object of every volition is to please himself; and to suppose a man to have any other object, that is, to will any thing that does not please him in itself, or in its circumstances, is absurd: it is to suppose him to will and not to will at the same time. He is *perfectly voluntary in his choice; but his willingness is the consequence of the view which his mind takes of the object presented to it, or of his prevailing disposition.*

"Those actions are free which are the effect of volition. In whatever manner the state of mind which gave rise to the volition has been produced, the liberty of the agent is neither greater nor less. It is the will alone which is to be considered, and not the means by which it has been determined. If God foreordained certain actions, and placed men in such circumstances that the actions would certainly take place, agreeably to the laws of the mind, men are, nevertheless, moral agents, because they act voluntarily, and are responsible for the actions which consent has made their own. *Liberty does not consist in the power of acting or not acting,* but in acting from choice. The choice is determined by something in the mind itself, or by something external influencing the mind; but, whatever is the cause, the choice makes the action free, and the agent accountable. If this definition of liberty be admitted, you will perceive that it is possible to reconcile the freedom of the will with absolute decrees; but we have not got rid of every difficulty. *By this theory, human actions appear to be as necessary as the motions of matter, according to the laws of gravitation and attraction: and man seems to be a machine, conscious of his movements, and consenting to them, but impelled by something different from himself.*"

If any thing further should be esteemed necessary upon this point, a few selections from Dr. Emmons, a distinguished divine of New England, and author of an elaborate work on theology, may supply the demand. He says, "Since the Scriptures ascribe all the actions of men to God, as well as to themselves, we may justly conclude that *the Divine agency is as much concerned in the bad as their good actions.* Many are disposed to make a distinction here, and to ascribe only the good actions of men to the Divine agency, while they ascribe their bad ones to the Divine permission. But there appears no ground for this distinction in Scripture or reason. Men are no more capable of acting independently of God in one instance than another. If they need any kind or degree of Divine agency in doing good, they need precisely the same kind and degree of Divine agency in doing evil.

"But there was no possible way in which he could dispose them to act right or wrong, but only by producing right or wrong volitions in their hearts. And if he produced their bad as well as good volitions, then his agency was concerned in precisely the same manner in their wrong as in their right actions. His agency making them act, necessarily connects his agency and theirs together, and lays a solid foundation for ascribing their actions either to him or them, or to both.

"But, since *mind* cannot act any more than *matter* can move, without a Divine agency, it is absurd to suppose that men can be left to the freedom of their own will, to act or not to act, independently of Divine influence. There must, therefore, be the exercise of Divine agency in every human action.

"By this invisible agency upon the minds, he governs all

their views, all their thoughts, all their determinations, and all their volitions, just as he pleases, and just according to his *secret* will, which they neither know beforehand, nor can resist, evade, or frustrate."

"The plain and obvious meaning of the words freedom and liberty, in common speech, is the power, opportunity, or advantage that any one has to do as he pleases; or, in other words, his being free from hinderances or impediments in the way of doing or conducting in any respect as he wills. And the contrary to liberty, whatever name we call that by, is a person's being hindered or unable to conduct as he will, or being necessitated to do otherwise.

"But one thing more I would observe, concerning what is vulgarly called liberty, namely, that power and opportunity for one to do and conduct as he will, or according to his choice, is all that is meant by it, without taking into the meaning of the word any thing of the cause of that choice, or at all considering how the person came to have such a volition—whether it was caused by some external motive, or internal, habitual bias—whether it was determined by some internal, antecedent volition, or whether it happened without a cause—whether it was necessarily connected with something foregoing, or not connected. Let the person come by his choice any how, yet, if he is able, and there is nothing in the way to hinder his pursuing and executing his will, the man is perfectly free, according to the primary and common notion of freedom." (Edwards on the Will, p. 12.)

"That every act of the will has some cause, and, consequently, has a necessary connection with its cause, and so is necessary, a necessity of connection and consequence is evident by this, that every act of the will whatsoever is excited by some motive.

"But if every act of the will is excited by a motive, then that motive is the cause of the act. If the acts of the will are excited by motives, *then motives are the cause of their being excited, or, what is the same thing, the cause of their existence.* And if so, the existence of the acts of the will is properly the effects of their motives. Motives do nothing, as motives or inducements, but by their influence; and so much as is done by their influence is the effect of them. For that is the motive of an effect, something that is brought to pass by the influence of something else. And if volitions are properly the effects of motives, then they are necessarily connected with their motives—every effect and event being, as was proved before, necessarily connected with that which is the proper ground and reason of its existence. Thus it is manifest, that volition is necessary, and is not from any self-determining power in the will; the volition which is caused by previous motive and inducement, is not caused by the will exercising a sovereign power over itself, to cause, determine, and excite volitions in itself." (Edwards on the Will, pp. 26, 27.)

The view given in this quotation, is the view elaborately sustained in Mr. Edwards' celebrated work on the will. The whole work is based, for the defense of this view, against Arminian notions of liberty. It will not be necessary to quote more largely upon this point, as our simple object, in these quotations, is to learn the view of the authors referred to, without examining their particular merits.

"The liberty of a moral agent consists in the power of acting according to his choice; and those actions are free which are performed without any external compulsion or restraint, in consequence of the determination of his own mind.

"The various changes upon matter, which are the events of the natural world, arise from a succession of operations, every one of which, being the effect of something previous, becomes, in its turn, the cause of something which follows.

The particular determinations of mind, which may be considered as events arising in the moral world, have their *causes*, also, which we are accustomed to call motives, that is, inducements to act in a particular manner, which arise from the objects presented to the mind, and the views of those objects which the mind entertains. The causes of the events in the natural world are efficient causes, which act upon matter; the causes of events in the moral world are final causes, with reference to which the mind, in which the action originates, proceeds voluntarily and deliberately to put forth its own powers. But the direction of the action toward its final cause is not less certain, than the direction of the motion produced in an inert, passive substance, by the form impressed upon it, which is the efficient cause of the motion." (Hill, pp. 551, 552.)

"It is essential to a soul to have a moral disposition, good or bad, or a mixture of both; and according to what is the prevailing moral disposition of the soul must be the moral actings of the will. [Query: How did a holy nature make an unholy volition?] Hence, there is a great difference in regard to the freedom of the will in the different states of man. In the state of innocence, the natural inclination of man's will was only to good; but it was liable to change through the influence of temptations, and, therefore, free to choose evil. In his natural corrupt state, man freely chooses evil; and he cannot do otherwise, being under bondage of sin. In the state of grace, he has a free will, partly to good and partly to evil. In this state there is a mixture of two opposite moral dispositions; and as sometimes the one and sometimes the other prevails, so the will sometimes chooses that which is good, and sometimes that which is evil." (Expositor of the Confession, p. 137.)

From the above quotations we make the following deductions:

1. Calvinists believe that every volition, or choice, is the

necessary result of an influence exerted upon the mind, through the agency of motives. In other words, they believe that such is the constitution of the human mind, that it cannot will at all without a motive, and that, when it does will, it cannot will otherwise under the circumstances, because the particular exercise of will is the necessary effect of the motives then operating upon the mind.

2. They believe that free agency consists, not in the power to originate and govern volitions, but in the power one has to do according to his volitions.

We insist that this view of the subject involves fatalism, and is entirely inconsistent with the free agency of man. And this must appear with the slightest examination.

The doctrine is, that, when a man makes a choice, or puts forth an exercise of will, he cannot, under the circumstances, make any other choice; the motives presented to his mind are such as to necessitate this particular choice, and to render any other impossible. Now, is it not manifest, that this renders man the victim of inexorable necessity. What he chooses he is coerced to choose, without the possibility of an opposite choice, by irresistible power. What matters it, though you say he acts from choice, or voluntarily, and is, therefore, free? Is it not certain that choice itself is forced upon him, and, hence, that he is not free?

I cannot do better here, than to quote from the distinguished Dr. Beecher: "Choice, in its very nature, implies the possibility of a different, or contrary election, to that which is made. There is always an alternative to that which the mind decides on, with the consciousness of choosing either. In the simplest form of alternative, it is to choose or not to choose, in a given way; but, in most cases, the alternatives lie between two or many objects of choice presented to the mind; and, if you deny to mind this alternative power—if you insist, that, by a constitution anterior to choice, of the nature of natural cause to its effect, the choice which takes place can come, and cannot but come, into being, and that none other than this can, by any possibility, exist, you *have as perfect a fatality of choice as ever Pagan, or Atheist, or Antinomian, conceived.* The question of free will is not whether man chooses—this is notorious—none deny it; but whether his choice is free, as opposed to a fatal necessity—as opposed to the laws of instinct and natural causation—whether it is the act of a mind so qualified for choice, as to decide between alternatives, uncaused by the energy of a natural cause to its effect—whether it is the act of an agent, who might have abstained from the choice he made, and made one which he did not. To speak of a choice as being free, which is produced by the laws of natural necessity, and which cannot but be when and what it is—more, that the effects of natural causes can govern the time, and manner, and qualities of their being—is a perversion of language.

"To illustrate the fatality of an agency, in which choice is the unavoidable effect of a natural, constitutional, and coercive causation, let us suppose an extended manufactory, all whose wheels, like those in Ezekiel's vision, were inspired with intelligence and instinct with life—some crying holy! holy! as they rolled, and others aloud blaspheming God—all voluntary in their praises and blasphemies; but the volitions, like the motions of the wheels themselves, produced by the great water-wheel and the various bands, which kept the motion, and the adoration, and the blasphemy agoing: how much accountability would attach to these praises and blasphemies produced by the laws of water-power? and what would it avail to say, as a reason for justifying God in punishing these blasphemies, O, but *they are free,* they are *voluntary,* they *choose* to blaspheme? Truly, indeed, they blaspheme voluntarily; but their choice to do so is necessary in the same sense that the motion of the great wheel, which the water, by the power of gravity, turns, is necessary, and just as destitute of accountability.

"Choice, without the possibility of other or contrary choice, is the immemorial doctrine of fatalism; the theory of choice, that it is what it is by a natural, constitutional necessity, and that a man cannot help choosing what he does choose, and can by no possibility choose otherwise, is the doctrine of fatalism in all its forms."

So writes one of the most venerable and learned living Presbyterian ministers, who has the boldness to think and speak his own sentiments. He sustains this view with an amount of learning worthy of himself and the subject.

The same point has been thus stated by Jouffroy, a distinguished French writer: "The principal propositions of the supporters of this system, are as follows: in the first place, they assert as a fact, that every volition has a motive; in the second place, they say, that if the motive which acts upon the will is a simple and single one, the motive will necessarily determine it; but if there are several motives operating at the same time, the strongest will determine it. Such, gentlemen, is the argument of the friends of this system." (P. 96.)

I have not thought it necessary, in this connection, to refer to the use of a variety of terms commonly incorporated in the controversy about the will. The only point we have deemed important to particularize, we find in the proposition, that "motives are causes of which volitions are effects." Upon this simple proposition, the whole controversy turns. If it is true, the Calvinian view of the will is true. If it is false, the Calvinian view of the will is false. It forms the direct issue.

It is presumed upon this point there will be no quibbling—no equivocation. We have already shown that the view thus stated, results consequentially from the doctrine of decrees, by showing that, if God decreed whatsoever comes to pass, he must have decreed what each distinct volition should be; and his decree being the necessity or necessitating cause of the thing decreed, it was, therefore, the cause of volitions. This we have shown before consequentially; and now, from a more direct examination of the doctrine of will, we learn that what was then a logical deduction, is, in fact, a matter of faith; the volition is determined by the force of motives—motives are arranged by the providence of God—and so the decree of God, with respect to volitions, is executed, or brought about by his providence.

This view is given as the most moderate and least objectionable. Many Calvinists have, indeed, asserted that voli tions are produced by the direct agency of God, and it might be shown that such is a legitimate consequence of other points of the system; but we select this as the explanation of the more moderate school, and the now prevailing sentiment of Calvinistic Churches.

Calvinists become angry with us when we accuse them of denying the free agency of man. Now, that there may be no mistake here, we call attention to this point. Calvinists do believe in free agency, according to their definition; that is, "the power or opportunity any one has to do as he pleases." They do believe that a man can do as he pleases when he is not prevented; but they do not believe that a man has any control over his choices—they do not believe that he is able to choose differently from what he does—they do not think that such a power is necessary to constitute free agency. Now, we shall show that all the consequences of sheer fatalism are included in their doctrine and definition of freedom; that, though they believe in what they are pleased to call free agency, yet they do not, in fact, include the idea of actual liberty therein, but leave it embarrassed with inexorable necessity.

That I have stated their views in the least objectionable

form, in the most moderate tone, I think must be admitted by all candid judges: it only remains, therefore, that I proceed to point out consequences, and then it will be for my readers to decide, whether the consequences thus deduced do actually flow or not.

1. And, first, I object to this doctrine of the will, that it is directly opposed to the consciousness of mankind. Here, again, I will employ the language of the venerable Dr. Beecher: 'Of nothing are men more thoroughly informed, or more competent to judge unerringly, than in respect to their voluntary action, as coerced or free. Testimony may mislead, and the sense, by disease, may deceive, but consciousness is the end of all controversy; its evidence cannot be increased, and, if it be distrusted, there is no alternative but universal skepticism. Our consciousness of the mode of mental action in choice, as uncoerced and free, equals our consciousness of existence itself; and the man who doubts either, gives indications of needing medical treatment, instead of argument. When a man does wrong, and then reflects upon the act, he feels that he was free, and is responsible; and so when he looks forward to a future action.

"And because this consciousness is in men, you never can reason them out of a sense of their accountability. Many have tried it, but none have effectually, or for any length of time, succeeded; and the reason is plain, there is nothing which the mind is more conscious of, than the fact of its own voluntary action with the power of acting right or wrong: the mind sees, and knows, and regrets, when it has done wrong. Take away this consciousness, and there is no remorse. You cannot produce remorse, as long as a man feels that his act was not his own—that it was not voluntary, but the effect of compulsion: he may dread the consequences, but you never can make him feel remorse for the act on its own account. This is the reason why men who have reasoned away the existence of God, and argued to prove that the soul is nothing but matter, know, as soon as they reflect, that all their reasoning is false. There is a lamp within they cannot extinguish; and, after all their metaphysics, they are conscious that they act freely, and that there is a God to whom they are accountable; and hence it is, that when they cross the ocean, and a storm comes on, and they expect to go to the bottom, they begin straightway to pray to God and confess their sins.

"The natural impossibility of choosing otherwise than we do choose, is contrary, then, not only to the common sense and intuitive perceptions of men, but contrary to their internal consciousness. There is a deep and universal consciousness in all men, as to the freedom of choice; and in denying this, you reverse God's constitution of man—you assume that God gave a deceptive constitution to mind, or a deceptive consciousness."

Upon this point, Mahan, in his excellent little work on the will—a complete refutation of Edwards—says, "We may pile demonstration upon demonstration in favor of the doctrine of necessity, still, as the mind falls back upon the spontaneous affirmations of its own intelligence, it finds, in the depths of its inner being, a higher demonstration of the fact, that that doctrine is, and must be, false—that man is not the agent which that doctrine affirms him to be."

It is still more elegantly expressed by Jouffroy: he says, "If there is one familiar feeling of which we are distinctly and vividly conscious, it surely is that which we experience when we make a choice. Whatever the force of the motive which we obey, we yet perceive a wide distinction between the influence of this motive, and any thing which can be called constraint. Indeed, we feel distinctly, that in yielding to this motive, that is to say, in resolving in conformity with it, we are entirely able not to form this resolve. If, for instance, when standing at a window, I determine not to throw myself into the street, I feel that it depends wholly upon myself to form an opposite determination; only, I say, I should then be a fool; and being rational, I remain where I am. But that I am free to be a fool, and to throw myself down, is to me most evident. If any of my audience are capable of confounding in their minds the fact, that a billiard ball on a table is put in motion by a stroke, with the fact, that a volition is produced in my mind when I seek to know what is my reasonable course of conduct, and think I discover it—if there are any here, who can see a similarity between the action of one ball on another, and the influence of a motive on my volition, then have I nothing more to say. But no one can imagine a similarity between the two; at least, no one who has not taken sides on the question, and given up his mind to some system, of which it is a consequence that some necessity must control our volition and acts, can confound two facts in their nature so dissimilar, as the action of one ball upon another, and the influence of a motive on the determinations of my will. The whole question—and I beg you again to remark it—depends upon the fact, whether you know that the influence which the motive exercises over the will is a constraining force or not. For myself, I say, that my inward feeling answers in the negative, and that, under the influence of all motives, I retain, in every case, a distinct consciousness of a power of acting in opposition to what they advise and direct.

"When I attempt thus to bring argument for the sake of proving that we are free, and that motives do not exercise a controlling force over us, I feel as uncomfortable as if I were answering one who should deny our power of moving or walking. To employ argument in refuting such an opinion, seems like some game of logic; for I have to oppose to this opinion a plain, decisive fact—a fact, the consciousness of which I can never lose, and which is in accordance with common forms of speech in all languages, with the universal faith, and with the established practices of mankind: and I smile to think, that when I can utterly destroy the system of necessity, by merely bringing it in conflict with this fact, I should be seeking superfluous trains of reasoning to oppose it with. This fact, which we cannot escape from, is one which consciousness bears witness to, when placed under the influence of the strongest possible motive, say, self-preservation. I feel, distinctly, that it depends upon myself, and only upon myself, whether I shall yield to or resist this motive, and do or refrain from what it recommends. I can conceive, indeed, that a man may deny this evident fact; for to what length of delusion will not the spirit of theory and system carry us? But I will ask him, am I not justified in not admitting this peculiar opinion of a small body of men, when I see that even they act and speak as if they agreed in my opinion—when I see the most logical among them form a scheme of ethics, and give rules for conduct—when I find in every tongue the words, right and wrong, punishment and reward, merit and demerit—when the whole human race agree in being indignant against him who does wrong, and in admiring him who does right—when, indeed, there is not an event in human life which does not imply, necessarily, and in a thousand different ways, this very freedom of will of which I feel so sensibly and deeply conscious? I have certainly some right to feel strengthened in my opinion by so many testimonies to its truth, and by its perfect accordance with what I see about me. And were there no stronger objections against the doctrine which denies human freedom, than this universal contradiction which it offers to all human belief, conduct, and language, to all judgments and feelings, it would, even then, be more completely answered than it deserves."

Thus we see that the Calvinian view of the will is opposed to the consciousness of mankind. When it is stated, every man feels within himself the consciousness that it is false—that it is not in accordance with his constitution. It may be mystified and drowned with bewildering terms, and encumbered with intricate speculations, and burdened with senseless distinctions, but deep beneath it all, the plain man and the scholar, all men alike, feel a consciousness that the will is essentially free—that volitions are not necessitated. This consciousness of mankind is not only detected by each man in his own bosom, but it is outwardly manifested and expressed, involuntarily and, in a great variety of ways, constantly by others; as, for instance, in the universal conviction of mankind, that their former course of conduct might have been different from what is. I will venture to affirm, that there is not a person on earth who has not this conviction resting upon his mind, in respect to his own past life. It is important to analyze this conviction, in order to mark distinctly its bearing upon our present inquiries. This conviction is not the belief, that, if our circumstances had been different, we might have acted differently from what we did; but a firm persuasion, that, under precisely the same circumstances, our volition and act might have been the precise contrary of what they were. This conviction, that, without any change of circumstances, our past course of life might have been different from what it was, rests upon every mind on earth, in which the remembrance of the past dwells. Now this universal conviction is totally false—and when, then, can consciousness be trusted?—if the doctrine of necessity is true. The doctrine of the liberty of the will must be true, or the universal intelligence is a perpetual falsehood.

In reference to all deliberate determinations of the will in time past, the remembrance of them is attended with a consciousness the most positive, that, in the same identical circumstances, determinations precisely opposite might have been originated. Let any one recall any such determination, and the consciousness of a power to have determined differently, will be just as distinctly recalled as the act itself. He cannot be more sure that he has willed at all, than he will be that he might have willed differently. But all these affirmations of consciousness are false, if the doctrine of liberty is not true.

The existence of such a consciousness is further evinced in the condemnation or approbation we exercise with respect to other men, in view of their determinations and acts. These are always accompanied with the conviction, arising from the consciousness of human freedom, that they might, under the circumstances, have acted and determined differently. And if this conviction could be displaced, we would no more condemn or approve them than we do an avalanche or earthquake, rain or sunshine.

But, further: not only with respect to the past, but with respect to the present, also, we are now distinctly conscious, that, with regard to the particular object submitted to our minds, under the identical circumstances existing, any one of a number of different determinations is equally or as certainly possible. Every man is as conscious of this as he is of his existence.

2. I object to this doctrine of the will, further, that it involves sheer fatalism—universal necessity. This point is thus expressed by Mahan: "If this doctrine is true, it is demonstrably evident, that in no instance, real or supposable, have men any power whatever, to will or to act differently from what they do. The connection between the determinations of the will and their consequents, external and internal, is absolutely necessary. Constituted as I now am, if I will, for example, a particular motion of my hand or arm, no other movement, in the circumstances, was possible, and this movement could not but take place. The same holds true of all consequents, external or internal of all acts of the will. Let us now suppose that

these acts of the will are themselves the necessary consequents of the circumstances in which they originate. In what conceivable sense, then, have men, in the circumstances in which Providence places them, power either to will or to act differently from what they do? Here, then, is absolute, universal necessity. The motive must produce the volition; the volition must produce the act; and all the circumstances taken together constitute the motive."

Well, now, the creature can have no control of the motives; that is, he cannot prearrange motives to produce in him certain volitions; because, to determine to make such a prearrangement is a volition, and this volition cannot take place without a motive to produce it; so he is utterly, and without mitigation, doomed to the despotism of such motives as exist, bringing in their train, as cause produces effects, other motives, and these producing their legitimate exercises of will. Fate runs through all. Every determination and act is immediately connected with a cause foregoing, which produces it as a necessary effect.

3. It follows from this system, not only that all things are necessary, but, also, that each individual thing is the best possible in its place and relations. God is the first mover—the first link in this endless chain of causation. From him, ultimately, all motion proceeds. All volitions and acts, therefore, have for their ultimate cause infinite Wisdom. All that has been, all that is, all that will be, are connected by an absolute necessity with the same great Source. There may be a million intermediate, transmitting links, but, through all, they trace back to the First Cause. It would be the height of absurdity to suppose it possible for any thing to be different from what it is, or to suppose that any change could make any thing better than what it is; for all that is, is by absolute necessity; and all that is, is just what and when infinite Wisdom has made it and disposed of it. No difference what it is, therefore—whether

murder, incest, idolatry, or what not—it is the best thing in that place, or the great First Cause is at fault. If that which we call evil in reality be evil, then it must be both necessary evil, and evil having its origin in infinite Wisdom. It is vain to say that man is the agent, in the strict acceptation of the word; he is—he can be no more than one of the links through which causation is traced back to God. Is not this fearful?

4. If this doctrine be true, man cannot be responsible or accountable for either his volitions or acts—cannot be subject of praise or blame. God himself is the only responsible being in the universe, as all causation—agency proper—terminates in him. This is so manifest, it is questionable whether any man, in the possession of his reason, can sincerely doubt it. The idea of obligation, of merit and demerit, and of the consequent propriety of rewards and punishments, are chimeras. To conceive of a being deserving praise or blame for volitions or actions, which occurred under circumstances in which none other were possible, and in which these could not possibly but be, is absolutely impossible. The human mind has not power to entertain such a conception. Let any one undertake it, and he will find it as impossible as to conceive of the annihilation of space, or of an event occurring without a cause. Human intelligence, as the consciousness of every one of my readers will attest, is incapable of affirming such a contradiction.

The ground of blameworthiness is not only the perception of the difference between right and wrong, and the conviction that the right ought to be done, but the possession of a power to do the right, and refrain from the wrong. But if every volition is fixed by absolute necessity, then neither can the individual be supposed to have power to do otherwise than he actually does, nor, all things considered, can it be supposed there could have been, at that present moment any other volition. The volition is fixed, and fixed by infinite Wisdom. We cannot escape from this difficulty, by perpetually ringing the changes of, "He can if he will," "he could if he would;" the thing is, he cannot will—he has no power competent to do the very thing which is required, and, hence, cannot be responsible.

Shall it be said, "that, in looking for the ground of accountability, men never go beyond the fact of voluntariness; they look not for the cause of volitions themselves; if the deed, whether good or evil, be voluntary, that satisfies? This is, no doubt, true; we are satisfied that men are accountable for acts which are voluntary; but this is because all men include, unfailingly, both in their theory and consciousness, the supposition of powers of agency unhindered and uncoerced by any fatal necessity. But convince them that choice is an effect, over which mind has no more control than over drops of rain, and the common sense of the world would revolt against the accountability of choice, merely because it was choice." The view of the will here offered, is, beyond all question, as diametrically opposed to accountability as it is to freedom; indeed, by the common consent of mankind—a consent founded in consciousness itself—these must stand or fall together, and cannot exist separately.

5. But if the foregoing be true, then men cannot be required to do differently from what they do; for to require this, is to require an absolute impossibility. Any law or lawgiver making such requirement, is the perfection of tyranny. There can be no cruelty, no oppression, more unreasonable, more unjust, than this. To imagine it, is blasphemously to cast inconceivable odium on the character of God. Dr. Beecher has well said upon this point, "God requires of his subjects only conformity to himself—to his own moral excellences—but he admits of no obligation on himself to work impossibilities; and does he impose obligations

on his subjects which he himself refuses to assume? He does not regard it as an excellence in himself to work impossibilities; does he command it as a virtue in his subjects? He has no desire to work impossibilities himself, why should he desire it in his creatures? He has never tried, and never will try, to work an impossibility; and why should he command his creatures to do what he neither desires nor tries to accomplish? He *cannot* work impossibilities; and how can it be thought that he will *require* of his creatures that which he *himself cannot do?*" Such is one of the fearful consequences to which this scheme inevitably leads. Either God cannot require men to do differently from what they do, and, if this be so, then he does not require them to obey his laws; for these laws enjoin a different conduct: or, if God does require men to do differently, then he requires them to do what is absolutely impossible—to do what Omnipotence cannot do—nay, to resist and overcome Omnipotence; for it is the causation emanating from Omnipotence which he is required to resist. Can a God of justice make such a requisition as this?

But if such a requirement cannot be made—if the idea is startling blasphemy—and who can think it is less—what must be our amazement to learn, not only that such requirements are made, but additionally for non-compliance, the wretch, who may be found guilty, is to be punished in hell throughout an endless eternity! Think of such a doom, and answer yourself the question, can God be a monster capable of such appalling ferocity? The devil that would torment his victim in flames through millions of years, for not annihilating the universe, with only power sufficient to crush a moth, would be the impersonation of mercy and loveliness compared with such a being as this.

If this doctrine is true, at the final judgment the conscience and intelligence of the universe must be on the side of the condemned. Suppose that when the conduct of the wicked shall be revealed at that day, another fact shall stand out with equal conspicuousness, namely, that God himself had placed these beings where but one course of conduct was open to them, and that course they could not but pursue—namely, the course which they did pursue—and that, having pursued this course, the only one possible, they are now to be punished with everlasting destruction from the presence of God and the glory of his power, must not the intelligence of the universe pronounce such a sentence unjust? Yet all this must be true, or the necessity false. Who can believe that the pillars of God's eternal government rest upon such a doctrine? A resort to blank Atheism, to hopeless death, would be a refuge from an existence under the inconceivable misrule and tormenting despotism of such a God.

6. I object, further, if this doctrine be true, probation is an infinite absurdity. We might, with the same propriety, represent the specimens in the laboratory of the chemist as on probation, as men, if their actions are the necessary result of the circumstances in which Omnipotence has placed them. What must intelligent beings think of probation for a state of eternal retribution, based on such principles? Is it not a mockery?

7. I object, if this doctrine be true, all the exhortations and persuasions which call upon the man to bestir himself—to think, to plan, to act—are inconsistent and absurd. In all such persuasions, the man is urged to will or put forth volitions, as if he were the author or determiner of volitions. It may be replied, that the man does will, that the volitions are *his* volitions. But, allowing them to be his in a certain sense, the point of difficulty is here: they are made his, by being wrought in him as a passive subject; they are not his in the sense of his being their prime cause. You exhort and persuade him to arouse himself to activity; but what is his real condition, according to this system? The

exhortations and persuasions do themselves contain the motive power; and, instead of *arousing himself* to action—the thing exhorted—he is absolutely and necessarily passive under the motive you present. If he does not act, he is not at fault, but the motive; the defect is in the motive, not in the man. He cannot act without a sufficient motive; and that he does not act, is proof that the motive is not sufficient. To blame him, therefore, is to blame him for not performing an impossibility. Whether he be moved or not as truly and as absolutely depends upon the motives you present, as the removing of any material mass depends upon the power or labor applied. When I bring motives before the minds of my fellow-beings in the proper relation, the volition is necessarily produced; but let me not forget, that, in bringing these motives, I put forth volitions, and that, of course—according to the system—I am myself moved under the necessity of some antecedent motive. My persuasions and exhortations are necessary sequents, as well as necessary antecedents. The water must run through the water course; the wheel must turn under the force of the current. I must exhort and persuade when motives determine me; the mind I address must yield, when the motives are properly selected and applied to it! Was there ever a more admirable system of fatalism than this? All volitions and actions, linked together in one endless chain of causation, reaching back to the first great Mover, as the sole and only cause! The connection between the volition and the strongest motive, is as absolute and necessary as the connection between any cause and its effect. The movements of mind, as a consequence of this system, are as absolutely fixed and rigidly necessary, as the movements of the material creation under the forces which cause its changes. How utterly absurd, therefore, to address exhortations, advices, and reproofs to men, with respect to their purposes and actions! Just with the same propriety might we urge and entreat the water-wheel to reverse its motion, and roll round against the current—the nerve to convey no sensation, under the most painful operation—the eye to look upon the full, blazing sun, without inconvenience—the earth itself to stand still, when Omnipotence urges it forward· the advice would be as proper in one case as the other. If it is manifestly absurd in the latter case, it is no more so than in the former. A mind, every one of whose determinations is absolutely fixed by the force of motives, can no more of itself make different determinations, than matter can, of itself, act contrary to the force which impels it. Therefore, if causation is in the motive, so is responsibility; and men would act wisely no more to exhort, advise, or reprove each other, but address themselves to the consideration alone of external causes. But is this so? Is man the thing here represented? the mere sport of outward influence, without power, without agency? He is, or Calvinism is radically false.

8. I object, further, to this doctrine, in the language of Tappan, "It is another consequence, that there can be nothing evil in itself. If infinite wisdom and goodness are the highest form of moral perfection, as, indeed, their very names imply, then all the necessary consequences of these must partake of their nature. Infinite wisdom and goodness, as principles, can only envelop parts of themselves. It would be the destruction of logic to deny this. It would annihilate every conclusion that has ever been drawn. If it be said, that infinite Wisdom has promulged a law which defines clearly what is essentially right, and that it is a fact that volitions do transgress this law, still this cannot affect what is said above. The promulgation of the law was but a necessary development of infinite Wisdom; and the volition which transgresses it, is a development of

the same nature. If this seems contradictory, I cannot help it. It is drawn from the system, and the system alone is responsible for its conclusions."

9. I object to the doctrine, that it is as fatal to freedom in the Divine as well as the human mind. I cannot better express this point than by substituting the language of Fisk: "It is argued, that to maintain the doctrine of spontaneous volition, independent of the control of motives, involves the absurdity, that 'our volitions are excited without any intelligent reason whatever, and as the effect, consequently, of nothing better than a mere brute or senseless mechanism.' Now, if this has any bearing on the question, it relates not to human mind and human volitions merely, *but to mind in general,* and must apply to the Divine mind. The same may be said, in fact, of most of the arguments that are brought in favor of this doctrine. Calvinists are convinced of this; and, hence, this, also, is a part of their creed. It was defended by Edwards, and is thus avowed by Upham in his system of Mental Philosophy. Speaking of the control of motives, he says: 'Our condition, in this respect, seems to be essentially the same with that of the supreme Being himself; he is *inevitably* governed in all his doings, by what, in the great range of events, is wisest and best.' Thus, the divine Being is, according to this theory, and by the express showing of the leading advocates of the theory, '*inevitably*' made a subordinate to a superior. It is believed there is no avoiding this conclusion; and, what then? Why, then, the doctrine makes God a necessary agent, and leads to Atheism! It is nearly, if not exactly, the same as the old heathen doctrine of fate. The ancient heathen supposed that Jupiter himself, the omnipotent father of the gods and men, must yield to fate. Modern Christians teach that there is a certain fitness of things, certain constitutional relations, existing independent of the Divine will, which

God himself cannot supersede, but to which he must yield. How does this sink at once both the natural and moral perfections of God! The exercises of his wisdom and goodness, are nothing more than the result of certain fixed and irresistible influences. Fixed, not by God himself, for that would be to give up the doctrine; for, in that case, in the order of cause and effect, the Divine mind must have acted without control of motives, if this law of motive influence did not exist until the Divine volition willed it into being; and if he could once act independent of this control, he might so act for ever, and the argument, built on the absurdity of volition without an intelligent reason, would be contradicted. But if that argument has any weight, it fixes, in the order of cause and effect, a paramount influence eternally antecedent to the exercise of the Divine mind, and controlling that mind with irresistible sway. This is fate! this is Atheism! Once set up an influence that controls the Divine mind, call that influence what you please—fitness of things, fate, energy of nature, or necessary relation—and that moment you make God a subordinate; you hurl him from his throne of sovereignty, and make him the instrument of a superior. Of what use is such a Deity? Might we not as well have none? nay, better, as it seems to me, if, under the control of his own motive influence, he is led to create beings susceptible of suffering, and fix the relations of those beings to the motives around them such, that, by a law of their nature, they are 'inevitably' led to sin and endless woe? Is it to be wondered at, that many Calvinists have become infidels? This doctrine of motives is the very essence of the system of Spinoza, whose deity was the *energy of nature*. The supreme, controlling power of Dr. Edwards and his followers, is the *energy of motives*, which exist in the nature of things, anterior to the will of God. Can any one point out an essential difference between the two systems?"

10. Fisk continues: "Another argument against the Calvinistic doctrine of motives, is that it leads to materialism. The doctrine, it will be recollected, is this: when the mind is brought into connection with objects of choice, it is inevitably led, by a law of its nature, to the selection of one rather than of the other, unless there is a perfect equality between them; in which case I suppose, of course, the mind must remain in equilibrium; for it moves only by the influence of motives, and to the same degree, and in the same direction, with motive influences; of course, when it is equally attracted in opposite directions, it must be at rest! It is on this ground that Leibnitz maintained that God could not make two particles of matter in all respects alike; because, in that case, being 'inevitably' governed by motives in his decisions, he could not determine where to place them, both having the same influence on his mind for a location in the same place! The same writer represents this motive influence, also, as frequently imperceptible, but not the less effectual, and not the less voluntary; and, to illustrate it, makes the following comparison: 'It is as if a needle, touched with a loadstone, were sensible of, and pleased with, its turning to the north; for it would believe that it turned itself independent of any other cause, not perceiving the insensible motives of the magnetic power.' This statement of Leibnitz, who had paid great attention to this philosophical theory, is important in several respects. It is, in the first place, an acknowledgment that consciousness is against the doctrine; and it is, also, a concession that the mind is imposed upon in this matter by the Creator. But, with respect to the argument that this doctrine leads to materialism, this quotation is important, because it shows that one of the most philosophical, if not one of the most evangelical, of the defenders of this doctrine, considered the law of motive influence similar to the law of magnetic attraction, differing only in

being accompanied by sensation and a deceptive consciousness. And what says its great evangelical champion in this country, Dr. Edwards? He compares our volitions to the vibrations of a scale-beam, the different ends of which are respectively elevated or depressed, as the opposite weights may chance to vary. What is this, but teaching that motions of mind are governed by the same fixed laws as those of matter, and that volitions are perfectly mechanical states of mind? What the advocates of this doctrine charge on the opposite theory, belongs, by their own showing, to their own system. They, not we, make choice the result of animal instinct. If the attractive power of motives over the mind is any thing different from the law of gravitation, or magnetic attraction, what is that difference? Should any one say, I cannot tell, I ask, then, how does he know but it is that very power for which Arminians contend? Most probably it is that power. Or will it be said the difference between motive influence and gravity is consciousness? I reply, consciousness is no part of the relation between motives and the power of choice. I see not, indeed, how it affects that relation at all. Look at the flowing stream; it hastens on most freely, and by the law of its own nature, down the gentle declivities or more precipitous slopes of its meandering channel. Suppose, now, that Omnipotence should impart consciousness to the particles of the continuous current, it would then wake up to perceive the action, and feel the pleasure of its own delightful motions. It would roll on still by the law of its own nature, and would feel that it was free to move according to its own inclination and voluntary tendency, for its will would, of course, be in the direction of its motive, or, in other words, its gravitating influence. But could it turn its course, and roll back its waters to their fountain? It could, if it was so inclined. But its present inclination is toward the bottom of the valley, or the bosom of the ocean; and thither, by the relation which exists between its particles and the gravitating influence of the earth, it rolls on with the utmost freedom, though with the utter impossibility of changing its own course, without the inversion of the gravitating power. Let the hand of Omnipotence invert the slope of the mountain, and, lo! with the same freedom these very same waters roll back again to their original fountains! Thus it is with the human mind: it is conscious of being free to move in the direction of its inclinations, but require it to turn its course, and move in the current of its volitions in an opposite direction, and it would be utterly impossible, until Omnipotence himself should change the motive influence. 'God is the determiner of perceptions, and perceptions are the determiners of choice.'

"We see, therefore, that this doctrine of motive influence leads to materialism; for it makes the analogy between mental and material action so complete, that it destroys all idea of intellectual power. Philosophically speaking, there is no power in the laws of nature. What we express by the power of attraction, repulsion, or decomposition, is nothing more than the uniformity of the Divine agency." The power of motives to excite volitions, is nothing else but the Divine energy operating through that mode to the accomplishment of a given end. God is the all-directing agent; mind, the passive recipient. From the theory, inertia becomes the law of mind as well as of matter; materialism is the unavoidable consequence.

Free agency, responsibility, and kindred vital doctrines, vanish before this theory, as mists before the sun. God becomes the sole and universal doer: all physical, intellectual, and moral results, emanate from and return to him. Human volitions are as really the effects of Divine agency, as the rising of the stars, the flight of the lightning, the tumult of the waters, or the light, which spreads itself like a garment over creation. Every volition of created mind is God's act, as really as any other effect in nature. We have seen how every volition is connected with its motive—how the motive lies in a preconstitution—how the series of antecedents and sequents necessarily runs back, and connects itself with the infinite wisdom. God's wisdom is his own act; the effect immediately produced by that volition is his own deed. Let that effect be the creation of man: the man, in all his powers and susceptibilities, is God's work; the objects around him are God's work; the correlation of the objects with the sensibility of man is God's work; the volition, which necessarily takes place as the result of this correlation, is God's work. The volition of the man is as strictly attributable to God, as, according to our common apprehensions, the blow which I give with the axe is attributable to me. What is true of the first man, is equally true of man removed to a thousand generations, for the intermediate links are all ordained of God, and form but so many parts of the same necessity. God is really the sole doer—the only efficient cause: all beings and things, all motions and volitions, are absolutely resolved into Divine volitions. God is the author of all beings, things, motions, and volitions, and as much the author of any one of these as any other, and the author of all in the same way, and in the same sense. All things exist in necessity; that necessity centres either in God, or in something which is above God; God himself is all and only, or he, like all things else, is but a link in the stupendous chain, which attaches to the blind fate which governs and directs him, together with the rest.

11. I object, further, to this doctrine, that it is not only contradictory to the reason and consciousness of mankind, but, also, to the word and revelation of God. It finds no favor in the Bible: every precept, exhortation, invitation,

entreaty, remonstrance of that book, is opposed to it: it is *anti-Bible.* This might be shown with the utmost ease, but it is so palpable as to need no such manifestation.

12. I object: it is contrary to the opinion of the early Christians. I refer my readers, for proof of this and the former point, given at length, to Beecher's Views in Theology, Tomlins' Refutation of Calvinism, Whitby on the Five Points, &c.

13. I object, that the whole theory of motive influence is without support, and depends upon vicious reasoning, or reasoning in a circle, for its proof. It asks to be believed upon unsound argumentation, and against the most overwhelming and conclusive evidence of its utter falsehood. When, for instance, we ask what determines the will, we are directly answered, it is the strongest motive; but when we ask what constitutes the strongest motive, we are answered, that which determines the will. The whole theory is reducible to this vicious circle—this absurd assumption. Edwards' celebrated work revolves in it from the beginning to the end. An unsupported assertion is made the basis of the whole, and upon the strength of this we are required to yield credence, against the testimony of consciousness, of reason, of nature itself, of the Bible, and of every thing else, within and without us, entitled to respect.

For a more extensive examination of this point, I must refer my readers to the following works: Dr. Beecher's Views in Theology, Mahan on the Will, Tappan's Review of Edwards, Bledsoe on the Will, Fisk, Jouffroy, &c. I take pleasure in acknowledging my obligations to these authors, as aids to the preparation of the present brief chapter. Had it been possible, I should gladly have made still more copious extracts from them. Let the studious inquirer refer to them, and he will find the subject thoroughly and sufficiently discussed. Had it been our purpose to write a treatise on the will, a more particular examination of the theory here objected to would have been made; such was not our plan, but simply to state the grounds or principles of the system, and name some of the many insuperable difficulties investing it. We leave the subject here: it will be for our readers to determine upon the question in debate. Is the view we have antagonized true or false? What is the answer? Let not prejudice make up the decision. What says reason—consciousness—the word of God? What says the language of mankind—the common, every day, and everywhere sentiments of the species? Does not every thing with which we are conversant—all law, all usage, all organizations of human society, all rational methods of government and influence—proceed upon the assumption that man is a free, voluntary agent, having power to determine his own choices, as well as actions? Such, it seems to me, must be the spontaneous response of mankind—of humanity, unbiased by prejudice, unfettered by false philosophy.

APPENDIX.

It will be proper to say, at this point, that what is here presented as an Appendix, is the substance of Dr. Rice's replies to my letters, with my rejoinders thereto. It will be seen by the reader, that our rejoinders are confined strictly to the points at issue between us. The reasons for this will be obvious. Had we permitted ourselves to be decoyed into irrelevant matters, we, and our readers, would have become bewildered and lost in the mazes of endless logomachy. This would, doubtless, have pleased our friend, as it would have served to divert attention from his system; but it did not suit us.

NUMBER I.

I am happy to be able to lay Dr. Rice's reply to my first and second letters before my readers. In its general tone and spirit it accords well with my expectations; and if it fails in argument, I find an apology *in the circumstances of the case.* The Doctor will make up for this hereafter.

"*Letters on Calvinism.*—We are decidedly of opinion, after reading two of Mr. Foster's Letters on Calvinism, that he really needs the assistance which, in his first letter, he so warmly invoked. His second letter urges the old objection, a thousand times made, and as often refuted, that the doctrine of decrees makes God *the author of sin.* This hackneyed objection is founded upon the idea, that '*God's decree is the necessity or necessitating cause of sin.*' Now, inasmuch as Presbyterians hold no such view, and would really depose any one of their ministers who should teach it, the objection is utterly without force. No Presbyterian holds, that God ever purposed or decreed to dispose or influence any man or angel to sin. If Mr.

Foster had taken the trouble to read the sixth chapter of the Westminster Confession of Faith, he would have found the following language concerning the fall of our first parents: 'This their sin God was pleased, according to his wise and holy counsel, to *permit*, having purposed to order it to his own glory.' He will scarcely assert, that God did not *permit* their sin, nor that by permitting it he forced them to it, and thus became the author of it. Nor, we presume, will he pretend, that God's purpose to order this sin to his own glory—to bring good out of evil—made him the author of sin. And yet this is precisely the doctrine of our Confession—that God purposed to permit the sins of men and angels, and so to bound, control, and order them, that his own wise plans shall be accomplished by their means. Any harm in this? Does not the Bible say, 'Surely the wrath of man shall praise thee: the remainder of wrath shalt thou restrain?' (Psalm lxxvi, 10.) Does it not say, that Jesus Christ was delivered to crucifixion, 'by the determinate counsel and foreknowledge of God?' (Acts ii, 23.) Come back, brother Foster, and start right, or your work will all be lost.

"There is another great defect in these letters. The real points of difference between Methodists and Presbyterians are not stated. One might conclude from all that Mr. Foster has yet said, that, according to Methodism, God has no purposes at all, certainly none that relate to men. What is the Methodist doctrine on this subject? Wherein, precisely, do they differ? The very first thing necessary to a satisfactory discussion of this subject, is a clear statement of the difference between the faith of Methodists and that of Presbyterians.

"We venture to suggest, whether it would not be well for Mr. Foster to let his first two letters go for nothing, as the boys say, and begin anew."

To so much of the above as purports to be an answer to

my letters, I now call attention. Irrelevant portions I must be excused from noticing. "His second letter," he says, "urges the old objection, a thousand times made, and as often refuted, that the doctrine of decrees makes God the author of sin." Now, Doctor, why did you not tell me how that old objection was refuted? That is precisely the thing I desire to know; and if it has been done so often, you, of course, will find it perfectly convenient to repeat it for my edification. Attend to this, if you please, as soon as you find leisure, by taking up and refuting my arguments.

"This hackneyed objection is founded upon the idea, that God's decree is the necessity or necessitating cause of sin. Now, inasmuch as Presbyterians hold no such views, and would really depose any one of their ministers who should teach it, the objection is utterly without force. No Presbyterian holds, that God ever purposed or decreed to influence any man or angel to sin. If Mr. Foster had taken the trouble to read the sixth chapter of the Westminster Confession of Faith, he would have found the following language concerning the fall of our first parents: 'This their sin God was pleased, according to his wise and holy counsel, to permit, having purposed to order it to his own glory.'" This language I can assure Dr. Rice I have often read, and much more to the same import, from various Calvinistic authors. But, as said in my second letter, this only convinces me that the different parts of the system clash, and they who embrace it embrace contradictions. It is certainly in vain to demur against a clear, logical conclusion. What the Doctor must do, is to point out where my logic is at fault, not to array disclaimers. His present course will only help me to another chapter of objections against his system; that is, that it is self-contradictory, which, in due time, I expect to prove.

But now to the question of fact. Dr. Rice asserts, that "no Presbyterian holds that God's decree is the necessity or necessitating cause of sin"—that "they would depose a minister who should teach it"—that "no Presbyterian holds, that God ever purposed or decreed to dispose or influence any man or angel to sin." Right upon this point I join issue with Dr. Rice. My reasons for making the charge are contained in my second letter, and his assertion must stand unsupported until these reasons are answered, and taken away. Will the Doctor remove them? Meantime we submit additional proofs upon this point.

1. This is the doctrine of the Confession itself, contained in the following language: "God, from all eternity, did, by the most wise and holy counsel of his own will, freely and unchangeably ordain whatsoever comes to pass. Although God knows whatsoever may or can come to pass upon all supposed conditions, yet hath he not decreed any thing because he foresaw it as future, or as that which would come to pass upon such supposed conditions." Here is a witness I introduce to the respectful attention of Dr. Rice: it is the Presbyterian Confession of Faith.

It testifies three things concerning God's decrees: 1. He decreed whatsoever comes to pass. 2. His decree was made from eternity. 3. His decree was unconditional—absolute.

Sin, then, as it has come to pass, was decreed to come to pass, from eternity, and without conditions. But that which is decreed to come to pass without conditions, cannot be said to be merely permitted, as it is manifest that to permit a thing supposes conditions, or reasons in the thing for so permitting it.

2. The expositor of the Confession says, "The foreknowledge of God will necessarily infer a decree; for God could not foreknow that things would be, unless he had decreed they *should be*"—not might be. Now,

according to this, either God did not know sin would be, or he decreed it *should be.* To deny the former is to deny the Divine omniscience—to admit, is to admit that he decreed sin *should* be. But the expositor of the Confession tells us explicitly, that the efficient cause of sinful actions is the decree of God. If the decree causes the act, does it not cause the sin?

3. Herman Witsius says, "The human will can produce no action of which God is not the author." Does sin reside in the will? Then God, who is the author of every act of the will, is author of every sin. With him agree Hill, Dick, Chalmers, and others, quoted in my third letter. I request my readers to refer to the numerous quotations contained in that letter upon this point.

4. "The will of the supreme Being is the *cause* of every thing that now exists, or is to exist at any future time." (Hill.) Does sin exist? Then, according to Hill, God's decrees caused it.

"The supreme Being selects those single objects and combinations of objects, which he chooses to bring into existence; and every circumstance in the manner of the existence of that which is to be, thus depending entirely on his will, is known to him because he decreed it *should* be"—not might be. "The Divine decree is the determination to *produce* the universe, that is, the whole series of *beings* and *events.*" (Ib.) Is it causing a thing to produce it—*create* it? Then the Divine decree, Mr. Hill says, caused sin.

5. "I say with Augustine, that the Lord created those who he certainly foreknew would fall into destruction, and that *this was actually* so because he willed it." (Calvin.) "I confess with Augustine, that God's decree is the necessity of things." (Ib.) Is sin something? Then Calvin says, God's decree is the necessity of it. "They further object, [we Arminians,] were they not, by the decree of

God antecedently predestinated to that corruption, which is now stated as the cause of condemnation? When they perish in their corruption therefor, they only suffer the punishment of that misery into which, in consequence of his predestination, Adam fell, and precipitated his posterity with him. I confess, indeed, that the descendants of Adam fell by *the Divine will;* and this is what I said at the beginning, that we must always return, at last, to the sovereign determination of God's will." (Ib.) "Nor should it be thought absurd to affirm, that God not only foresaw the fall of the first man, and the ruin of his posterity in him, but also arranged all by the determination of his will." (Ib.) "It should be considered as indubitably certain, that all the revolutions in the world *proceed from the secret exertion of the Divine power.* What God decrees, must *necessarily* come to *pass.*" (Ib.) Does this look like permission, Doctor? "It is not probable that man procured his own destruction, by the mere permission, and without the appointment of God." (Ib.) Not much favor for your idea of permission here, Doctor. "We make God the arbiter and governor of all things, who, in his own wisdom, has, from the remotest eternity, decreed what he would do, and now by his *own power executes* what he has decreed. Whence we assert, that not only the heavens, and earth, and inanimate creatures, *but also the deliberations and volitions of men are so governed by his providence, as to be directed to the end appointed by it.*" (Ib.) "They therefore evade the difficulty, by alledging that it happens only by the permission, and not by the will of God; but God himself, by the most unequivocal declarations, rejects this subterfuge." (Ib.) It would seem, Doctor, that Calvin was not well pleased with your *subterfuge* of permission. "The whole may be summed up thus: that, as the will of God is said to be the *cause* of all things, his providence is established as the governor in all the counsels and works of men, so that it not only exerts its power in the elect, who are influenced by the Holy Spirit, but also compels the compliance of the reprobate. . . . For the first man fell, because the Lord had determined that it was so expedient." (Ib.)

I commend these quotations from Calvin especially to the attention of Dr. Rice. Will he give us light upon them?

6. To Dr. Rice's retreat from my arguments, under the pretense that Presbyterians do not attach the idea of necessity to decree, but bare permission, I object, further, that it is not only contrary to the teaching of those distinguished Calvinists already referred to, but it is also absurd in itself, and antagonistic to the whole system essentially.

It is contrary to the signification of the terms employed. Decree, purpose, predestinate, ordain, predetermine, and such terms, exclusively used, do not contain the idea of permission, but are precisely the opposite of such idea, and contain alone the idea of appointment, establishment, fixedness, to set, to appoint, to establish, to prepurpose, to procure by edict, by authority; and with no consistency whatever, can that which is barely permitted be said to be decreed.

Is it said the decree was to permit sin; that is, God appointed, fixed in purpose, decreed, that he would permit sin? I answer, such a construction shows clearly that he did not decree sin, but only decreed what his own action would be in respect to it, should it be about to occur: he decreed that in such a case he would not prevent it—he would allow it to take place. Is this decreeing sin? The decree did not respect the sin, but simply himself; so that, if God simply permitted sin to exist, he did not decree its existence. But then Dr. Rice is reduced to this dilemma. If he says God simply permitted sin, he admits that he did not decree it; and so he admits that his Confession is in error, when it says God decreed whatsoever comes to pass. If he says God decreed sin, he retreats from the position he has already made, that he simply permits it.

7. But I object, further, to Dr. Rice, that, when he says God did not procure sin by his decree, he antagonizes his system in another particular. It is contended by all Calvinists, that God's foreknowledge is consequent upon his decree; he foreknows things will be, because he has decreed they shall be. How can this be, if the occurrence of the thing is not somehow dependent upon the decree? If it might occur without being decreed, might it not be known to an omniscient God? If it could not occur by any possibility without being decreed, then is not the intervention of decree supposed to be the essential thing in order to its occurrence, or the cause of it?

8. I object, further, to Dr. Rice's doctrine of permission, that it is contrary to his doctrine of the will. He does not believe that the human will can act of itself—he will admit this—he cannot deny. The will, he believes, always and necessarily acts from the force of motives. The strongest motive must prevail. The will must accord with the strongest motive, as the needle must turn to the pole—as the scale must descend with the preponderating weight. He believes that these motives, whatever they may be, are all arranged of God, and brought to bear upon the will, by a decree as old as eternity. But how now, if he has made the action of the will subject to motives, and if he has appointed all the motives, can it be said he permits the action of the will? Is it not manifest that he causes it, as directly as though he controlled it by positive agency?

The foregoing reasons, together with the quotations and arguments previously given, I assign as sustaining the charge made in my second letter, that Calvinism makes God the author of sin. Will the Doctor point out in what particular they fail to sustain the charge? To these, a variety of additional quotations from other authors and arguments, will be submitted as occasion may require.

NUMBER II.

Dr. Rice thus notices my letters, after reading the fourth: "The first objection urged by Mr. Foster, of the Methodist Church, against the Calvinistic doctrine of Divine decree, is that it makes God the author of sin, by making him the necessitating cause of sin; the second is, that it destroys the free agency of man; and the third, that it destroys the accountability of man. These three objections are so nearly identical, that they properly make but one, and they are all based upon a view of the doctrine not taught in the Westminster Confession of Faith, and not held by any Presbyterian. The whole of his arguments, therefore, are nothing more nor less than an entire misrepresentation of the doctrine. This being the case, no particular notice need be taken of them."

I am here charged with misrepresenting Calvinism. Upon this ground the Doctor declines noticing my letters further.

The charge that I have misrepresented Calvinism, to me seems strange. Why, I have not represented it at all—I have only *presented* it. I have quoted only from their own standards. If they are misrepresented, they have misrepresented themselves. I have drawn inferences from their authors quoted, it is true, and deduced consequences. If in this I have been unfair or illogical—if I have misunderstood the authors cited, I can assure the Doctor it has been unintentional, and I only ask him to correct my honest and sincere misapprehensions. My sole object, in addressing these letters to Dr. Rice, was that I might have the benefit of his explanations. Now, why does he decline? He cannot think I have been unkind—he cannot look upon the matter with indifference—he cannot plead disinclination to such controversies. Why, then, will he at this point abruptly leave me under all the misapprehensions and consequent difficulties of mind I experience in regard to his system? I was in hopes, and still am, that explanations could be made, which would discover that we are not so wide apart as we sometimes have thought. I have stated my views of the system, always giving the authorities upon which they were founded, and then raised my objections to the system as I understood it, on purpose that such explanations might be made, expecting that Dr. Rice would—particularly after pledging himself to my aid—point out my mistakes, and lead me to a better view. And now he stops still, and meets me with the blank reply, that my "letters are an entire misrepresentation." Is this magnanimous? I will not say it is not. Dr. Rice will perceive the propriety of a second thought, and will return to my aid—particularly as he will have the opportunity of correcting the erroneous views of at least 40,000 readers of the Advocate, with respect to his system.

Dr. Rice says that I misrepresent Calvinism on this point—that it renders the decree of God "the necessitating cause of sin." Now, if I had made that charge in so many words, on my own authority, it would be sufficient for Dr. Rice to deny. This would satisfy our readers. But I have stated my reasons for making the charge. These reasons are either good or bad: if good, they sustain the charge, and the system is liable; if bad, it can be made to appear.

The Doctor says no Presbyterian believes the doctrine! I quote his own Confession and many authors—standard with his Church—against him, and sustaining my charge. Now, these quotations sustain my charge, or they do not. If they do, I have not misrepresented Calvinism; if they do not, it can be shown.

The Doctor has made the issue with me himself upon this point. Why now does he decline it? He certainly cannot suppose that his bare denial will be sufficient in this case.

I will not complain of the Doctor, that he charges me of *misrepresenting* Calvinism to thousands of his readers, without letting me be heard—thereby producing the impression that I have done them a great wrong. I make no complaint. It may be right to hold a man up as a false accuser, without giving the particulars of his accusation. If the Doctor was under no obligation to notice these letters in the first instance—having made an issue with us voluntarily—he must certainly see the propriety of sustaining his own issue. After all that has appeared from Dr. Rice's pen, and in his columns, it must seem strange for him to retire at this juncture. We, however, leave him to pursue his own pleasure; and, having commenced, we shall go on with our letters, exposing what we conceive to be the errors of Calvinism. Whenever Dr. Rice shall redeem his pledge, we shall be glad to treat him with due courtesy; but whether or not, we shall proceed in the same good spirit to perfect the work we have undertaken.

That Calvinists are inextricably involved in the doctrine of necessity, as charged, and so liable to all the objections urged against them, particularly the three expressly disclaimed by Dr. Rice, will appear still further by the following considerations:

1. The expositor of the Confession, in his notes on the article respecting the will, holds this language: "According to Calvinists, the liberty of a moral agent consists in the power of acting according to his choice; and those actions are free which are performed without external compulsion—physical compulsion—in consequence of the determination of his own mind. The necessity of man's willing and acting, according to his apprehension and disposition, is, in their opinion, fully consistent with the highest liberty which can belong to a rational nature. . . . As nothing can

ever come to pass without a cause, the acts of the will are never without necessity; understanding, by necessity, an infallible connection with something foregoing." This I understand to be the doctrine of all Calvinists respecting the will of man, as well before as since the fall; it is often expressed in stronger language.

Now, this view of the will utterly discards this idea of liberty—power to choose either of two alternatives. Here is the real point of difference between us and them: with them liberty is necessity to choose one way according to the motive, but not power to make an opposite choice: with us it is the power to choose either of the various alternatives presented to the mind. Now, upon their doctrine of the will, I base an argument that its decisions are necessitated, and not free; and, hence, that it is absurd for a Calvinist to contend for freedom. Take man in a state of innocence—for we desire to give the advocates of the system the most favorable opportunity to defend themselves—the question is, Was man capacitated with freedom to stand or fall, in the circumstances? And, according to the Calvinian system, the answer must be, he was not; for he was so constituted that he must yield to the prevailing disposition or strongest motive. He could not avoid this; it was his nature. He had no control of these motives, and when they came upon him he as necessarily was moved by them, as the needle is moved to the pole; it matters not that he chose to move with the influence; for the want of liberty and the fact of necessity were found in the circumstance, that he had no control of his choice: he made his choice necessarily.

Now, I ask Dr. Rice, what does control the choice? He must answer, whatever goes to constitute the prevailing motive. But, then, I ask, who controls and governs these motives? And he must answer, that all things are arranged and governed by God himself: God controls the motives; the motives control the man. He sins, necessitated by the motive. And, now, where do we find the first cause? Not in the choice; for it was an effect: not in the motives; for they were under the government and control of God. Here, then, we trace the operations of man's will back to God: not as permitted, but procured. If the Calvinists can trace it beyond God, they may free their system from making God the first cause of sin!

2. I derive an argument from the Calvinian view of providence. Two things are included in the notion of providence—the preservation and the government of all things. "God governs all things by *directing and disposing them to the end for which he designed them.* . . . The providence of God extends to all creatures, *actions,* and things, from the greatest even to the least." This is the doctrine of providence, taught by the expositor of the Confession. According to it, God's providence extends to all *actions,* from the greatest to the least; and while it regards all actions, it consists in directing all to the end for which he designed them, so that all actions come to the very end for which God designed. Are any sinful, he designed them as such; and, by his providence, disposed and directed them in their causes and development. "To solve the difficulty connected with this point," says Mr. Shaw, "theologians distinguish between an *action* and *its quality.* The *action, abstractly considered, is from God,* for *no action* can be performed without the concurrence of Providence; but the sinfulness of the action proceeds entirely from the creature." The first part of this sentence declares the faith of Calvinists; the second part disclaims a consequence of their faith. It is for us to see whether such a disclaimer is rational and consistent, or the contrary. The proposition is, that the action, abstractly considered, is from God—God is its author—for the reason that no action can be performed without his concurrence or agency. Now, I insist that the

proposition positively asserts, that, just so far as sins are actions, God is their author. There can be no controversy here. The act of murder and adultery, and what not, is God's act, so far forth as it is an act. Now, if the act is his, I leave it to the metaphysics of Calvinists to determine whose is the sin. For more particular argumentation upon this point, I refer to my second letter.

3. The same conclusion is inferred from the Calvinian doctrine of a Divine plan. "The whole universe derives the reason of its existence from the will of its Creator, and every particular being and event in the universe has that connection with something going before it, by which it forms a part of the plan of Providence." If sin is an event, Mr. Hill thus asserts that it derives the reason or cause of its existence from the will of God. Its cause is in God's will, and yet is not God its author. Every event in the universe has connection with something before it—it is an effect; and, as such, forms a part of the plan of Providence; which plan is the cause of all, or that something going before all, and emanating from the Divine will, which is the only cause.

In accordance with this view, all things are directly and repeatedly ascribed to the necessary operations of God's plan by Calvinists—even the reprobation and damnation of sinners, with the causes leading thereto.

"Whom God passes by, therefore, he reprobates, and for no other cause than his determination to exclude them from the inheritance which he predestines for his children." (Calvin.) How explicit this language! how impossible to misunderstand it! Whom God passes by—does not include in the decree of election—he reprobates. Not because of their sins—not for any thing he foresees in them; but for no other *cause* than his determination to exclude them from the inheritance of his children. Thus honest John Calvin—and with him agree many authors quoted—scorns to seek any other cause for the reprobation and consequent damnation of some men, than the sovereign purpose of God How absurd and ridiculous for his followers to attempt to deny and demur, when we charge this consequence upon them—when it is thus explicitly declared and extensively elaborated by their great leader—in the conclusion of which argument he says, "Whence it follows that the cause of hardening—the sinner in his sins, or working his sins in him as an occasion of damnation—is the secret counsel of God!" First, the sinner is reprobated for no other cause but the purpose of God. Thus reprobated, he is established in sin by the secret will of God, operating to that purpose; and then he is damned, because of his previous reprobation and hardening.

Hear Calvin again: "That the reprobates obey not the word of God when made known to them, is justly imputed to the wickedness and depravity of their hearts, provided it be at the same time stated that they are abandoned to this depravity, because they have been raised up, by a just but inscrutable judgment of God, to display his glory in their condemnation." Observe this passage. The disobedience of the reprobates may be attributed to their depravity, but their depravity is attributable to the fact that God raised them up, fitted them for destruction; so both their actual disobedience and natural depravity is ascribable to God's purpose in raising them up, even their eternal destruction.

Presbyterians of the nineteenth century, do you believe this? Can you believe a system necessarily involving it? Yet I show you that such is the miserable doctrine of your Confession, and your standard authors—a consequence from which there is no escape, but by a total abandonment of the whole. And will you be content, when you see, by fair logical deductions, such consequences fastened upon you—consequences at which your reason and piety equally revolt? Will you be content, when the only reply attempted by your leaders to fair and unavoidable arguments and proofs, is, "We *don't* believe it?" Will this mode of defense satisfy Presbyterians? Is your Confession capable of no better a support? And still will you cling to a system, beset and encompassed with consequences, at the announcement of which you are stunned—which I do not marvel that you spurn with indignant vehemence? But why shall you cling to premises, necessarily involving such conclusions?

4. That God necessitates the sinful acts of men, is unavoidable upon the Calvinian view of foreknowledge. Calvinists hold that God cannot foreknow any event as future, only as he perceives it connected with some other thing as a cause infallibly and necessarily to produce it—all future things are foreknown as effects springing from a first cause by successive links of attachment, or as a succession of causes and effects. According to this, it is manifest that the first cause is the actual and real cause of every successive link. But each sin is a link, and therefore the first cause is the actual cause of each sin. It matters not though they be separated by ten thousand intervening links, scattered through as many ages.

5. The same fact is deducible from the reasonings of Calvinists, in regard to the Arminian doctrine, that the mind originates its own volitions. It is said by Edwards, and it is common to Calvinists to say so, that such a view renders the volitions of men an effect without a cause. By which they deny the mind of man to possess the nature of a cause; or, in other words, they thus deny its agency, and assert its mere passivity. All its motions are mere effects, of which it is the passive instrument: it causes no volition itself. Where is the cause? It is not in mind. It is finally in God! But if God causes the motion, and the motion is sinful, who causes the sin?

"If the determinations of moral agents are thus certainly directed by motives, it is plain that the Almighty, whose will gave existence to the universe, and by whose pleasure every cause operates, and every effect is produced, *gives their origin to these determinations*, by the execution of the great plan of his providence; for as there entered into his plan, all those efficient causes, whose successive operations produce the motions and changes of the material world, so there are brought forward in succession, by the *execution* of his plan, all those objects which present themselves to the mind as final causes." (Hill.)

This quotation first assumes that the determinations of moral agents are created by motives, as final causes. It is then assumed that the Almighty, by whose will all such final causes operate, causes the determinations produced by them; and this efficiently, inasmuch as all such motives—final causes—are brought forward by the execution or direct operation of his providence. Well, now, are these determinations sinful? If so, and God caused the determination, who caused the sin?

"For according to the view of the Divine foreknowledge, which is essential to the Calvinistic system, all things are brought into being by the execution of the Divine decree, so that no circumstance, in the manner of the existence of any individual, can depend upon the conduct of that individual; but all that distinguishes him from others, must *originate in the mind that formed the decree.*" (Hill.) Every thing peculiar in the conduct or character of the individual—of each and every individual—originates in the mind that formed the decree. If he is sinful, therefore this originated with God!

In the trial of Dr. Beecher, Dr. Beecher accuses Dr. Wilson as follows: "Dr. Wilson has made a distinct avowal, that free agency and moral obligation to obey law, do not *include any ability of any kind.*" To which

Dr. Wilson replied directly in so many words, "With respect to fallen man I do!" "Now," says Dr. Wilson, "let us look at the doctrine of the Confession with this principle in view, that the *state of the man determines the will. The will is always at liberty: choice is an effect always, and not a cause!* It is always produced freely. When the mind chooses, it always chooses freely. There is no such thing as bound will. Hence, all do what is good or evil voluntarily, in view of *a motive,* and according to the state of mind in which they are. Take man in a state of innocence. God made him upright; in his own image; his choice is free, and he chooses what is right; but not *from any power in the will.* The will, as I have said, has no power to operate on any thing but the body. His uprightness was in the right state of the affections, and the luminous state of the understanding, in the correct state of the memory, and in his entire moral rectitude in the Divine image. *His will was free to do good while no temptation was presented to it.* He had no motive but his accountableness to God, and his love to God. His will operated according to the state of the man. But now look at him in another state—the state of temptation. Motives are now presented to him by the arch tempter, but not to his will at all; they are presented to his understanding and appetites—to his taste for beauty. The fruit is pleasant to the eye; and what was the effect? The will was not trapped in any other way than this: the temptation addressed to these powers was so strong, that it overcame the dictates of judgment, and the man chose wrong. Volition moves the body: the mind moves the will; and the mind is moved by that without, which is adapted to its constitution." Now who moved that without, and made the constitution?

The foregoing is the language of Dr. Wilson, who, for forty years, occupied the First Presbyterian Church in this city, and during his long life a prominent man in the Church in the west: certainly, for ability and opportunity, inferior to none of his school, and therefore as reliable an exponent as any other. But now observe his honest and candid admission, on an occasion when, of all others, he would be most accurate, and on a point where he would be most critically prepared: "Free agency and moral obligation to obey law, with respect to fallen man, do not *include any ability of any kind!*" According to this, free agency, as held by Calvinists, does not include ability of any kind. A man is a free agent, though he have no power at all! He is also responsible to obey law, though he have no ability of *any kind* to do so!

But he more fully unfolds his view, as above; and no one can read the quotation, it seems to me, without sympathizing with the sincere and able author, in the manifest confusion and self-contradiction in which he involves himself. "The will is always at liberty;" yet its choice is always caused by a foreign agent! "When the mind chooses, it always chooses freely;" yet it has no kind of ability whatever, but is ruled by the motives in every case! "There is no such thing as bound will;" but it is always an effect, and not a cause! Observe, further, his philosophy of the will Dr. Wilson carries back beyond or behind the fall. Of man, in innocence, he says, "His will *was free to do good, while no temptation was presented to it;*" but what is implied in this? When temptation came, the will was not free to do good, but bound to do evil, or to yield. This, indeed, he does not leave us to infer, but expressly states that the temptation presented to the first pair was such that it overcame, by its strength, the mind—"the mind moves the will, and was itself moved by that without; and thus man fell under the force of a temptation which he had no power to resist. He fell, therefore, when, under the circumstances, he had no power to stand!

And yet he was free in doing what he had no power to avoid!

Dr. Twisse, the Prolocutor of the Westminster Assembly, in conformity to whose views the Confession of Faith was formed, holds the following language: "All things come to pass by the efficacious and irresistible will of God." Again: "It is *impossible that any thing should ever be done but that to which God impels the will of man.*" Again: "God is the author of that action which is sinful, by his irresistible will."

Piscator: "God made Adam and Eve to this very purpose, that they might be tempted and led into sin; and by force of his decree, it could not otherwise be but they must sin."

Again: "God foresees nothing but what he has decreed, and his decree precedes his knowledge."

Again: "For we neither can do more good than we do, nor less evil than we do, because God, from eternity, has precisely decreed that both the good and the evil should be so done."

Again: "God procures adultery, cursing, lyings." Again: "The reprobates who were predestinated to damnation, and the causes of damnation, are created to that end, that they may live wickedly, and be vessels full of the dregs of sin."

Peter Martyr: "God cannot be termed the author of sin, though he is the cause of those actions which are sins. . . . He supplies wicked men with opportunities of sinning, and inclines their hearts thereto. He blinds, deceives, and seduces them. He, by his working on their hearts, bends and stirs them up to do evil."

Zanchius: "God's first constitution was, that some should be destined to eternal ruin; and to this end their sins were ordained, and denial of grace in order to their sins. . . . Both the elect and the reprobates were foreordained to sin, as sin, that the glory of God might be declared thereby."

Zuinglius: "When God makes angels or men sin, he does not sin himself, because he does not break any law."

Witsius, in summing up his reasonings, uses the following language: "If all these truths thus demonstrated be joined and linked together, they will produce that conclusion which we laid down—namely, from all this may be inferred, by plain consequence, that man *could not but* fall on account of the infallibility of the Divine prescience, and of that necessity which they call a necessity of consequences. For it is inconsistent with the divine perfection, that any decree of God should be rendered void, or that the event should not be answerable to it. For if all creatures depend on God in acting—if he not only concurs with them when they act, but *excites them to act*—if *that excitation be so powerful as that on supposing it the effect cannot but follow*—if God, with that same *efficacy, influences vicious actions* so far as they are physical—if the creature cannot give its actions their due moral goodness without God, *it infallibly follows that Adam, God himself moving him to understand, will, and eat, could not but understand, will, and eat, and God not giving goodness to those actions, man could not understand, will, and eat in a right manner.*" Honest Witsius! worthy of imitation! He, you see, does not hesitate, with Calvin, his illustrious model, to confess that, in regard to the first, as well as all other vicious acts, man acts only as coerced by Divine influence.

How, in the face of all these declarations, and the many others cited in foregoing letters, can Calvinists, with any candor, accuse us of misrepresenting them, or attempt themselves to frame an escape by a resort to the doctrine of permissive decrees? I confess I am at a loss to understand how good men reconcile their conduct on this point; but the wrong I must believe is not in the heart, however difficult it may be to ascribe it to the head.

NUMBER III.

In the Presbyterian of the West, Dr. Rice honors me with a notice, which I herewith subjoin. It is all given, but in paragraphs, followed by replies, to render the answer more direct.

"*Foster on Calvinism.*—We have not intended to enter into a regular discussion with Mr. Foster on Calvinism. The reasons are obvious. We were previously engaged in a discussion with Dr. Simpson, on some other points of difference between Methodists and Presbyterians; and we considered Mr. Foster's letters simply as a plan to divert attention from the weak points of his faith we are exposing. We do not choose to permit the plan to succeed."

Doctor, you must excuse us for smiling at this. It is impolite, I know; but nature will out. "A plan to divert attention from the weak points of our faith *you are exposing!*" Truly, we have great need to be alarmed! Your assault is so *potent,* and your success is so *signal!*

"If Mr. Foster desired a discussion with us, courtesy, as we think, would have required him to wait till we were through with Dr. Simpson. Besides, if he desired a discussion with us, he would have proposed it, and allowed us to have some hand in arranging preliminaries; and have made an arrangement to have both sides published in both papers. Having thrust himself forward, whilst a discussion with Dr. Simpson was pending, and without making any of the usual arrangement of preliminaries, it is rather surprising with what confidence and with what vaunting he has claimed our particular notice."

"If Mr. Foster desired a discussion with us!" Strange, Doctor—I had almost said, shame! Do you not know that your own imprudent intermeddling with your neighbors provoked the whole controversy, which now engrosses our columns? Why, now, do you talk as though we sought controversy with you. When a man repels the assassin, does he court the fight? Have you forgotten your haughty replies to our published deprecations of the whole matter?—that even in the commencement of these letters, you were in exceeding good heart? That your tune has changed, is not without cause. That courtesy should have induced me to wait till you were done with Dr. Simpson, I am almost inclined to admit; for your troubles ought not to be increased. But, then, did you not court it? Did you not proclaim your readiness and resources? As to the matter of preliminaries, did you stop to make preliminary arrangements when you commenced your abusive misrepresentations of Methodism? And why did you not think of this before, when you promised, at the appearance of my first letter, to assist me in the discussion? There was no complaint then! And you talk about arranging to publish our articles in both papers! Do you not know that nothing could induce you to publish my letters in your columns? And have you forgotten that I promised to publish your replies, whether you would insert my letters or not, if you would attempt a candid examination of the subject? This attempt of yours to present matters in a false light, and to elicit sympathy, comes with a poor grace from Dr. Rice. You are surprised that I address myself so confidently to you! Did you not tell us that you were the man? Have you not put yourself forward as the great champion? Have you not assailed us? and, then, does it surprise you when we take up your vaunting challenge, and repel your virulent attacks? O, sir, it is too late to *supplicate pity!*

"We propose, however, in connection with our preceding articles on Divine decrees, to pay our respects briefly to Mr. Foster. He has quoted brief extracts from the Confession of Faith, and from Calvinistic writers; but it is easy for one who takes up a doctrine without understanding it, to make quotations from writers, so partial, or so completely severed from explanations and qualifications given, as entirely to misrepresent them. This Mr. Foster has done—we do not say intentionally."

"He has quoted brief sections of the Confession." Do you not know that I have quoted whole chapters of your Confession, without the omission of a word? How can you, in sight of this fact, print, to be read by your readers, who will never see my letters, that I have garbled your Confession? Why have you done this? You say, I have misrepresented your authors. Will you point out a single instance? Will you take any quotation I have made, and show that I have put a meaning on it contrary to the meaning of the author? Do this, or your readers may have occasion to question your accuracy, not to say candor.

"From his quotations, he comes to the conclusion that, according to the faith of Calvinists, the decree of God is the efficient cause, not only of the acts of men and angels, but of the affections and passions under which they are performed. Hence he concludes that men can no more avoid the murders, blasphemies, etc., which they commit, than they could resist the fiat of Omnipotence, or subvert the purposes of the Almighty—that sin results as an effect from the Divine decree as its cause. It is upon this grossly false view of the subject that all his objections to Calvinism are based, such as that, according to this doctrine, 'God is the author of sin; man's free agency is destroyed,' etc. The correction of the false view of the doctrine, of course, destroys the force of his objections."

"From his quotation, he comes to the conclusion," etc. Now, Doctor, the question here is, did the quotations warrant the conclusion I came to? If they did, Calvinism is guilty. If not, will you please make it appear? This is the point in a nutshell. No dodging here. Come up squarely to the work.

"Upon this grossly false view of the subject all his objections are based." Why don't you show that I have taken a false view of the subject? Why assert and reiterate this for the ten thousandth time? Are *assertions* arguments among Calvinists?

"The correction of this false view of the doctrine, of course, destroys the force of his objections." Exactly so, Doctor; but will you correct this false view, not by cant, but by reasoning? This is precisely what we want! Don't waste your time; I know it is precious.

"On the general subject we make the following remarks: 1. If Mr. Foster desired a fair and intelligible discussion of the difference between Methodists and Presbyterians, he should have stated precisely wherein they differ. But, though he has attempted to state the doctrine of Presbyterians, he gave no account of that of the Methodists. Do the latter hold that God has no purposes or decrees at all? Do they deny that God foreordained any one event which was to be fulfilled by the free agency of man? Why does Mr. Foster give us no light on this subject? How can we determine which of two systems is the better, or more accordant with Scripture truth, unless we have them fairly stated, that we may compare them? Why had Mr. Foster no desire to make the public acquainted with the Methodist faith on this important subject?"

This would be rather amusing, if it were not unkind to be amused at the vexation and confusion of a fellow-worm. It is now the third time you have turned attention to this subject, and one of your correspondents condoles with you in your distress; it has evidently perplexed you not a little. But, Doctor, how came you to imagine that I ought to write about Methodist doctrine? I assure you I had no such intention; I saw no occasion for it. My object was simply to examine your faith, and show my objections to it. If you have any desire to know what Methodism is, no one will question your right; and, if you find objections, in due time, we will most probably assist you to examine them

This absurd struggle to keep away from the issues, and to escape from an examination of the objections I have made to your system, is fruitless; men will understand it, and attribute it to its proper cause. Put an end to all this loss of time, and labor, and self-confusion, and come up to the work like a man; take up my letters consecutively, and demolish them; you say it is an easy work. Many of your readers, to my personal knowledge, are extremely anxious to see it done. Many of mine are anxious to see if it can be done. You have every facility; my arguments and authorities are before you. When you have done this, you will have sustained Calvinism. If, then, you desire to examine other subjects connected with the doctrines of Methodism, you will find no foreign matters introduced; no evasion; no special pleading. You have provoked this controversy. Nothing else would do you. Now, then, let there be a direct, candid, Christian, thorough work made of it.

"The faith of the Presbyterian Church is clearly stated in the Westminster Confession. Whatever individuals may have said, more than is there written, or different from it, our Church is not responsible for. We make this remark, not because we believe that any one of the writers quoted by Mr. Foster has materially departed from the doctrine, as there stated, but because a discussion concerning the views of each of them would fill a volume, instead of a few columns of a newspaper."

I agree with you here, Doctor, that the Westminster Confession is the standard of your faith. Hence, in making my statements of your doctrine, I have invariably quoted from it *fully* first, and I have called in other authors of great authority among you—Calvin, Hill, Witsius, Dwight, Edwards, Boston, Shaw, Dickinson, Ridgley, Chalmers, Toplady, Zanchius, etc.—simply to show the common view taken of these doctrines by yourselves. I was not willing to venture an interpretation of your faith without your own sanction, knowing what a wonderful facility you have in the use of such epithets as "*misrepresentation, ignorance, do not understand,*" etc. My deductions are all based upon the Confession of Faith, as interpreted by these authors; *and, if you will show that they are not, I promise a public recantation of the charges made against you.* But let me remind you again, that the question is not, whether your Confession and these authors teach an opposite doctrine to that which I have derived from them, but *do they teach this?* When you attempt to derive an opposite doctrine from them, without correcting and removing my reasonings and quotations, you only prove that you have a contradictory creed, liable to all the objections I bring against it, and, the more grievous than all the rest, that it diametrically contradicts itself, and its defenders destroy themselves. First, show that the arguments with which I sustain my interpretation are faulty, and then favor us with your new *translation.*

"Now, in the Confession of Faith, we have first the general declaration, that 'God, from all eternity, did, by the most wise and holy counsel of his own will, freely and unchangeably ordain whatsoever comes to pass; yet so as thereby neither is God the author of sin, nor is violence offered to the will of the creatures, nor is the liberty or contingency of second causes taken away, but rather established.' (Chap. iii, sec. i.) We have a particular explanation of the doctrine. The shorter Catechism teaches that God executeth his decrees in the works of creative providence. The fourth chapter of the Confession states what God did, in fulfillment of his decrees in creation. To the doctrine of this chapter Mr. Foster has taken no exception. In the fifth chapter, we have stated the fulfillment of the Divine decrees by the providence of God. After stating that God upholds, directs, disposes, and governs all creatures, actions, and things, to his own glory, it employs the following language: 'The almighty power, unsearchable wisdom, and infinite goodness of God, so far manifest themselves in his providence, that it extendeth itself even to the first fall, and all other sins of angels and men, and that not by a *bare permission*, but such as hath joined with it a most wise and powerful *bounding*, and *otherwise ordering and governing* them, in a manifold dispensation to his own holy ends; yet so as the sinfulness thereof proceedeth only from the creature, and not from God!' How did the providence of God extend to the fall of man? The sixth chapter answers: 'This their sin God was pleased to permit, according to his wise and holy counsel, having proposed to order it according to his own glory.'

"Now, concerning the sin of our first parents, and all sins of men and angels, the Confession states two things: 1. God decreed, or chose to permit them. 2. That he not only determined to permit them to have sinful inclinations, but powerfully to bound, order, and govern their actions, so as to bring to pass his own wise designs. God knew the design of Satan to tempt Eve. He had power to prevent it. For wise reasons, he chose to permit him to tempt her, and to permit her to sin. Was her free agency destroyed by this permission? Or was it destroyed by the purpose of God to bring good out of the evil designs of Satan and the sin of Eve? Or did either of these things make God the author of her sin? God decreed to harden the heart of Pharaoh, so that he would not let the Israelites go out of Egypt, and he did harden it. (Exodus iv, 21, and vii, 13.) By this hardening, the purposes of God are fulfilled. Was the free agency of Pharaoh destroyed? Did God become the author of his sins? God decreed to send the Assyrian king against the rebellious Jews, to chastise them, and he did send him. (Isaiah x, 5–15.) And yet he punished the king for his sins, committed in that very war against the Jews. Will Mr. Foster tell us how he explains this plain Bible fact?

"God permits the sinful dispositions of men; and he so controls them that he accomplishes by them his holy purposes; and this is precisely what he decreed to do, and no more. Francis Turretine has long been used as a standard author, by Presbyterians. How does he answer the objection that the doctrine of Divine decrees makes God the author of sin? He says, 'The decree does not flow into the thing, and is not effective of the evil, but only permissive and directive! God simply permits and directs, or controls, and, therefore, is not the author of sin; or, as Solomon says, "A man's heart deviseth his way, but the Lord directeth his steps."'

"When the doctrine is thus correctly and briefly stated, all the potent objections so triumphantly urged by Mr. Foster become, not only powerless, but almost *ridiculous*. More on this subject hereafter, if we are spared."

Here, Doctor, you reiterate an argument for the third time, in support of the doctrine of Divine decrees. I must, therefore, notice it, to save your printers the trouble of setting up the type again, or, perhaps, you might lay it aside to insert from week to week, to avoid the trouble and expense of composition. I cannot help but think it remarkable, Doctor, that, though you have written, directly and indirectly, five lengthy articles upon my letters, you have not named one of my arguments or quotations! For some cause, you *cannot help* but write, though with evident irresolution and dispiritedness; and, for some other cause, you cannot venture to attack one of my arguments, by way of examination and refutation. Why is this, Doctor? Can you tell? You seek to avoid all the objections I alledge against your doctrine of decrees, by assuming that I misrepresent you. I quote from your distinguished authors, to show you that the view I take is their view. You don't examine my quotations at all! I show you that these authors are against you. You answer not a word! I make an argument, from the language of the Confession itself, against your interpretation. You say nothing in reply! I show, from the system, that your interpretation is discordant. Not a response do you make!

You know very well that, before you can defend your doctrine of decrees, it must be defined. The whole controversy, at present, is upon this point. What is your doctrine? I have defined it. You disagree with me. I quote from your authors to prove that I am correct, and make additional arguments to the same point. Now, manifestly, the first thing to do, is to settle this point. Will you attend to this? No evasions. And the way to settle it, is to show that the arguments which I employ, to sustain my interpretation, are not competent. When you examine foregoing arguments, you shall have others, and if you can unsettle my interpretation, you gain your point. Come, sir, with good heart; the path is plain before you. Your present course is like the Irishman's, when brought before the court, on charge of a trifling theft. It being proved that Paddy was guilty, the judge proceeded to condemn him, on the testimony of some witness who had actually seen him perpetrate the theft. Whereupon Paddy very quickly replied, with all the vivacity of his countrymen, "May it plase yer honor, I can bring fifty men that didn't see me take the thing at all, at all, so I can."

But in dismissing this subject, one word more to you. I am heartily glad that you renew your promise to attend to this matter hereafter. Don't forget this promise; and attend to it right. I shall not promise to notice any future equivocations. If you desire to discuss, and will do so, we shall find great pleasure in having your co-operation, both with respect to your doctrine and our own; but, in any event, we shall progress with our letters, and not complain at you, whatever course you may deem best in the defense. I doubt not you know perfectly well which is the wisest course for you to pursue. I had almost said, I can but admire your *shrewdness.*

Four questions:

1. Do you not know that a decree, or purpose to permit whatsoever comes to pass, is not a decree that the things should come to pass?

2. Do you not know that when you assume the doctrine of permission, you become an Arminian, and desert Calvinism?

3. Do you not know that all your questions and Scriptural arguments, in the above, have no bearing whatever on the points between you and myself, and are mere subterfuges and evasions?

4. Do you not know that I defend the doctrine of permission, against you, who deny it?

God permits whatsoever comes to pass! Is this Calvinism? or have I not proved that your doctrine is, that he necessitates whatsoever comes to pass? Come, Doctor, no equivocation. Meet the matter squarely; let us get at the truth.

NUMBER IV.

"*Foster on Calvinism.*—As already we have proved, the Presbyterian Confession teaches, concerning the sins of angels and men, that God decreed, or purposed to *permit* and to *direct.* This is all. Mr. Foster, however, is in difficulty about two points, (see his 2d Letter,) namely, 1. He is under the impression that sin is a *thing.* He reasons thus: 'God's decree [according to Calvinists] is the necessity of things; but sin is something; therefore, God's decree is the necessity, or necessitating cause of sin.' We reply, that sin is not a *thing,* but a *quality;* and, therefore, when it is said, that God's decree is the necessity of *things,* it does not follow, that it is the necessitating cause of *sin.*

Such a blunder looks badly in a man who evidently glories in his acuteness and in his logical powers. Again, he says, 'God decreed whatsoever comes to pass; but sin comes to pass; therefore, God decreed sin.' We answer, this is a gross abuse of language. It is not true, that *sin comes to pass*. It is true, that *events* come to pass, in connection with which men commit sin. Mr. Foster proves, that Calvinists make God's decree the necessitating cause of sin, by assuming what every one ought to know is untrue, that sin is an *event* or a *thing!* Having thus perverted their language, he proceeds to do battle against a doctrine despised by every enlightened Calvinist on earth."

Dr. Rice commences, by stating that he has already proved, that "the Presbyterian Confession teaches, concerning the sins of angels and men, that God decreed, or purposed to permit and direct. This is all." To this I reply, Dr. Rice has proved nothing more than was stated and *admitted* in my letters—nothing but what is subversive of his own creed; but he has overlooked the real issue, and he seeks to keep it from the view of his readers. *It is this:* I have proved, by several arguments, which the Doctor is too cunning to notice, that his Confession and standard authors teach, that God has efficiently decreed whatsoever comes to pass—that he causes, not permits, all things. To this he makes no reply. He well knows that he has adopted an interpretation of his system which cannot be sustained; and for this very reason he will not meet me here. Not a word will he say on this subject. He knows that the doctrine of permission is an abandonment of the doctrine of decrees, as taught by his Church—that it is Arminianism, and not Calvinism. He escapes the difficulties I bring against him by deserting his creed!—by turning Arminian! Calvinism says, God decrees whatsoever comes to pass. Arminianism says, God permits whatsoever comes to pass. *Where is Dr. Rice?*

To my argument, "God's decree is the necessity of things; but sin is something; therefore, God's decree is the necessity, or necessitating cause of sin," he replies, "*Sin is not a thing, but a quality.*"

Again: to my argument, "God decreed whatsoever comes to pass; but sin comes to pass; therefore, God decreed sin," he replies, that "*this is a gross abuse of language. It is not true, that sin comes to pass. Mr. Foster proves that Calvinists make God's decree the necessitating cause of sin, by assuming what every one ought to know is untrue, that sin is an event or a thing.*"

Sin is not a thing! Not an event! *It does not come to pass! It is a quality!* Therefore, though God decreed all things and events, with whatsoever comes to pass, yet he did not decree sin! A cardinal's cap for the learned Doctor! If sin is a thing, or an event, or if it comes to pass, the Doctor will admit my argument. Very well, then. Is sin a thing? What is a thing? Webster says, a "thing is an *event or action;* that which happens or falls out; that which is done, told, or purposed."

Now, what is sin? John says, "*Sin is the transgression of the law.*" But is it an act to transgress the law? Then sin is an action. But perhaps John is mistaken. I have a better authority with Dr. Rice—the Confession of Faith. "Every sin, both original and actual, being a transgression of the righteous law of God," etc. "Sin is any want of conformity unto, or transgression of any law of God." But what now? May be transgression is a *quality!* Webster says, "transgression is the *act* of passing over or beyond any law or rule of moral duty; the *violation* of law or known principle of rectitude; *breach* of command." So, between John and Webster, we find that sin is an act—an act is a thing; so sin is a thing!

Again: nothing is more common than for ministers, authorized by the Bible, to warn men against *committing, doing, performing* sins! Now, do they warn them against committing *qualities* or *actions?*

Again: will Dr. Rice inform us what a quality is, separate from a thing? or what a thing is, separate from its qualities?

But sin is not an event! What is an event? "Event," says Webster, "is that which comes, arrives, or happens; that which falls out; any incident, good or bad."

Well, now, what is sin? "Sin is the transgression of the law." Query: Did it ever occur that the law was transgressed? or, if Dr. Rice prefers it, did it never happen that an act occurred embracing a sinful quality? if so, was this an event? Then sin is an event! But, again, either all sin is eternal, or sins do come to pass in time, or there is no sin. But Dr. Rice says, sin does not come to pass in time; therefore, there is no sin, or all sins are eternal. Which will the Doctor choose?

But again: Dr. Rice quotes the Confession of Faith, to prove that the Presbyterian Church believe that God permitted sin. What does he mean by this? Permitted sin—how? in what sense? Permitted it to come to pass? Can he mean any thing else? But he says, it is an abuse of language to say sin came to pass! Will the gentleman help us here?

He says, also, concerning sin, "that God decreed to order, govern, and bound them." What does he mean by this? That God bounds and governs *qualities*, or *events* and *things*—the acts of men and angels?

But I have perpetrated a great blunder—am guilty of a great abuse of language—in making sin a thing—an event—in saying it comes to pass! It is not any thing! It is not an event! It never did come to pass! So says Dr. Rice, *and he ought to know.* Henceforth let it be known, *sin is a quality!* an abstraction! It is an abuse of language to say, men commit sin, or to speak of it as a thing that is effected or brought to pass? What men do, or think, or purpose, are not sins—nothing could be more unscholarly than to say they are.

But, now, if it should seem to my readers, after all, that sin is something, and not nothing, my argument, by tacit admission of Dr. Rice, bears unanswerably against his system.

I could very easily show, that all his authors, the Confession, and God himself, speak of sin in the same manner in which I speak of it—as an event—an action; of course, the action nor event are ever stripped of their qualities. But really this is too ridiculous: it shows to what an extremity a man will permit himself to be driven in support of a bad cause. I have met with many attempts to escape the difficulty; but this last, I must admit, in justice to my distinguished antagonist, is the *climacteric.* He admits that God decreed all acts and events, but not their quality. Now, look at this. He decreed every blasphemy, every murder, every theft, every enormity, with every intention—and his decree necessitated their occurrence; but he did not decree sin, and his decree did not necessitate the occurrence of sin. Very well. Now, admit that sin is a *quality* separate from all these acts and intentions—the idea of which is preposterous—yet can the acts and intentions exist without the sins? Will Dr. Rice say they can? If they cannot, if the thing is impossible, does not the decree, which necessitates the act and intention, necessitate the quality of sin, also?

I this moment observe, that Dr. Rice speaks of sin as action in this very connection, showing how error causes its advocates to blunder and fall in its defense. He says, "It is true that events come to pass, in connection with which men *commit* sin." What does this mean, Doctor? Do men commit *qualities,* or *acts?* Sin is not an event—

not an act. When men commit sin, what do they *commit? something* or *nothing?*

Doctor, what do you suppose candid, thoughtful men must think of a system admitting no better defense than you find yourself able to make here? In all candor, are you not ashamed of such quibbling yourself! Come, sir, come, put it away—discuss this subject, for once, in a manner worthy of yourself and worthy of it.

But I thank you for admitting that God has decreed all events and actions, in a manner which necessitates their existence. This is making some progress, and looks as though you were about to give up your subterfuge of permission, and come out an up and down Calvinist. Stick to this, and you will fare much better than by attempting to defend two contradictory systems.

"2. Mr. Foster is wholly unable to understand, that God may direct certain *acts,* without being chargeable with the *sin* men commit in performing those acts; and he is quite certain, that if the *act* can be attributed to God, the *feeling* or *motive* which prompts it, must also be attributed to him. Strange that a man should so stumble and blunder concerning a principle perfectly familiar to every thinking mind. Joseph's brethren hated him, and determined to kill him; but Reuben persuaded them to put him in a pit, 'that he might rid him out of their hands, and deliver him to his father again.' (Genesis xxxvii, 21, 22.) Now, was not Reuben the author, in an important sense, of the act of putting Joseph into the pit? But for his influence that act would not have been performed. But was he chargeable with the sin committed by his brothers in performing the act? They were influenced by malignant feelings; he by benevolent feelings. The act, so far as Reuben was concerned, was good; so far as his brothers were concerned, it was bad. They would have killed him; Reuben persuaded them to do a different thing, which, though it gratified their revenge, offered the prospect of saving him."

Here follows a number of quotations from the Bible; but as they do not bear on the point in dispute, and as what is given is a specimen, we need not insert them in full.

The Doctor here takes up what he calls my second difficulty; and he says "it is to understand how God may direct to certain acts, without being chargeable with the sin men commit in performing those acts." Query: Why did not Dr. Rice state my difficulty in my own language? Why does he scrupulously avoid giving my arguments in his replies? Can any body guess? Does the Doctor know? Does the Doctor know why he will not examine my replies even, if he supposes himself able, triumphantly, to defend his cause?

My difficulty, which the Doctor is here trying to state and remove, is this: not to distinguish between an act and its morality, but to separate morality from *an act and its intention.* My language is this: "There is a discrimination between the sinful act and the sin of the act. This is correct. An act and its sinfulness are certainly distinct. (Act is here spoken of as free from the intention.) Sin resides in the intention, not the act. Well, then, is this the meaning of our Calvinistic brethren, that, though God's decree is the efficient cause of the sinful act, as an act, it is not the cause of its sin; for the sin is in the sinner's intention in committing it? But, then, a question arises right here: Was not the sinner's intention decreed? If you answer me no, then there is something which comes to pass which was not decreed. If you answer yes, and the sin was in the intention, then God, who was the author of the intention, was author of the sin."

Now, Dr. Rice must know that the point I make here is this: that God has decreed all acts, with the intentions that produced these acts, and, hence, that he decreed sin, because the act and the intention do constitute the sin—the sinful quality must necessarily belong to them—they are the sin itself.

It would be a useless task to take up the cases he introduces to assist him, because they do not touch the point in dispute between us; but to show you how superficial they are, we will take up the first. To show that an act may be bad or good, in itself considered—a thing not disputed—and, hence, to decree an act is not to decree its quality, he takes up the case of Joseph's brethren. He says, "Now, was not Reuben the author, in an important sense, of the act of putting Joseph into the pit? But was he chargeable with the sins committed [that is, *qualities* committed] by his brothers in performing the act? They were influenced by malignant feelings; he, by benevolent feelings. The act, so far as Reuben was concerned, was good; but, so far as his brothers were concerned, it was bad." Now, with this statement of the Doctor I agree perfectly. But, now, mark. Why was the act good in Reuben? Because his intention was good. Why was the *act bad*—acts, you see, are sins—in his brothers? Because their intention was bad. But whence came that intention? Dr. Rice says God decreed it, in a manner to necessitate its existence. If God's decree was the cause of the intention, and sin was in the intention, who caused the sin? Doctor, will you tell us? Every other case admits of the same easy answer, in a word.

"The Scriptures abound in such facts—facts which Mr. Foster, soaring aloft in the airy regions of abstract logic, did not think worth while to notice. His arguments are not against Calvinism—they are against the inspiration of the Bible. In his zeal to pull down Calvinism, he has struck at the foundations of Christianity. In his anxiety to furnish his Methodist brethren with arguments, he has furnished the *infidel* with arguments no less conclusive. If we were an infidel, we could desire no better arguments against the truth of the Bible than those of Mr. Foster, if they are at all sound. With those arguments we would prove, not that *Calvinism* destroys man's free agency and accountability, and makes God the author of sin, but that the Bible is liable to these charges!"

The Doctor does not like my logic. I do not wonder at this. It is very natural he should not. But I am at some loss to know how the truths of logic and the truths of Scripture conflict with each other. Perhaps the Doctor will enlighten us here. And as for Scripture facts, I am prepared to examine any that shall be submitted upon the real points at issue; and I further boldly deny, that Dr. Rice can find any passage of Scripture sustaining what I object to. I defy the gentleman to produce it. Let him do so, before he accuses me of using logic in opposition to the Bible. He says, "My arguments are not against Calvinism—they are against the inspiration of the Bible. In his zeal to pull down Calvinism, he has struck at the foundations of Christianity." I suppose the Doctor means *Calvinism* is Christianity! I cannot perceive how otherwise his strange charge is to be understood. But what a posture is this for *Dr. Rice*, the champion of Calvinism! How are the mighty fallen! He finds he cannot answer my logic, and, hence, deprecates its use. My arguments are unanswerable; and he cries the ark is in danger—"to your tents, O Israel!" He says, "With those arguments we would prove, not that Calvinism destroys man's free agency and accountability, and makes God the author of sin, but that the Bible is liable to these charges." Does the gentleman mean that the Bible is liable to these charges? If so, of course he believes them; for he believes the Bible. If not, of course he does not believe the arguments sufficient to convict the Bible; and why, then, would he use them against it? But who, besides Dr. Rice, has ever imagined that my letters assailed the Bible?

"Mr. Foster seems wholly unable to comprehend, what is perfectly plain, that the same moral feeling may lead to the commission of any one of fifty acts. And hence he argues, that if God decreed to bring to pass a certain event, he must have decreed to *produce* in the heart the moral feeling by which that event is brought to pass. A man *hates* another. Under the influence of that hatred he may *slander* him; he may injure his *property;* he may institute vexatious *civil suits;* he may *insult* him; he may *strike* him. A man is *ambitious;* and his ambition may be gratified in many ways. To what particular acts it may lead him, will depend entirely upon the circumstances in which he may be placed. A man is *covetous.* His covetousness makes him desire to accumulate money and property; but there are many ways in which this may be done. What particular acts his love of money may lead him to perform, depends upon what moral principle he has, and by what circumstances he may be surrounded. Now, all that Calvinists hold on this subject, is simply, that God decreed to *permit* the fall and sinfulness of men, and that he decreed so to *control* their sinful dispositions, as to bring to pass his wise and holy ends. That he did permit the fall and the depravity of men, Mr. Foster will not deny. That he exercises a controlling providence over the wicked, the Bible most abundantly teaches.

"The enlightened Calvinist has no insuperable difficulty in finding a satisfactory explanation of these things. God purposed to *permit* the temptation and the fall of our first parents. In consequence of that event all their posterity are sinful. God, withdrawing from them his divine influence, *permits* them to be so; but he does not allow them to wander abroad *uncontrolled.* In its native freedom, 'the heart of a man deviseth his way;' but in his divine sovereignty 'the Lord directeth his steps.'"

This paragraph is, if possible, still more remarkable than

either of the former. I have read from Dr. Rice's pen for some years; but the inaccuracies of this letter are more unaccountable than in any of his former writing that has come under my observation. I attribute this to the badness of his cause, and his evident confusion. He says, "Mr. Foster seems wholly unable to comprehend, what is perfectly plain, that the same moral feelings may lead to the commission of any one of fifty acts." Where did you learn this, Doctor? I assure you it is news to me. I have many difficulties, upon some of which I have asked your assistance; but this I never dreamed of in my life. "And hence," he says, "he argues, that if God decreed to bring to pass a certain event, he must have decreed to produce in the heart the moral feeling by which that event is brought to pass. A man hates another. Under the influence of that hatred he may slander; he may injure his property; he may institute vexatious civil suits," etc. I suppose the Doctor means that I argue, that if God decreed the event or act, he decreed the sin. If this is his meaning, I answer yes. For if God decreed all things whatsoever come to pass, he decreed the act and the intention, and the state of heart that produced them; for these all come to pass. If he decreed that a man should slander another, or kill, or any otherwise injure, and if these things proceed from intention, and this intention springs from hatred, and all these come to pass, he decreed them all; for he decreed whatsoever comes to pass.

The Doctor does not seem to remember, that though a great diversity of bad acts can flow from one bad feeling, yet not one of them can flow, as a bad act, without the feeling.

He says, "The enlightened Calvinist has no insuperable difficulty in finding a satisfactory explanation of these things. God purposed to permit the temptation and fall of our first parents." Is permitting it decreeing it, Doctor? I ask you this short question. You will never answer it! You cannot! Its answer is fatal to Calvinism.

"Such arguments are proper weapons of infidelity; they look exceeding badly in a Christian minister. Let him come down from his airy logic, and grapple with Bible facts, and we will hear him patiently." When Dr. Rice shows that my logic is bad, it will then be time to attend to Bible facts. First let us know what the system is; then inquire whether it is found in the Bible. I am ready, however, at any time, to hear Dr. Rice prove Calvinism from the Bible. Will he ever do it? I have no fear that any of our readers will suppose that I have less reverence for that book than my friend has. I am ready to show that the Scriptures sustain against his system all the objections I have laid. If the system is logically liable, it cannot escape. This is the first question. In conclusion, I repeat that I am now noticing Dr. Rice's seventh letter, direct and indirect, and as yet he wavers as to the mode and point of attack. Will he ever come up to it?

NUMBER V.

Dr. Rice notices me in two columns of his last issue. He reiterates the charges of slander, and misrepresentation, but, as usual, without bringing a solitary proof to sustain it, or attempting to refute or correct a single statement I have made. But my readers will remember that I have not made a single charge against him which I have not sustained by numerous arguments and authorities. Why does not the gentleman attend to these?

It is a plain case. Do I sustain my charges against him? If I do, he is not slandered. If I do not, cannot Dr. Rice, the *acute polemic*, expose the fallacy? I regret to see ebullitions of feeling upon the part of the gentleman; but I can only remind him of former times, when he was in a better humor with himself—he may find comfort in the reference. His appeal to Presbyterian ministers is amusing.

What, sir, have we not your Confession of Faith, and the works of your great men, living and dead? Are not these the exponents of your creed? The question between us, and at the bar of the public, is simply this: Have I correctly stated these authorities? What are the logical consequences flowing from them? This is a question easily settled. That you would be glad to have a jury of *Presbyterian preachers* to settle the matter between us, I have no doubt. *I have great respect for these brethren, but will excuse them, on the same principle that relatives are excused in important civil suits.* But I must protest that I neither think them vile nor unlearned, but believe them generally a pious and worthy class of men. I further believe that, if they were the court, they would admit that I have correctly stated their system. But they will disclaim the consequences I deduce. But the point is not to disclaim, but to disprove. This, sir, troublesome as it is—and I know it exceedingly vexes you—is what you must do.

He repeats in this number the *learned argument* (*!*) about *sin not being a thing or event.* What has been said above will satisfy the gentleman on this subject; but I predict he will never show it to his readers.

He next gives a long list of quotations from Calvin, disclaiming the consequences charged against him. *But are disclaimers arguments?* Suppose a volume of such quotations were given—a thing I could easily do myself, and so I notified my readers at first—what avail would it be? If Calvin, and all Calvinistic authors, teach *contradictory doctrines*, or *embrace premises, but deny the logical consequences*, are they, for this reason, to stand acquit, and those who show the consequences to be accounted slanderers? Such letters as Dr. Rice's may *satisfy his people*—this is their object. He may persuade them that somebody is greatly traducing their faith; but what will all candid men think of such defense by such a man? What a strange reluctance

Dr. Rice has to make a definite issue on any point or argument! Why is this? He accuses me of slander—he deals in generals—he stands aloof from all issues. Presbyterians, what do you think of such defense? Many of you will think for yourselves. Will you be content with this? Is this the strength of your champion? *Here I distinctly challenge Dr. Rice: he accuses me of misrepresentation; I challenge him to specify in what particular. I have stated his system, and then I have deduced logical consequences. I defy the gentleman to make good his charge of misrepresentation.* Now let him do it—*let him specify.* Eight replies, direct and indirect, and no issue yet! What must be the confusion and trouble of Dr. Rice when such is the case! What must the strength of the argument be which keeps him thus in abeyance!

NUMBER VI.

The course of Dr. Rice, with respect to my letters, thus far, has, at least, afforded some amusement to many observers. The amusement may, indeed, in many instances, have amounted to innocent merriment. His confusion and flounderings—his bold and resolute assaults and rapid retreats—his fruitless effort to escape, or cover up the points in debate—his boastings, and pious horrors, and suppliant entreaties—his evident bad spirits, with his endeavor to seem in good heart—all taken together, combined with the recollection of the man who enacts the scene, constitute an exhibition provoking, at the same time, an involuntary smile and a sense of *pity.*

First he ridicules; then he becomes demure and morose; then he commences a *stately* defense, in articles regularly numbered; then he stops still; then he turns round, and commences anew at No. 1 again; then he denies and disclaims; then he attacks: thus he runs through eleven letters, without making a single intelligible issue with a single proposition I have made. His best performances I have quoted fully to my readers, and they can judge about the correctness of this representation. Verily, Calvinism has found but a feeble defense in this instance. But it is not Dr. Rice's fault—he wants neither the will nor the ability to defend it to the utmost it will admit of—it is the fault of the system. He has done nobly. What more could he have done? Has he not cried "misrepresentation?" Has he not refused to meet all the issues? Has he not faithfully kept all my charges from his people? Has he not done his best to divert attention? Has he not praised the system, and told his readers what could be done, and what has been done a thousand times? Has he not quoted sentiments, from his authors, precisely contradictory to the sentiments I quoted from the same authors? Has he not declaimed against logic as a weapon of infidelity? Nay, more: has he not assumed to be an outright Arminian? What more could the gentleman have done? I say again, if it all fails, it is not his fault. He has struggled nobly, and with his accustomed tact. The system alone is to blame. I hope Presbyterians will understand this. Let not your wrath come down upon the Doctor. He has done all that mortal could do, and you should do your utmost to comfort him. Make the best of a bad cause.

In his last, with admirable precision, he runs the same *old round* of his former nine. First, he enters a denial of my charges, and declares me a false accuser; but not a word, not an allusion, to my arguments or authorities! A conclusive mode of reasoning, as you all know! It tears arguments and authorities right up by the roots! It is good old Calvinistic, Geneva logic! Then he quotes disclaimers from the authorities employed by us! An admirable method of meeting logical consequences! Nothing could be more to the point than this! "A man," says John Smith, "is a murderer; and whoever murders deserves to be hanged." A listener says, "Then John Smith deserves to be hanged." The former speaker becomes enraged; says he is misrepresented—he never said *John Smith* deserved the fate of hanging! It's logic! He is not accountable for logic! It is an infidel weapon! He does not believe what is charged against him! He does not believe, more than his accuser, that *John Smith* ought to be hanged! Of course, the disclaimer annihilates the logic! Nobody will presume to doubt it! Nobody will believe that he said or thought that John Smith ought to be hanged!

The Doctor follows his declamation with this fatal admission: "We denounce that doctrine [the doctrine I charged upon Calvinists] as unequivocally as he does; and we readily admit that he has proved it perfectly absurd and *blasphemous*." Thus, it will be perceived, the cogency and correctness of my arguments is admitted. The doctrines I antagonize, it is confessed, are shown to be perfectly absurd and *blasphemous!* This is Dr. Rice's judgment. Well, now, my readers know perfectly well, that these very doctrines are quoted *alone* and *only* from the Confession of Faith, and such authors as Calvin, Edwards, Buck, Witsius, Dick, etc. Are these Calvinistic authorities, or not? If so, the doctrines proved to be perfectly absurd and *blasphemous*, Dr. Rice himself being judge, are Calvinistic; and so Calvinism, in the judgment of its champion, is *absurd* and *blasphemous!* What worse than this have I said of it?

He next introduces, as wont, the doctrine of permission, but, *of course*, without alluding to the fact that I have triumphantly exposed the fallacy. He has no idea of letting his readers know what weakness marks his defense—what contradictions he is involved in. He knows too much, as an old and practiced polemic, to quote arguments which he cannot answer, or to admit replies which uncover his nakedness. He never will do this.

The learned Doctor, having thus *lucidly*, and *creditably* to himself, defended his own system, proceeds, in answer to the inquiry, "Are our Methodist brethren free from difficulty upon this subject?" to make quotations from Wesley and Watson, which, we infer, he supposes involve us in similar difficulties to those besetting his own system, which he admits is shown to be absurd and blasphemous; but I confess I have not discernment enough to perceive the difficulty. I find nothing objectional in the quotations. I find no logical consequences that give me a moment's uneasiness. When the gentleman names consequences, or premises, which he deems objectional, we may help him. He promises to do this. In the meantime, will he attend to the matters in hand? Will he relieve his own system? Come, Doctor, keep in good heart. You have a troublous task, it is true; but keep up your spirits—don't get out of humor—do the best you can, and, for your encouragement, always remember, nobody will censure you in the event of failure and defeat. Your abilities are admitted, and it will be set down to the fact that you have a bad cause.

NUMBER VII.

This letter, as the former, starts out with the stereotyped charge of misrepresentation. The point here named is this: he says that I attach to the word necessity the idea of compulsion; although Calvinistic writers have been careful to say that they use it in no such sense—that by the word necessity they mean only certainty. To this statement I reply, 1. It is not correct in point of fact. Calvinists do not attach the simple idea of certainty to necessity—and here I will join particular issue with Dr. Rice whenever he chooses—but they do attach to their use of the term necessity the idea of an inevitable effect following a preceding cause. 2. I deny that Calvinists, as a class, have been careful to state that they use it in no such sense. 3. I assert, they cannot, in consistency with their system, employ it *simply* in this sense. Dr. Rice cannot sustain his issue. Let him try it.

He next proceeds to discuss the doctrine of election. He makes his statement of the doctrine; and, though there is an evident effort to obscure or vail its fiercer features, he admits all that we could desire, to warrant *our* statement of this point, deduced from other and more distinguished authors. He says, "What is the doctrine of election? 1. Not that God, *from eternity,* determined to save any of the human race in their sins, but that he *determined to work in a great number* to will and to do—to call them, by his word and Spirit, out of darkness into his marvelous light—to sanctify and to save them. 2. Not that he determined to prevent others from repenting and believing in Christ, but *simply to pass them by, leaving them to their own free choice.* 3. Not that he determined to punish any, without regard to their moral character, but only for their sins. 4. Not that God has not the best reasons for choosing some to life, and passing by others, but that the reasons are not found in the foreseen goodness of the former, and are not revealed to us. 5. Not that the atonement of Christ is not, in its nature, sufficient for all, or is not offered to all who hear the Gospel, *but that he particularly designed by it to redeem to himself a peculiar people, zealous of good works.*" Every one will admire the prudence and precaution, not to say timidity, with which the Doctor has selected his ground. But, in despite of all his pains to cover it up with a lamb's skin, or invest it in a doye's feathers, the claws and teeth of the monster will appear. He does nobly to keep them out of view; but it is of no avail. After all, it is the same old monster, which the honest Calvin exhibited without a covering, labeled election and reprobation, which he admitted himself was most horrible. Election, Dr. Rice says, "is the determination, from eternity, to work in a great number to will and to do—to sanctify and save them." Of course, their salvation is inevitable, or the determination of God must fail. All the consequences charged in my letters follow. But, again: election is the determination, from eternity, "to *pass by*" those not elected, "leaving them to their own choice." Of course, if they were passed by, they could not be saved; and, if they could not be saved, they must necessarily and inevitably be damned; and so, again, all the consequences charged in my letters follow. If they are punished simply for their sins, they are punished for what was inevitable to them; because, being passed by, they could not avoid sinning. So the Doctor, notwithstanding all his effort to soften down the asperities of the doctrine, believes outright in eternal election and reprobation; that is, that a certain definite number of the human race were elected, by a determination which cannot fail, to be saved—that another definite number were reprobated to be damned, being so passed by, that they could not, by any possibility, avoid damnation. The gentleman has committed himself here; and now, how perfectly ridiculous his former disclaimers, when, by his own statement, he is involved in the very worst consequences charged upon him! But, again: election "is not that the atonement is not sufficient for all, but that he particularly designed by it to redeem to himself a peculiar people." Here, again, in defiance of an effort to keep in the dark his beloved tenet of limited atonement, it will exhibit its deformities. The atonement, though sufficient in itself for all, was not made or designed for any but the peculiar people—the *elect;* for the residue it was not an atonement, though sufficient to be of unlimited efficacy—it was not limited in its sufficiency, but in the will of God. All the consequences charged in my letters follow. Those for whom it was not designed cannot enjoy it—they are under an eternal necessity to be damned. The gentleman never will state my objections on this point, and attempt to remove them. His policy will be to strike at them in a general manner, without letting his readers know what they are, and close by telling them that he has entirely met them.

Let the reader now remember, that Dr. Rice is convicted upon his own statement—and I defy the gentleman to escape—of believing and teaching, that, by a determination of God, from eternity, a certain number of men were assigned to eternal life, and a certain other number to eternal death, in a way that the event must answer the determination: then let him refer to the many objections urged in our letters against him, and it will be seen how dreadful is his system, and how hopelessly he is involved in contradictions, or, as he has unwittingly admitted, on another point, in *absurdity* and *blasphemy*.

He proceeds, having stated the doctrine of election, as given above, to inquire how far Methodists and Calvinists are agreed upon the subject. Upon this point I find no occasion to make any remarks. *If they agreed exactly, it would not, in the slightest degree, relieve his system.* But though the statement he makes is, to some extent, inaccurate, it is so innocent it needs no correction. If he wishes to involve Methodism in the dilemmas which encompass himself, he must strike more severely than this. We have not been able yet even to feel the thrust. When he premonished us several times of the "bottled thunder" he had in reservation for us, we began to think, may-be, he had discovered some crevice, or seam, where he would make deadly onset; but, when the threatened storm bursts, it is but the cooing of the dove! We find no alarm! Twist your cords again, Doctor, and lay on harder, or we shall not realize that the attack has commenced.

Having run the parallel, he next proceeds to take up the objections urged in my letters. For once, he seems really as though he were going to work like a man. He commences at objection first; and you would imagine that now comes the tug of war; but, lo! without delaying for a moment to make battle, he says, "This objection is based upon the false view of the doctrine of decrees," and, with this masterly blow, flies from it as from the face of pestilence. What a Hercules! How masterly this mode of argumentation!

He then takes up objection second; but here, as he cannot but perceive, the point of the argument is misstated. Our point is this: that persons are elected to salvation, and decreed to damnation, irrespective of any conditions; so that, as an unavoidable consequence, the event of their salvation or damnation is in no sense under their control, but is inevitably fixed, independently of them. They have nothing whatever to do with it, as it was all fixed before they had an existence, and for causes independent of them. Let the gentleman meet this point, and he will meet one point of difficulty. Will he grapple this objection? If he admits the point I make, he admits that neither sin nor holiness were taken into the account, in the decree of election and reprobation, unless sin and holiness are inevitable to the subjects of them. If he denies the point, he, by necessary consequence, admits that the decree proceeded upon foresight, and in consequence of some voluntary act of the creature. The former involves him in all that I charged in my letters—the latter is a desertion of Calvinism. He says, "All that our Confession teaches upon the subject is, that God chose to pass *them* by, and punish them for their sins." This is all we ask to justify all the objections we have urged—this is unconditional reprobation enough for us; and the gentleman will struggle till doomsday to escape, and struggle in vain. Hear his feeble attempt to sustain this position. I give it because it resembles the forms of an argument, and looks as if he had not forgotten that there is such a thing as reasoning.

"Now, was it unjust to pass them by, and not renew

their hearts? If so, God is bound to offer salvation to men, and to exert upon them divine influence to induce them to accept it; and then the whole plan is simply a matter of justice, and not of grace toward men. If not, who has the right to object to it as unjust?" This is a refreshing specimen, I say, because it looks as though the gentleman had some respect to rules of reasoning. But, upon examination, it will appear that his logic is about as objectionable as his theology. In the first place, the premise does not contain the issue. It is not pretended in our letters that it is unjust "to pass them by, *and not renew their hearts;*" but this is the point where injustice is charged—the *passing men by, and leaving them in a state in which it is impossible for them to have their hearts renewed, and then damning them for not performing the impossibility.* This correction of the premises being made, the "if so," and "if not," of course, are not legitimate, and the attempted argument falls to the ground. The plan of salvation is not a scheme of mere justice, and such a consequence cannot be shown to result from the premises; but if it is not a plan of mere justice, so neither is it contrary to justice—it is a scheme of mercy in harmony with justice. The plan of Calvinists, as is abundantly shown, is neither a plan of justice nor mercy, but is alike cruel and unjust. Take another specimen of logic. I do not wonder that the gentleman is on bad terms with logic! I think it is on no better terms with him! He says, "Again: either the finally impenitent will deserve eternal punishment for their sins, or they will not. If not, the penalty of God's law, which will be executed upon them, is unjust; if so, Mr. Foster represents it as horrible that God should do what is perfectly just." What is this argument intended and competent to prove? This: that the final destruction of the impenitent will be perfectly just. Who has ever questioned this? No Arminian. Not a word in my letters. On the contrary,

I contend that the damnation of the finally impenitent will be perfectly just; and, because it will, I contend that Calvinism is totally false. The gentleman supplies me with a premise which overthrows his system. Here is my argument: the damnation of the finally impenitent is perfectly just. But if that damnation were for a cause over which the subject of it had no possible control, then it would be unjust; for it would be damnation for not performing an impossibility. But Calvinism teaches that the sinner's damnation is for sins which he had no power to avoid; hence, that it is unjust. Therefore, Calvinism is false, because it makes the sinner's damnation unjust. Doctor, try your hand on this logic: see how it suits you.

He next takes up my third objection, "that the doctrine makes God a partial being, and destroys entirely the foundation for the doctrine of grace;" and he *absolutely* refers to my letter! He says, "See Letter VIII!" but where shall his readers find it? He is too shrewd to show them any part of it! He never would have told them to see it, only he knew that most of them could not, and that his reference would seem to imply a willingness on his part, if it were possible—a show of confidence. To the objection, that his doctrine makes God a partial being, he attempts an answer, by giving Walker's definition of partial: "A partial being is one who is inclined to favor one party or person above another without reason." He denies that God favors one above another without a reason. My readers must judge of this themselves, seeing what the system actually teaches, namely, that God viewed all men as sinners, without a particle of difference between them—in all respects exactly alike; and thus beholding them, he chose A., B., C., and D. to eternal life, and consigned E., F., G., and H. to an eternal hell. Now, if this does not imply partiality, then I admit Calvinism does not make God partial—he has not favored one person above another without reasons, such as acquit him from partiality—he has been equally kind to all. It is a plain case: you will judge for yourselves.

He next attempts to show that the difficulty lies against Methodism. Now, if he could sustain this, he does not help his own case; and his attempt shows evidence of conscious weakness. He denies that his creed shows partiality in God. He then endeavors to show that Methodism is as liable as himself; but what he charges to Methodism he believes, and *much more:* how then can he pretend that Methodism is guilty, when he assumes that he is not? But his attempt to involve Methodism in this, as in the former case, is fruitless. The particular in his creed, on which we base the charge of partiality, Methodists do not believe. If the charge lays against it justly, it does not lay against Methodists, for Methodists do not embrace it. If there are other things which the Methodists do believe, in common with Calvinists, against which the charge of partiality justly lays, then my objection is still true, for the Calvinists are guilty with the Methodists. But I defy the gentleman to sustain the charge against Methodism, even in common with himself—much more do I defy him to escape the odium of the charge, as bearing specially against the doctrine of Calvinian election and reprobation. The gentleman asks, in view of the fact admitted by all, that there is a manifest difference in the condition of men and nations, "How great a difference may God make before he is chargeable with partiality?" He asks this question as though he thought it would be difficult to answer, and as if it bore more upon others than himself. I will answer it for him. God, as an impartial being, is bound to deal with all men upon the same great, immutable principles of wisdom, goodness, and justice—never to deal unwisely, unkindly, or unjustly by any one—not to be influenced by one set of principles toward one, and another set toward another. If the gentleman will show that such is not the fact, he will show that God is a partial being. I have shown that his system teaches that such is not the fact, and, hence, that it is liable to the charge of making God partial. If he will show any thing in Methodism that renders us liable, he will involve us, together with himself, but will not relieve himself in the slightest degree. The point for Dr. Rice, at present, is either to admit the truth of my charge or escape from it. But he never will do either.

I could wish, for the sake of Dr. Rice's reputation, and the edification of our readers, that he would, in a more sturdy manner, meet arguments; but I suppose this is like requiring impossibilities, and I must not do this. The character of his replies must explain the style of my rejoinders.

NUMBER VIII.

In the first part of this letter, the Doctor continues to urge that Methodists are not free from difficulties on the subject of election. To this I paid sufficient attention in my last letter, as it forms no part of the present issue. Indeed, as yet I see no occasion to vindicate our views upon this subject—his remarks are so perfectly harmless. When we see Methodism trembling under potent assault, we might even turn aside from the point in debate to defend it; but we cannot be decoyed without something more serious than has yet been submitted. Our apprehensions are yet all asleep.

The Doctor continues: "Mr. Foster, in his ninth letter, presses with great earnestness the objection, that the doctrine of election is inconsistent with all those passages of Scripture which teach that Christ died for all men. Now, he ought to know that the word *for*, like all other prepositions, has a number of meanings. What, then, does he mean, when he affirms that Christ died for all men? Does he mean, simply, that the atonement made by Christ is sufficient to save all men, if they would believe? If so, we heartily agree with him. Does he mean that God designed freely to offer salvation to all men, without distinction, through the atonement? If so, we have no controversy with him." To the above interrogations, abating the word simply, as it occurs in them, I will answer, yes. We believe that, in this sense, Christ died for all. But we believe more than this. But, as our faith is not the matter in controversy, we need not name it. It is known of all men; it has no equivocations; it is simple and one. We are under no necessity to resort to far-fetched explanations to protect it, or make it understood. But I shall now show you what difficulty he has involved himself in by his admissions. He states just what I stated for him, in my regular letter on this point; and all the difficulties there named bear against him, and I defy the gentleman to escape them. Corroborating the statement above, and immediately following it, he says: "The Calvinistic doctrine of election is, 1. The atonement of Christ is of infinite value. 2 . Salvation, through Christ, is freely offered to all." He admits these two propositions. But, now, mark: he believes, 3. That Christ died only for the elect, in the eternal purpose of God—in other words, that his death was limited, in the design of God, to a part of mankind, and did not extend to the rest, in such a sense as to make their salvation possible under the circumstances. I defy the gentleman to deny this statement. He dares not do it. He dares not say that Christ died for all men in such manner, all the circumstances included, as to make their salvation possible. Will he come out here? Here is the precise point where we call upon him for light.

But, now, mark the difficulties resulting from his admissions. "He believes that the atonement is of infinite value, sufficient for all, if they would believe." What does the gentleman mean, when he says the atonement is of infinite value—is sufficient for all? Does he mean that it was sufficient to remove all the hinderances in the way of the salvation of all?—that it was competent to save all? Then the question arises, why does it not save all? The gentleman must answer, because it was not designed for all; the limitation, then, is in the design of God. Is this so? then the damnation of some arises purely from the sovereign design, or will of God, that they should be damned. Look at this. There was a sufficient atonement for all; nothing more was necessary. But God, of his own will, limited what was sufficient for all to a part. Is it withheld from any? it is because it is the will of God. Are they consequently damned? it is because it is the will of God. But, again: what does he mean when he says, "if they would believe?" Does he know and teach that they cannot believe, because Christ did not die for them? Why, then, does he speak of faith in them as possible, "if they would believe," when he knows they cannot? That very want of faith is, according to his creed, the proof that Christ did not die for them. His death was sufficient, but it never was intended for them; God limited it to these, not to them. It was no more possible to the reprobates than to the devils; it was no more an atonement for them, than it was for the devils. Now, Dr. Rice, no dodging here. If you have the courage, come out and meet this point candidly, and in such a way, as to show where you stand. Sir, at the risk of being called *immodest*, I say, you will not dare to defend your ground here. You cannot escape by an old trick—and it is well to remind you of it—by saying that they are not saved because of unbelief. For, according to your system, the very reason why they do not believe, is, Christ did not die for them. Their unbelief is an effect of the previous cause, that they were not atoned for—the first cause why they are not saved is the want of an atonement for them.

And now, sir, we come to the second point: "Salvation is freely offered to all who hear the Gospel." You believe all are invited to come to Christ. I ask, *how* they can be invited to come, when Christ did not die for them; you answer, "All *may* come, and all are, therefore, invited." Now, here, again, I urge you, by your love of truth and consistency, to meet this point openly and fairly. You say that "*all are invited* to come to Christ, because *all may* come." Dr. Rice, hear me patiently, when I say you do not believe this proposition; you *cannot;* you have imposed upon yourself. In your zeal to reconcile your creed with the Scriptures which antagonize it, you have overstepped yourself—not intentionally, but certainly. This will appear to yourself, if you will attempt to answer *to yourself*—and I should like for you to answer them to the public—a few questions. Is it possible for all men to come to Christ and be saved? If you answer, yes, then it must be possible for all men to have the will to come; for no man can come without the will, and if any cannot have the will to come, they cannot come. But you do not believe it possible for all to have the will to come, unless you believe that it is possible for some to have a will different from that which they actually have, under the circumstances, which you know is not your faith. But, again: do you not believe that, though the atonement is sufficient for all in itself, yet that it is limited, in the design of God, to a part—and that another part are passed by, to whom it is not purposed to be applied? To this you must answer, yes. Well, if it is limited, in the design of God, to a part, can those to whom it is not extended ever enjoy it? If you say, yes, then the design of God must change or fail. If you say, no, then you admit they cannot come. But, again: do you not believe that the atonement is sovereignly applied to those for whom it was made, before they can come to Christ, in their regeneration? You must answer, yes. Well, then, can those to whom it is not thus applied come to him? If you say, yes, you say a man may turn himself to God and be saved; if you say, no, you say that none but those to whom it is sovereignly applied can come.

But, again: some of the human race will finally be lost. Do you believe that those persons, who will so be lost, ever had the power to come to Christ and be saved, under the circumstances and influences in which they were placed? If you answer, yes, then you admit that their salvation was in their own power, and might have been achieved by their own exertions. If you answer, no, you admit that these persons never could come to Christ.

But, again: you believe that a definite number of the human race were elected unto everlasting life, and a definite number not elected. Now, answer me this question: do you believe that any but the elect can be saved? You must answer me, no or yes. If yes, then a man may be saved whom God passed by, and never chose to be saved; if no, then those passed by could not, cannot, come to Christ, to be saved; the thing is impossible.

If you still say the thing is impossible, because of the will, I charge you, as you dread to mislead and deceive the ignorant, that you say, at the same time, that the will to come is not possible to the creature unless it is given; and it is only given to those for whom Christ died, and, therefore, that those who have not the will, have it not because Christ did not die for them.

Sir, *you know, that those for whom Christ did not die, in the purpose of God, cannot come to him.* How, then, I ask you, in the name of all that a Christian, above all, a Christian minister, should hold dear—how can you say you invite them, because they may come? There is a feast spread for a thousand guests, but is designed for only five hundred particular persons: it is impossible that any others should come. These five hundred are yonder, in an assemblage of a thousand. Now, how can the master of the feast send his servant to invite the thousand, without the charge of insincerity? Again: suppose that, of the one thousand, the five hundred for whom the feast is not intended are chained, so that they cannot move until the master of the feast unloose them—how can they be invited to come without sheer mockery? The cases are precisely analogous if you add, that, for not complying with the base, heartless invitation, those who refuse are to be doomed to nameless tortures!

But if Christ did not die for all, why are reprobates commanded to believe? Dr. Rice undertakes to answer this question He says, "Because it is their duty to believe." Let us look at this. What is it that is required of the reprobates? To believe on Jesus Christ, in order to salvation. This, Dr. Rice says, is their duty. Now, if Jesus Christ did not, in the design of God, die for these persons, which Dr. Rice contends is the fact, then it is certain he is not their Savior—he has no salvation for them. If he has, it is contrary to the design of God; but if he has not, then, Dr. Rice says, it is the duty of reprobates to believe a lie; and, for not believing a lie, they are damned! Will the gentleman inform us how he escapes this? But, further, if it is the duty of reprobates to believe in Christ, they either can believe, or they cannot. If they can, they may come to Christ; and they will be either saved or not. If they will be saved, they will be saved by believing a lie, and by a Savior who never died for them; if not, they will falsify Dr. Rice's creed and the Scriptures, which equally teach that whosoever believeth shall be saved! Will the Doctor help us here? If they are not able to believe in Christ, and yet it is made their duty to believe in him, then it is made their duty to do an impossibility; and if they are damned for not performing their duty, they are damned for not doing an impossibility!

What a most remarkable sentence is the following, to come from the pen of Dr. Rice! "Since salvation is freely offered to all, and all are free to accept or reject it, there is no inconsistency in inviting all, and no injustice in the condemnation of those who abide in unbelief." Look at this. If salvation is freely offered to all, and if Christ did not die for all, then salvation is freely offered to some for whom there is no salvation, or else there is salvation for some for whom Christ did not die! What an offer is this! Is it not hypocritical and empty? Can it be any thing else? And who makes it? The God worshiped by Dr. Rice!

But, again: are all free to accept it? Then are some free to accept what has no existence! What absurdities beset this most miserable system at every point! When will Dr. Rice extricate himself from the difficulties he has thus invested himself with? Never! He will not try—he knows the thing is impossible! But this comes of his fruitless effort so far. It is now proved by himself, that my statements of his creed were true and correct, and that the difficulties alledged are insuperable.

The Doctor proceeds to state, in his bland and Christian manner, that "a more outrageous misrepresentation of Calvinism was never made—more glaring injustice to authors was never done. Our business has been that of correction much more than argument; for the correction of misrepresentations is the best answer to arguments founded upon them." Now, to this statement I find but one objection. Its style and spirit, of course, are unobjectionable! Shall I say commendable? The objection I make is this: it is quite a small matter—it only relates to one word—the Doctor, I think, will admit it, and then it will be a fine paragraph. Let him strike out the word *correction*, and substitute *assertion;* then it will be perfect. It will read, "My business has been that of *assertion* much more than argument." That is true, Doctor. No one who has been at the pains to read your singular replies, will doubt it for a moment. But as for corrections, I have yet to find a single one. I defy you, sir, to name it. You have repeatedly asserted that I misrepresented you, but, sir, you have not corrected one of my statements; unless you consider your assertions corrections! I suppose this is your meaning.

In closing up this volume, I cannot avoid expressing astonishment, that Calvinism should find favor and advocacy with wise and good men. It is most strange that it should be so. No system is so encompassed with serious difficulties. It is not less beset with contradictions than Atheism itself. It is less defensible than Deism or Universalism. Blind, universal skepticism would be a refuge to reason and religion compared with it. Let it be understood, we now speak of Calvinism proper—not of the systems of faith in which it is included—not of the communities embracing it. Calvinism, in the creeds of the various Churches entertaining it, is surrounded with many wholesome and saving truths—with, indeed, whatever is essential to be believed; but itself is an unmitigated blotch.

This is the reason why an effort is always made by its advocates to disguise it—to explain it away—to mystify it. This is the reason why it is reserved for special occasions—why it is kept for the study, not for the pulpit—why, when persons become troubled on account of it, they are told that it is not a suitable subject for them to seek to understand—why it is not made a condition of membership in the Church—why, in a word, it has been debated by its defenders whether or not it ought to be preached. This is the reason why Dr. Rice has been so anxious to escape from its examination—why he has perpetually declaimed about our misrepresentation—why he has avoided to discuss the case upon its merits. He knows full well it will not bear the light—that it can only be kept in countenance by keeping the deceptive cover on it—that to state it is to damn it. Hence his fruitless attempt at defense. His abilities—great, confessedly—have failed him in the support of such a cause. The cause has put him to shame.

It has been no pleasure, but, on the contrary, extremely painful to me, to make the plain statements contained in the foregoing pages. Nothing but a provocation, which it would have been unchristian to endure longer, could have induced it—unchristian, because truth and righteousness were suffering, and likely to suffer more by silence. We would have been content to let this controversy slumber for ever, leaving truth to work out error by a peaceable process, which it was doing, rather than to have caused pain to a single disciple of Christ—much more, rather than to involve two large Christian bodies in unpleasant conflict. We were willing for our friends to hold their opinions, though we believed them erroneous, rather than to insult and wound them, and provoke unkind feelings between those who ought to be friends, leaving time and progress to correct them. But nothing would do but controversy. We, therefore, reluctantly yielded to the necessity. We have spoken plainly, that we might be understood, and sometimes, it would seem, severely; but God is our witness, we have not intended to be unkind—we do not feel it in our hearts. We do not call in question the piety of our opponents. They hold much truth. Many of them have been, in the Church, high and shining lights. But as the sun may have its spots, and yet be brilliant, so may the wise and good err in judgment. We love the Presbyterian Church, and will still try to love it, and the reverend Doctor with whom we have been engaged, just as well as though nothing had passed.

We believe them in error, and have given our reasons; but we claim no infallibility—we dogmatize our opinions upon nobody—they are uttered only in self-defense, and in defense of what we believe to be truth. Our readers will judge for themselves of the merits of the performance. And, now, may God bless our humble endeavors to do good, and bring both writer and reader to that world, where we shall see as we are seen, and know as we are known! Amen.

THE END.